Contents

Edges of Empire

New Interventions in Art History

Series editor: Dana Arnold, *University of Southampton*

New Interventions in Art History is a series of textbook mini-companions – published in connection with the Association of Art Historians – that aims to provide innovative approaches to, and new perspectives on, the study of art history. Each volume focuses on a specific area of the discipline of art history – here used in the broadest sense to include painting, sculpture, architecture, graphic arts, and film – and aims to identify the key factors that have shaped the artistic phenomenon under scrutiny. Particular attention is paid to the social and political context and the historiography of the artistic cultures or movements under review. In this way, the essays that comprise each volume cohere around the central theme while providing insights into the broader problematics of a given historical moment.

Art and Thought
edited by *Dana Arnold and Margaret Iversen* (published)

Art and its Publics: Museum Studies at the Millennium
edited by *Andrew McClellan* (published)

Architectures: Modernism and After
edited by *Andrew Ballantyne* (published)

After Criticism: New Responses to Art and Performance
edited by *Gavin Butt* (published)

Envisioning the Past: Archaeology and the Image
edited by *Sam Smiles and Stephanie Moser* (published)

Edges of Empire: Orientalism and Visual Culture
edited by *Jocelyn Hackforth-Jones and Mary Roberts* (published)

Psychoanalysis and the Image
edited by *Griselda Pollock* (forthcoming)

Exhibition Experiments
edited by *Sharon MacDonald* (forthcoming)

Pop Culture and Post-War American Taste
edited by *Patricia Morton* (forthcoming)

Material Identities
edited by *Joanna Sofaer Derevenski* (forthcoming)

Edges of Empire

Orientalism and Visual Culture

Edited by
Jocelyn Hackforth-Jones
and
Mary Roberts

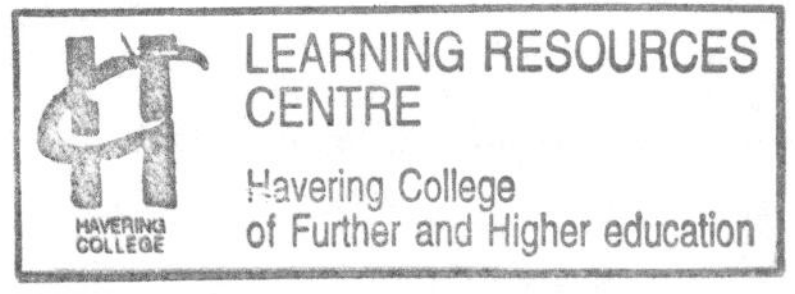

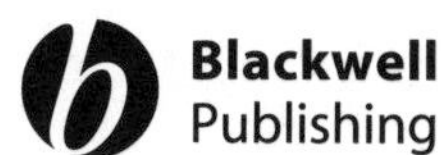

BLACKWELL PUBLISHING
350 Main Street, Malden, MA 02148-5020, USA
9600 Garsington Road, Oxford OX4 2DQ, UK
550 Swanston Street, Carlton, Victoria 3053, Australia

First published 2005 by Blackwell Publishing Ltd

1 2005

Library of Congress Cataloging-in-Publication Data

Edges of empire: orientalism and visual culture / edited by Jocelyn Hackforth–Jones and Mary Roberts.

p. cm. — (New interventions in art history)
Includes bibliographical references and index.
ISBN–13: 978–1–4051–1688–6 (hard cover: alk. paper)
ISBN–10: 1–4051–1688–9 (hard cover: alk. paper)
ISBN–13: 978–1–4051–1689–3 (pbk. : alk. paper)
ISBN–10: 1–4051–1689–7 (pbk. : alk. paper)
1. Intercultural communication in art. 2. Orientalism in art. 3. Art, European—19th century. 4. Art, Middle Eastern—European influences. 5. Art, North African—European influences. I. Hackforth-Jones, Jocelyn. II. Roberts, Mary, 1965– III. Series.
N7429.E34 2005
303.48′21821056′09034—dc22

205004886

A catalogue record for this title is available from the British Library.

Set in 10.5/13pt Minion
by SPI Publisher Services, Pondicherry, India
Printed and bound in the United Kingdom
by TJ International, Padstow, Cornwall

The publisher's policy is to use permanent paper from mills that operate a sustainable forestry policy, and which has been manufactured from pulp processed using acid-free and elementary chlorine-free practices. Furthermore, the publisher ensures that the text paper and cover board used have met acceptable environmental accreditation standards.

For further information on
Blackwell Publishing, visit our website:
www.blackwellpublishing.com

Series Editor's Preface

New Interventions in Art History was established to provide a forum for innovative approaches to and perspectives on the study of art history in all its complexities. This volume represents a timely contribution to the fast-growing body of work on Orientalism in nineteenth- and twentieth-century visual culture. It is the necessary "next stage" in moving on from a Western-dominated art/cultural history to something more pluralist and nuanced.

Edges of Empire combines the work of major players in the Orientalism debate with new voices to present a refreshingly coherent collection of essays. The chapters are well focused and each makes an individually significant and new contribution. Taken together the writings combine to make an important intervention in the field as a whole. The interrelationship of the essays is a strength of the volume as different aspects of the same cultural area – for instance turn-of-the-century Turkey or turn-of-the-century Paris – present different aspects of the topics discussed that are mutually informative. *Edges of Empire* will be of interest to all who work on the social, cultural, and visual history of Europe and the eastern Mediterranean in the nineteenth and twentieth centuries.

Edges of Empire pushes studies of Orientalism a step further towards a more nuanced reading of this most complex of discursive formations. And I have no doubt that it offers the reader an extended space for considering the dialog between East and West that is so often absent from standard Westernized accounts. It is, then, a most appropriate and welcome addition to this series, which seeks to encourage interventions in art history such as this that truly expand the field.

Dana Arnold
London 2005

List of Illustrations

Notes on Contributors

Roger Benjamin is J. W. Power Professor of Art History and Visual Culture at the University of Sydney. His earlier research focused on the art and writings of Henri Matisse. Since the 1990s his work on Orientalism has resulted in two international exhibitions and a monograph, published in 2003.

Frederick N. Bohrer is Associate Professor of Art at Hood College in Frederick, Maryland. He is the author of *Orientalism and Visual Culture: Imagining Mesopotamia in Nineteenth-Century Europe* (2003) and editor of *Sevruguin and the Persian Image: Photographs of Iran, 1870–1930* (1999). His current research deals with the relation of Middle Eastern archaeology and photography during the nineteenth century.

Zeynep Çelik is Professor of Architecture at the New Jersey Institute of Architecture. She has published widely on cross-cultural topics. Her publications include *The Remaking of Istanbul* (1986; 1993), *Displaying the Orient* (1993), *Urban Forms and Colonial Confrontations: Algiers under French Rule* (1997), and *Streets: Critical Perspectives on Public Space* (co-edited with Diane Favro and Richard Ingersoll; 1993). She served as the editor of the *Journal of the Society of Architectural Historians* (2000–3) and is currently working on a book entitled *Other Modernisms: Architecture and the City in the Middle East and North Africa.*

Darcy Grimaldo Grigsby is Associate Professor of the History of Art at the University of California, Berkeley, and author of *Extremities: Painting Empire in Post-Revolutionary France* (2002). She is currently completing a book entitled *Colossal Engineering (Reconnecting the Suez Canal, Statue of Liberty, Eiffel Tower and Panama Canal).*

Jos Hackforth-Jones is Professor of Art History and Provost at Richmond, The American International University in London. Before taking up her present position she directed an intercultural MA at Richmond. She has published widely on travel art, landscape painting and intercultural issues, including most recently *(Re)Forming Identities: Intercultural Education and the Visual Arts* (1998). She is currently working on an exhibition for the National Portrait Gallery, London, which considers eighteenth- and nineteenth-century visual representations of non-European visitors to that capital.

Reina Lewis is Senior Lecturer in Cultural Studies at the University of East London. She is author of *Gendering Orientalism: Race, Femininity and Representation* (1996) and *Rethinking Orientalism: Women, Travel and the Ottoman Harem* (2004). She is also co-editor, with Sara Mills, of *Feminist Postcolonial Theory: A Reader* (2003), and series editor, with Teresa Heffernan, of *Cultures in Dialogue*, a multi-volume project republishing Eastern and Western women's writing from the eighteenth to the twentieth centuries.

Sally MacDonald is Manager of the Petrie Museum of Egyptian Archaeology, University College London. She has worked in a range of decorative art, social history, and community museums, including Croydon Clocktower, where she established a new museum service that won many awards.

Mary Roberts is the John Schaeffer Senior Lecturer in British Art at the University of Sydney She specializes in nineteenth-century British Orientalism, gender, and the culture of travel. She has co-edited two books: *Orientalism's Interlocutors: Painting, Architecture, Photography* (2002) and *Refracting Vision: Essays on the Writings of Michael Fried* (2000), and is currently writing a book entitled *Intimate Outsiders.*

Alastair Wright is Assistant Professor of Art History at Princeton University. He was the recipient of a Getty Research Institute Postdoctoral Fellowship and has delivered papers in Europe, America, and Asia. He has also worked as a research and curatorial assistant at the Metropolitan Museum of Art, New York, and the Minneapolis Institute of Arts. He is the author of the forthcoming *Matisse and the Subject of Modernism* (2004).

Acknowledgments

A number of individuals were enthusiastic about and supported this project from its earliest manifestation as a conference entitled "Occidents Will Happen" held at Tate Britain in April 2002, which considered ways in which Orientalist visual culture is enriched and made more complex by the inclusion of indigenous artists and patrons. At Tate Britain, warm thanks are due to Richard Humphreys for his initial enthusiasm and to Joanna Banham for ensuring the success of the conference. We are happy to acknowledge the grant from the Paul Mellon Centre for Studies in British Art which secured this event. Richard Resch, formerly Provost at Richmond, The American International University in London, gave his support to the conference and we thank him, students, and faculty at Richmond. Heartfelt thanks also to Brian Allen, Sam Smiles, and Jonathan Watkins.

We are grateful to Dana Arnold for her advice, professionalism, and collegiality. Her interest and support have been intrinsic to the metamorphosis of this project into *Edges of Empire*. Jayne Fargnoli's engagement with the project and continuing support have been invaluable. In addition we thank Ken Provencher and Janet Moth for bringing this work to fruition.

We would also like to thank a number of key individuals whose contributions have enriched this book: Jananne Al-Ani, Jill Beaulieu, Roger Benjamin, Lissant Bolton, Laura Brown, Peter Funnell, Kaveh Golestan, Michael Hatt, Helen Pether, Zineb Sedira, Chris Spring, Susan Strong and Hannah Williams. In addition we thank Martin Neild and Tessa Kerwood, who generously lent us their house in Oxfordshire so that we could complete much of the editing process free from interruptions.

We gratefully acknowledge the financial support of the Australian Academy of Humanities in Canberra and the Faculty of Arts at the

University of Sydney, for the provision of grant fundings for the illustrations in this volume.

Finally we thank our contributors, who cheerfully engaged in a rigorous editing process, responded to deadlines with professionalism, and have written papers that we acknowledge as significant contributions to the field.

JH-J and MR

Introduction: Visualizing Culture across the Edges of Empires

Mary Roberts and Jocelyn Hackforth-Jones

This anthology stresses the movement of objects, artists, and iconography across the edges of empires, between European, North African, and Ottoman cultures. Rather than critiquing the stasis and fixity of the colonial stereotype, this volume emphasizes the processes of translation that occur as artists, artworks, and iconographic conventions shift across the boundaries between East and West. From this perspective the borders between cultures are treated not solely as sites of antagonism and constraint, but also as sites of transformation and innovation where resistant indigenous perspectives emerged. The emphasis here is on movements that occur in both directions between Europe and the Near East: on European artists traveling to North Africa and the Ottoman empire as well as Ottoman and Maghrebin artists visiting Europe.

When iconography shifts across these cultural boundaries from one context to another, some surprising connections and cross-fertilizations are revealed. Essays in this anthology explore the implications of such transactions. In Zeynep Çelik's essay, for example, a monument celebrating the French colonial presence in Algiers is an unexpected inspiration for an Ottoman monument in Damascus celebrating modernity and a pan-Islamic identity. Another instance of this shift is to be found in Darcy Grimaldo Grigsby's analysis of an unrealized design celebrating the opening of the Suez Canal, in which a monumental statue of the Egyptian fellaheen emerges as a precedent for the Statue of Liberty in the United States of America. What comes into view as a result of the focus on these processes of exchange are the varying agendas of painters, sculptors, photographers, and architects as well as the distinctive contexts and audiences for their practice. European Orientalist practice is dislodged from its centrality in defining the exotic other, and the focus shifts to Ottoman and Maghrebin artists forging new definitions of self through their encounter with an other – Europe.

As such, this anthology develops the current debate within the field of Orientalist studies wherein the significance of Orientalist visual culture is being reassessed through the recognition of its heterogeneity and susceptibility to reinterpretation beyond the framework of colonial ideology.[1] In recent years there has been a major shift, as Western Orientalist visual culture is resituated within an expanded field that encompasses non-Western artists and patrons. A reassessment of the central terms in the Orientalism debate has gone hand in hand with this crucial project of historical recovery.

These reassessments have not only taken place within the domain of the fine arts, the critique has emerged within a broader field of visual culture that encompasses photographic history, architecture, urban geography, archaeology, and museology. Such has been the impact of this shift in recent years that it would be impossible to exhaustively map the new contours of the field here; however, it is important to mention some of these to indicate the diverse range of concerns that they encompass. In art history, recent studies of Algeria and Ottoman Turkey have encompassed indigenous as well as European artists and patrons. Emphasizing the divergent outcomes of the colonial encounter in French North Africa, Roger Benjamin's research brings colonial cultural institutions into dialog with the work of contemporaneous Algerian artists.[2] Such considerations of local responses to imported European culture are further evident in recent exhibitions and books emerging from Istanbul which address the very different political circumstances of Ottoman Turkey. For instance, in Semra Germaner and Zeynep İnankur's book on art in nineteenth-century Istanbul and in numerous exhibitions held at the Topkapı Palace Museum, the work of European artists is analyzed in conjunction with changing traditions within Ottoman painting, and both are considered in relation to the patronal influence of the Ottoman court.[3] Photography has also been subject to such revisionary approaches in recent years, being analyzed as not exclusively a technology of European colonial authority but also a vehicle for indigenous self-expression. Fred Bohrer's exhibition of Sevruguin's photographs of Qajar Iran and Bahattin Öztuncay's monograph on one of the key photographers to the Ottoman court, Vassilaki Kargopoulo, exemplify such revisionary approaches.[4] In the field of architecture and urban geography the impact on the built environment of struggles between local cultural traditions and colonial ideologies is examined by scholars such as Zeynep Çelik in her studies of Istanbul and Algeria and by Mark Crinson's comparative analysis of Egypt, Palestine, and Turkey.[5] Nineteenth-century Eyptology has also been subject to such reassessments. Donald Malcolm Reid, for instance, explores the connections between Egyptology and an emergent Egyptian nationalism through a study of previously neglected nineteenth-century Egyptian archaeologists.[6] Nineteenth-century museology is another area in which such debates about the transplantation and modification of European institutions and ideas have been influential. This has been explored, for example, by Wendy Shaw in her book analyzing the ways in which selectively imported museological practices were modified to articulate Ottoman identity in late nineteenth-century Istanbul.[7]

There is much to be learnt from the transposition of ideas from one disciplinary field to another. Such a strategy has been exemplified in the writing of Zeynep Çelik, who seeks to draw together a series of case studies from diverse mediums and geographical contexts.[8] In her essays, distinctive colonial projects are counterpointed with diverse strategies of "speaking back" in such a way that each is utilized to illuminate the others while, at the same time, the complexities of their particular manifestations are kept in view. Recent anthologies, such as *Orientalism Transposed* and *Orientalism's Interlocutors*, have been instrumental in orchestrating these cross-disciplinary dialogs by drawing together a diverse range of scholars. The first reassesses the history of the Easternization of Britain and the latter instigates a focus on indigenous adaptations of European conventions of representation and initiates new directions in the study of gender and Orientalism.[9]

Edges of Empire continues this strategy of innovative interdisciplinary dialog by contributing to these debates through a focus on the nexus between modernization, modernism, and the cultural politics of empire. In the nineteenth and early twentieth centuries, North Africa and the Middle East experienced profound social change as a result of an engagement with European modernity. Whether through external imposition in a colonial context, or by a self-determined engagement, cultures of the Middle East responded by adapting, appropriating, or resisting modernizing processes that largely came from the West. Such profound social changes, which impacted in particular on the major urban centers of

Algiers, Istanbul, Alexandria, and Cairo, are rarely represented in Western Orientalist imagery, which tended to favor a vision of a timeless and exotic East (itself the antithesis of the upheavals experienced in the European metropolitan centers). As a consequence, in the realm of the visual arts, the very act of representing the processes of modernizing reform within Islamic cultures had the potential to challenge exotic stereotypes.[10]

In various ways, essays in this volume extend further this exploration of the relationship between processes of modernization and visual culture. Across this anthology there is a sustained focus on the urban centers of Istanbul, Alexandria, and Cairo as key sites of change in the nineteenth century. In the essays by Çelik and Grigsby, memorials as markers of place are interpreted as a response to the changing identities of key urban centers in the region. Similarly, contested views of the city of Istanbul emerge through Fred Bohrer's analysis of representations of the well-known pleasure grounds of the city. By investigating divergent local definitions of place, essays in this volume make a significant contribution to our understanding of contested spatial histories of the region.

Changing definitions of the self (of both the individual and the state) were enmeshed in these processes of modernization and they find expression through visual culture. In Ottoman Turkey for example, as Wendy Shaw argues, in the Tanzimat era of reform, "new modes of cultural self-identification [were invented] that would naturalize and nativize these reforms for an increasingly inclusive body of citizenry and increasingly exclusive formulation of the national ideal."[11] To date, the role of visual culture in mediating reform within Maghrebin and Ottoman societies has received relatively little scholarly attention. Çelik identifies precisely such a nativizing of the reform process in her essay here on the Ottoman monument to the telegraph tower in Damascus, which celebrates this modernizing reform while simultaneously articulating an invented pan-Islamic, shared Ottoman identity. Competing definitions of identity are a consistent theme throughout this anthology, again coming into focus in the private realm of the Ottoman harem in the essays by Mary Roberts and Reina Lewis. Roberts analyzes cultural cross-dressing as a mechanism for articulating contested claims for identity. Pushing the debate about cultural cross-dressing across the boundaries between East and West, Roberts reveals some surprising results, particularly in her analysis of the highly educated "modernized" elite Ottoman women who, through cross-dressing, parody the Western harem stereotype, thereby refuting a self-consolidating Western Orientalist identity. Reina Lewis develops her intensive studies of women's Orientalism in her essay here on Ottoman women's harem literature which reveals the ways in which, for these writers, an engagement with Europe became a vehicle for dissent and critique of their own culture.

A study of modernizing processes carries with it implications about the modernizing culture's relationship to tradition. A number of the essays in this anthology expand our understanding of the role of Orientalist representations in redefining tradition. This can entail an engagement with a culture's own past, or that of other cultures through which self-definition is forged. Roger Benjamin, for example, analyzes the function of historical reconstruction through a study of the representation of Moorish Andalusian history at the Paris Exposition of 1900 which, as he argues, became the focus for projected anxieties about contemporary French colonialism in Algiers. This claim on Moorish tradition is counterpointed with the celebration of Islamic Moorish Andalusian heritage in the art of the Maghrebin painter Mohammed Racim. What becomes clear through this analysis is that the expression of tradition is as riven with complexities as the processes of modernization. Sally MacDonald addresses the contemporary dimensions of such problems from the point of view of a museum professional assessing museological practices at the Petrie Museum in London. Acknowledging that displays of ancient Near Eastern artifacts in this small London museum are intimately bound up with the museum's colonial history and persistent Orientalist stereotypes of the contemporary Near and Middle East, McDonald faces the challenge of how to present alternate narratives of ancient history. Through this dual contemporary and historical focus, these essays establish the complex ways that traditions are transmuted, refashioned, or invented to serve present cultural and political agendas.

Just as this volume explores the ramifications of modernizing processes beyond the Western metropolis, so it also analyzes the refracted influence of modernism. Modernism continues to be one of the most hotly contested terms within art-historical studies in general. In recent years, one of the most potent challenges to received histories of European avant-garde visual culture has come from a post-colonial perspective. This standpoint critiques the view that prioritizes formal innovation over political contextual considerations and valorizes a teleological interpretation of an emergent avant-garde in Europe. A post-colonial analysis also questions a reductive approach to modernism that persistently dismisses regional modernisms as derivative and belated. The dynamic which privileges esthetic developments in European centers over cultures on the periphery is so defining in this sphere of art-historical inquiry that even those sympathetic to post-colonial critiques often inadvertently perpetuate the reductive assessment or occlusion of regional modernisms. Yet the challenge is not just to include modernist practices that emerged in Turkey, Algeria, or Japan in the histories of avant-garde practice in Paris (and later New York), but also to rethink the very terms through which canonical status is secured.[12] The challenge, as Benjamin puts it in his book, *Orientalist Aesthetics*, is how to recontextualize "modernism from the periphery."[13] Alastair Wright engages with this question in his essay in the present volume through an analysis of Turkish modernism. Not only analyzing the process of this shift in focus, Wright's essay actually stages this shift, from questions determined at the center to an inquiry that accounts for the priorities of a local Turkish context of reception for modernist practices.

Moving across geographical boundaries and traversing the edges of disciplinary practices, this anthology questions key assumptions that have long held sway within the Orientalism debate. As the essays in this volume highlight, a movement out from the center to the peripheries not only broadens the parameters of discussion, it also enables a reassessment of the terrain itself through the introduction of unfamiliar players and their divergent perspectives. In distinctive ways each of the essays in this volume takes up this challenge of how to interpret visual cultures from the periphery, in turn prompting us to reinterpret the center from the edges of empire.

* * *

In her essay, Zeynep Çelik addresses the question of cultural influence across cultural boundaries, across the edges of empires, and in doing so enables us to expand our definition of modernism in relation to architecture and city planning. Çelik achieves this via a case study that focuses on the refracted influence of design ideas from French colonial Algiers to the Ottoman empire. Significantly it was Viollet-le-Duc's non-modernist monument celebrating the visit of Napoleon III to Algiers in 1865, an unrealized project that has been sidelined in the oeuvre of this French modernist architect, which inspired an Ottoman monument that celebrated modernity: the telegraph tower in Marja Square, Damascus, in 1904.

The symbolism of Viollet-le-Duc's eclectic design, mixing French and Islamic forms, articulated Napoleon III's aspirations towards a *royaume arabe.* Napoleon's policies refashioned French imperial rule through the exercise of principles of reconciliation, protection, and association and yet it continued to affirm hierarchical relations between French colonizers and their subject peoples. By contrast, the later Ottoman monument in Damascus responded to the very different political needs of an Ottoman empire asserting its shared bonds under Islam while embracing modern technology in an effort to rejuvenate itself. This monument, heralding such a vital form of modern communication (the telegraph), affirmed the pan-Islamic sentiments of its commissioner, Ottoman Sultan Abdülhamid II, while also articulating the importance of the empire on the world stage. As Çelik argues, the combined symbolic references inscribed on the telegraph tower monument signal the empire's embrace of modern technology and the shared Islamic affiliations of territory within the Ottoman empire.

Çelik indicates that, significantly, this is not so much an act of appropriation of French architectural forms as their reinterpretation. Through this case study of traveling iconography, Çelik argues for a more encompassing definition of modernism in architecture and city planning, moving beyond familiar Western parameters toward a "dialectical process" that operates "across physical and social space to reveal hitherto ignored links."

Darcy Grimaldo Grigsby also engages with the implications of traveling iconography in her study of the little-known Egyptian precedent for Bartholdi's famous Statue of Liberty. As with Çelik's monument, it is an unrealized project developed in one context that is transmuted into another project serving alternative political agendas. Grigsby tracks a surprising lineage from a proposed monumental sculpted Egyptian fellaheen form, intended as a lighthouse (to celebrate the opening of the Suez Canal), to the Statue of Liberty in New York. That is, a remarkable shift from "fellah" to "liberty." The proposed Egyptian statue, and its failure to materialize, provides the occasion for the analysis of a confluence of concerns; these include the desires and frustrations of the artist. In the political arena, the priorities of the Egyptian patron Khedive Ismaïl Pasha clearly excluded the kind of statuary Bartholdi was planning. Most interestingly, it appears that the connotations of the original drawing of the Egyptian fellaheen, its associations with an ancient, unchanging, and static Egypt, made it an unsuitable precedent for the figure of Liberty, and this is perhaps one reason why the connection between the two projects has not been in the public domain until recently. Another is clearly political. Bartholdi himself contested an accusation that he had clandestinely and opportunistically recycled "a failed Egyptian project into an American success."

When one considers modernization as a theme, Bartholdi's monumental, frozen image of the fellaheen has a complex relationship to the feat of modern engineering it was designed to celebrate. As Grigsby argues, the proposed statue of the fellaheen celebrated the Suez Canal and yet masked the Egyptian labor so crucial in the early years of its construction. After 1863, the 40,000 fellaheen initially enlisted as indentured labor to dig the canal were supplanted by machinery. Grigsby argues that "modernization had exploited fellaheen labor but it had also moved beyond it. To be fully realized technologically, the remapping of Egypt required the loss of its 'slaves' and the return of the fellaheen to their 'timeless' role as agricultural workers." The visual arts participated in this remapping. Grigsby finds a striking parallel between Bartholdi's proposed monument, with its relationship to site, and Charles Landelle's painting of the fellah woman (acting as guard or hostess) positioned above a relief map of the Suez Canal at the 1867 Paris exhibition. Both representations of the fellaheen promised a timeless representation, sublimating the role of the fellah in the recent history of the canal's construction, as they functioned to celebrate this landmark feat of modernization.

Grigsby's nuanced account emphasizes the limitations of the various media in which Bartholdi worked and the processes of translation between them. It is this emphasis on the processes of translation that allows for other resistant voices to be registered: the laughter of the fellaheen that thwarted the artist's efforts to still action into monumental form, and the vulnerability of photography "to the agency of other persons." But, above all others, it is Ismaïl Pasha's refusal to commission the sculpture that is the most powerful act of resistance.

These two essays by Çelik and Grigsby provoke a reassessment of the political interpretation of monuments to empire because they challenge us to consider their mutable significance in Ottoman territories. Recent writings have explored the symbolism of monuments in the European imperial capitals, for example Tim Barringer's analysis of the Albert Memorial in London as an expression of Victorian imperial ideals.[14] Other writers have explored the significance of monuments in colonial cities, for example Zeynep Çelik's important study of the contested history of the Place d'Armes in Algiers. The placement of the statue of the Duke of Orleans in this square in 1845 was a powerful symbol of French colonial rule, and equally significant was the counterclaim to the space with the statue's removal in 1962 following Algerian independence. Çelik examines the way memory and identity were contested in these claims and counterclaims between colonizer and colonized in the struggle to redefine the urban topography of Algiers.[15] A very different power dynamic is, however, addressed by Çelik and Grigsby in their essays for this anthology because they are dealing with Ottoman patrons for the monuments they analyze. Rather than focus exclusively on mutually defining relations between colonizer and colonized, Çelik here examines the participation of the Ottoman empire in shaping their own "universal imperial iconography... [and thereby] creating a universal culture that belonged to the 'connected world of empires.'"

Mary Roberts's essay provides another intriguing contribution to our understanding of the processes of identity formation through cultural exchange in her analysis of Ottomans and European Orientalists engaged in the practice of cultural cross-dressing. Recent post-colonial writers have explored European cultural cross-dressing as a means of establishing the authority of the Western traveler in the East.[16] Roberts extends this further by considering Ottoman engagement with this sartorial strategy as a playful and parodic response to Western misconceptions of Ottoman culture. Three case studies reveal the complexities of these processes of cross-gender and cross-cultural engagement.

In her first case study, Roberts analyzes the mythology that developed around the British painter John Frederick Lewis resulting from William Makepeace Thackeray's account of the artist's life in Cairo in the 1840s. Thackeray's text describes the transformation of the British dandy into a venerable eastern Bey, ensconced in a traditional Ottoman house. Roberts argues that it is the performative element of metropolitan dandyism which enables Lewis to so effectively assume his Oriental guise. She explores the utility of this myth of the Eastern Lewis within art-historical literature, where an uncritical reiteration of Thackeray's account has established the veracity of the artist's Eastern paintings as a result of his presumed intimacy with harem life. This powerful myth, which ensures the authority of the British artist and provides an imaginary point of identification for other British men, is counterpointed with Roberts's second case study – the astonishing tale of a harem parody recounted in the diary of British harem governess Emmeline Lott.

In this instance Western men visiting Constantinople became the target of an elaborate charade. Convinced that they had bribed one of the eunuchs to gain access to the sultan's harem, the British gentlemen were instead duped by eunuchs masquerading as odalisques. Here the gap between performer and performance reinforces the distance between the

Western fantasy of the sultan's seraglio and the household of the venerated Ottoman dynasty. According to Lott's account, this humorous cross-gender performance was designed by Kaleb, one of the eunuchs at the Ottoman court, in order to profit financially from the duped Englishmen while also exacting a symbolic revenge for the transgressions of that other famous traveler, Richard Burton. Burton's cross-cultural disguise had enabled him to violate Islamic religious customs by penetrating the sacred cities of Mecca and Medina. By retelling this parody in her published travelogue, Lott emphasizes her privilege as an intermediary between the secluded world of the harem and the world beyond its boundaries. Surprisingly, this Englishwoman allies herself with the harem eunuchs as she delights in this parody of her countrymen who fantasized about visiting harems. Yet another parodic response to Western attitudes is evident in Roberts's third case study of an intriguing pair of photographs of the Ottoman Egyptian Princess Nazli Hanım. This time it is a harem woman herself who utilizes the strategies of gendered and cultural cross-dressing. Nazli's honorific portrait in contemporary European fashion presents a resolutely modern image of the princess, thus implicitly resisting the Western harem stereotype which Nazli more explicitly parodies in the companion photograph where she assumes the guise of harem master.

These sartorial parodies from inside the elite harems of Constantinople and Cairo highlight a sophisticated understanding of the West and its preconceptions of Ottoman culture. In an intriguing twist, inhabiting the Western stereotype becomes a vehicle for indigenous agency. Rather than refute the Western stereotype, Princess Nazli and the harem eunuchs in Lott's tale defuse its power through parody, thereby usurping the position of mastery. In effect the stereotype becomes masquerade.

Like Roberts, Reina Lewis considers ways in which Ottoman women contested Orientalist knowledge and manipulated Western cultural codes. In her essay, Lewis examines a range of Ottoman women's harem writings published in Europe from the 1870s to the early years of the Turkish Republic. This is an eclectic selection of texts that interweave autobiography with fiction. Empowered by the process of writing, these Ottoman authors often consciously addressed their writings to two distinct audiences in Britain and Turkey. As Lewis characterizes it, these authors represented harem life to a Western audience, addressing their preconceptions, which were based on fantasies of claustration and erotic intrigue, while simultaneously engaging with local Ottoman debates about the changing social circumstances for Ottoman women as a result of modernization.

Both Roberts and Lewis consider the profound changes that were taking place inside the elite Ottoman harems by the late nineteenth century as a result of the increasing engagement with European culture, and explore ways in which these are represented to the West (or alternatively suppressed for strategic purposes). The responses of these Ottoman women are varied and inventive. These include Lewis's visually evocative image of the heavily veiled Zeynep and Melek Hanım submissively greeting the French writer Loti in their "borrowed" traditional Ottoman apartment, deliberately choosing not to assert their "modern" metropolitan identity. Instead they manipulated Loti by appealing to the European stereotype of the traditional Turkish *hanım*. This performance has its parallels with the eunuchs' masquerade for the duped Englishmen in Roberts's essay. Both of these studies emphasize the richness of this material and the sophisticated levels of cross-cultural engagement undertaken by harem inhabitants.

Lewis extends her inquiry to consider the author function in relation to the cultural authority of these texts and the particular challenges this raises for feminist analysis. For a Western audience, the authority and veracity of a harem testament was premised on the secure cultural identity of its author. Lewis is particularly drawn to those texts with disputed and unverifiable authorship because they reveal the particular contours and investments of this genre. In examining them, she addresses the vital issue of how one deals with sources that slip between the cracks of conventional historical evidence.

The author Vaka Brown, a woman of Greek Christian family who grew up as an Ottoman subject, provides a fascinating example of the way the reception history of this harem literature is caught up in differing definitions of Ottoman identity. Vaka Brown's Ottoman identity was disputed by the Western readership, with its rigid distinctions premised on religious and ethnic identities, whereas her designation as Ottoman was uncontested within Ottoman society because of its broader and more inclusive definition. Even more intriguing are the challenges presented by the uncertain authorial attribution of harem literature published under the designation "Une Circassienne." This limit case enables Lewis to explore the protocols of this genre, and in particular to uncover her own, and other contemporary critical theorists', continuing investment in establishing authenticity.

From a focus on the private realm of the elite Ottoman households in the essays by Roberts and Lewis, we shift to public realm of Istanbul's parks, pleasure grounds, and art museums in the essays by Fred Bohrer and Alastair Wright. As with the other essays in this book, Bohrer and Wright's analyses are written against the idea of a fixed, binary model of cultural exchange, emphasizing instead the processes of movement of people and images across boundaries and the permeability of those borders.

The city of Istanbul, which straddles Europe and Asia, provides a striking geographic metaphor for the meeting of East and West. Precisely how that geography is inscribed in the European and Ottoman imaginary and the disputed nature of such geographic imaginings is the focus for Fred Bohrer's essay. Bohrer courts the complexity of those inscriptions through the analysis of contested Ottoman and European representations of two key sites of leisure: the "Sweet Waters of Asia" and the "Sweet Waters of Europe." Through this analysis, Bohrer reveals the divergent investment of its various claimants and the consequences of such differences for the status of Orientalist representation.

The European naming of these two sites, which privileges binary distinctions between East and West, is counterpointed with Ottoman naming from which such divisions are absent. This divergent logic is reiterated in the realm of visual representation. European artists expressed a clear exoticizing preference for the site on the Asian shore of Istanbul, whereas the Abdülhamid II albums, an Ottoman project to present a modernized image of the empire, privileged the Sweet Waters of Europe. Similarly the representation of the Sweet Waters of Asia as an Orientalist pleasure ground, exemplified for Bohrer in the art of Wittmer and the writing of Gautier, is resisted by the Ottoman Sébah's prosaic photographic representation of the architecture of the site, in which local inhabitants stare confrontingly at the viewer.

Further complexities emerge when Bohrer considers distinctions between the representations of the site by the German painter and the French writer. Wittmer's "Sweet Waters" is an aristocratic leisure ground where European and Ottoman elites mingle. It is a souvenir of Crown Prince Maximilian's visit and, with its inclusion of Europeans and emphasis on cultural mixing, it is markedly different from Gautier's representation of the "Sweet Waters" as a voyeuristic pageant, an "open-air harem" for the European male. Bohrer argues for a more encompassing examination of European Orientalism that does not exclusively focus on Britain and France and instead attends to the distinctions between the various different European Orientalisms, thereby "enlarging the scope of European renderings."

Bohrer's analysis of these divergent representations not only addresses the partial and incomplete imaging of the site but also reflects on the epistemological status of Orientalist representation, arguing that it is "incomplete as representation." Here complex distinctions across a range of media undermine the claim of each particular medium to a self-sufficient realism. As Bohrer argues, this play of difference reveals the insufficiency and incommensurability of each medium.

Alastair Wright's essay is about journeying and border crossings as he tracks the emergence of Turkish modernism in the art of Mehmet Ruhi Arel and his artistic circle, the "Generation of 1914." This essay focuses on transformations across the cultural boundaries of Turkey and Europe with this group of Turkish artists who fray a path between European modernism and local tradition. The richly allusive narrative style that Wright mixes with a more conventional art-historical voice suggests that this essay is about a confluence of journeys – historical and theoretical as well as artistic. Confronted by a photograph of Ruhi and his compatriots in Paris in 1909, Wright is prompted to ask several key questions that frame his journey of inquiry into their modernist practice: "What, then, did it mean for Ruhi, born on the shores of the Bosphorus, to travel to Paris, to learn his craft at the epicenter of advanced European art? What was at stake as he painted the *Stonebreakers* in the first year of the republic? What are we to make of this translation from one culture to another?" Wright moves us through a range of different answers to these questions.

In the movement of his prose, we witness Wright's own journey from an imperative to interpret Ruhi's art, and Turkish modernist painting, via European modernist precedents, to an approach that focuses on processes of translation within a Turkish context of production and reception for this art. This is a shift from discerning the imitative relation of Ruhi's *Stonebreakers* to European precedents in the art of Courbet, Millet, and Cézanne, to a consideration of its significance for a Turkish audience in the context of shifting attitudes towards Western cultural influence.

For artists in Istanbul in these crucial transitional years of the formation of the republic, an engagement with European modernist painting is bound up with debates about nationalism and attitudes to European culture operating in a dialectic that vacillates between selective embrace and strategic refusal. One of the intriguing insights of Wright's analysis is that the imperative to assert a clear divide between East and West, in this instance, was coming from the Turkish side of this cultural divide. Such distinctions took place against the backdrop of a long history of cultural exchange as the nationalists sought to distance themselves from the late nineteenth-century Ottoman sultans, whom they perceived as detrimentally "Europhilic" in their cultural and political allegiances.

In the subject and style of Ruhi's art, Wright discerns processes of translation into the vernacular in response to the circumstances of the newly formed Turkish republic. The role of visual culture in national identity is at stake here, as Turkish artists were called upon to respond to a strong desire to "imagine a visual language free of foreign accents." And yet, as Wright argues, Ruhi's art continues to echo other voices in a polysemy that cannot be contained by a single language: "even as it pushes towards an essentialized national identity, it speaks otherwise." A similar complexity is discernible in the temporality of this art, which claims to speak an "unchanging Turkish idiom" and yet does so through a language of the modern. This collation of the timeless and modern, Wright argues, typifies the rhetoric of nation-building.

It is significant that the first port of call for Wright's imaginary journey is the Museum of Painting and Sculpture in Istanbul. In this, Wright invites us to reflect upon the museum as a context for our encounter with visual culture. This emphasis on museology and the cultural priorities articulated through practices of display becomes the focus for essays by Sally MacDonald and Roger Benjamin. As a museum curator, MacDonald brings a different perspective to these issues, which are addressed via empiric studies of audience reactions to the archaeological representation of Egypt at the Petrie Museum in London. She outlines the problems in European perceptions of ancient Egypt as well as analyzing curatorial strategies for conveying alternate historical narratives.

Like Darcy Grimaldo Grigsby's study, Sally MacDonald's essay engages with European perceptions of ancient Egypt as a static and unchanging culture. MacDonald, however, raises the issue of the way in which contemporary non-African audiences at the Petrie Museum regard modern Egypt via the lens of ancient Egypt (resulting in striking stereotypes). MacDonald notes the tendency to perceive ancient Egypt as an appropriated, largely Western heritage with little connection made between ancient and modern Egypt. Such persisting European responses today, as emphasized by Donald Malcolm Reid, remind us that archaeology and imperialism have long operated in tandem, and that contemporary responses to ancient Egypt have earlier resonances. From the nineteenth century, Egyptology was largely, although not exclusively, the preserve of Europeans in whose studies an exclusive focus on ancient Egypt occluded both Islamic and modern Egypt.[17] In a broader sense, fantasies of Egypt's past acted as a lens for encounters with the present. Thus, upon coming ashore in Egypt, in one vast exotic sweep, Florence Nightingale was able to imagine herself in the land of the pharaohs, the Bible, the Greeks and the Romans, the Quran, and the Arabian Nights.[18]

Many of the examples in the following essays, drawn from archaeology, architectural monuments, sculpture, painting, and photography, put perceptual processes under critical scrutiny, in particular examining the immediacy of the visual. In his book *Orientalism and Visual Culture* Fred Bohrer invokes Riegl's notion of "age-value" to describe the way in which objects "speak" to the viewer across the ages by seemingly making themselves immediately accessible to perception "in a way prior to any scholarly knowledge or conventional education."[19] Sally MacDonald examines the contemporary legacy of this mode of apprehending ancient objects that emerged in the nineteenth century. She observes that the modern museum visitor, who experiences a sense of wonderment on viewing antiquities, uncritically apprehends them as part of a shared European heritage, and refuses to make connections with contemporary Egyptian culture. MacDonald notes that such preconceptions have been fueled by Hollywood films, Bible stories, and computer games.

MacDonald argues that, in order to challenge such powerful preconceptions amongst much of the museum's European audience, the museum's strategic plan now includes within its target audiences groups hitherto largely excluded: that is, Egyptians, Sudanese, and people of African descent. MacDonald's project at the Petrie Museum has been to research these perceptions and address such limited understandings through audience research specifically including black African and Egyptian responses to the exhibit. She also outlines other strategies, such as the inclusion of indigenous expertise in the editing of catalog entries for the thousands of Coptic and Islamic objects. Egyptian scholars collaborate with British curators, thereby assisting their understanding of the nuances of contemporary meanings of objects. This essay also reinscribes the long history of black scholarship on ancient Egypt and its relationship to the rest of Africa. Afro-Caribbean and Egyptian outreach staff act as intermediaries to explain the exhibit to diverse audiences, with the result that participants are made aware of the vital link between ancient and modern cultures in Egypt and the Sudan. Finally, interventions by artists, such as the Egyptian novelist Ahdah Souef, act as a powerful tool for engaging the participation of visitors and invite them to question the role of history, and of archaeology itself, in the formation of the exhibit. Such a project has wide ramifications extending beyond museum education to the National Curriculum (where the stereotypes of ancient Egypt are insufficiently challenged).

Roger Benjamin takes up questions about the politics of display in his essay on the historical reconstruction of *Andalusia in the Time of the Moors* orchestrated by entrepreneur J. H. Roseyro for the Paris Exposition of 1900. The temporal collisions that occur within this historical reconstruction are highlighted, and Benjamin characterizes the effect of this fairground mélange as a "lamination of time." Errors of chronology that suffuse the display are interpreted symptomatically, thus revealing a web of intersecting political investments. Benjamin's richly contextualized analysis addresses French and Spanish as well as Maghrebin cultural identities.

The collage of architectural references to Moorish culture at Roseyro's *Andalusia* enabled visitors to be imaginatively transported to another place and time, and the site was enlivened by a series of performances included to provide local flavor. An eclectic range of references were at play. Contemporary Maghrebins (French colonial subjects) were involved as actors in events that ranged from Muslim cortèges and Catholic processions to fantasias, tournaments between Moors and Christian knights, Gypsy marriages, and gazelle hunts. As Benjamin argues, these events were drawing on continuing, long-standing Spanish traditions of symbolic representation of the struggle between Christian and Muslim powers as well as being inflected with contemporary French North African colonial politics.

The contemporary concerns of empire met historical reconstruction in this pavilion, but they did so in such a way that some surprising displacements and disruptions are evident. Medieval Moorish Andalusia was far removed from the concerns of the modern French empire and yet its representation at the 1900 exhibition is, according to Benjamin, a manifestation of imperial "bad conscience." The performance reconstruction became a screen for projecting anxieties about colonization, including a romantic nostalgia for a lost era. This mourning for the lost time of the Moors at some level inscribes colonial regret through a recognition that "imperial expansion entails the destruction or mutation of cultures potentially richer than those that replace them." The figure of Boabdil, the last Moorish king of Granada, emerges as a powerful distillation of these mixed sentiments of triumph, nostalgia, and loss within French culture.

An actor dressed as Boabdil presided over events at the reconstructed *Andalusia*; in doing so he functioned as an uncanny witness to events. As Benjamin points out, Boabdil was a particularly resonant figure within French culture. He could function as an allegory of the submission of Islamic forces of the Maghreb to contemporary French armies. However, he also had the potential to evoke cultural sympathy rather than imperial triumph, as is evident in Dehodencq's painting of this historical figure in 1868.

Benjamin's essay is an imaginative reconstruction of this ephemeral event, exploring its historical and contemporary resonances within French and Spanish culture. Benjamin also pushes this idea further by invoking contemporaneous Maghrebin historical imaginings of Moorish Andalusia. The defiant triumphalism of the first caliph of Cordoba, Abderrahman, celebrated in the art of the Algerian painter Mohammed Racim, forms a powerful counterpoint to French nostalgia for the last caliph, Boabdil, from whom power slips away and whose defeat signaled the end of Moorish rule in southern Spain. Racim's painterly reconstructions of Moorish Spain are symptomatic of an alternate view of this history, a nostalgia amongst Maghrebins for the loss of Al-Andaluz to the Spanish, for whom this period was seen as a golden age of Moorish culture. Such claims for tradition were crucial in articulating modern notions of pan-Islamic and Algerian national identity. The complex interweaving of French, Spanish, and Maghrebin claims on medieval Moorish history in Benjamin's essay is indicative of the contested visual histories that this anthology addresses.

The essays in this volume share a commitment to re-examine what Bayly and Fawaz have referred to, in another context, as the "connected world of empires."[20] That is to say, these essays uncover connections between cultures that have been overlooked when focus is narrowly constrained with the parameters of European imperial culture. In particular, each of these essays examines the role of visual culture in managing the impact of modernization on European, Ottoman, and Maghrebin cultures, whether that be through a redefinition of tradition or through a refashioning of individual and collective identities. As a consequence, what comes into view are unfamiliar definitions of individuals, nations, and supranational identities through visual culture, and European visual culture no longer has a privileged hold on our understanding of the processes of modernization in the nineteenth and early twentieth centuries. By resituating European responses to modernity within a broader network of relations between North African and Ottoman cultures, the essays in this anthology work to reshape our understanding of the visual cultures of modernity.

Notes

1 This body of literature is now quite extensive. For a summary of these debates and some of the major contributors see Jill Beaulieu and Mary Roberts, "Orientalism's Interlocutors," in J. Beaulieu and M. Roberts (eds.), *Orientalism's Interlocutors: Painting, Architecture, Photography* (Durham, NC: Duke University Press, 2002), 1–18, especially the section "Rethinking Interlocution."

2 R. Benjamin, *Orientalist Aesthetics: Art, Colonialism, and French North Africa, 1880–1930* (Berkeley: University of California Press, 2003).

3 S. Germaner and Z. İnankur, *Constantinople and the Orientalists* (Istanbul: İşbank, 2002); *The Sultan's Portrait: Picturing the House of Osman*, Topkapı Palace Museum (Istanbul: İşbank, 2000); D. Bull et al., *An Eyewitness of the Tulip Era: Jean-Baptiste Vanmour*, Topkapı Palace Museum and Rijksmuseum (Istanbul: Koçbank, 2003).

4 F. N. Bohrer (ed.), *Sevruguin and the Persian Image: Photographs of Iran, 1870–1930* (Washington, DC: Arthur M. Sackler Gallery, Smithsonian Institution, 1999); B. Öztuncay, *Vassilaki Kargopoulo: Photographer to His Majesty the Sultan* (Istanbul: Birieşik Oksijen Sanayi A. Ş., 2000).

5 Z. Çelik, *The Remaking of Istanbul: Portrait of an Ottoman City in the Nineteenth Century* (Berkeley: University of California Press, 1993); Z. Çelik, *Urban Forms and Colonial Confrontations: Algiers under French Rule* (Berkeley: University of California Press, 1997); M. Crinson, *Empire Building: Orientalism and Victorian Architecture* (London: Routledge, 1996).

6 D. M. Reid, *Whose Pharaohs? Archaeology, Museums and Egyptian National Identity from Napoleon to World War I* (Berkeley: University of California Press, 2002).

7 W. M. K. Shaw, *Possessors and Possessed: Museums, Archaeology, and the Visualization of History in the Late Ottoman Empire* (Berkeley: University of California Press, 2003).

8 See Z. Çelik, "Colonialism, Orientalism and the Canon," *Art Bulletin*, 78/2 (1996), 201–5; Z. Çelik, "Speaking Back to Orientalist Discourse," in Beaulieu and Roberts (eds.), *Orientalism's Interlocutors*, 26–31.

9 J. F. Codell and D. S. Macleod (eds.), *Orientalism Transposed: The Impact of the Colonies on British Culture* (Aldershot: Ashgate, 1998); Beaulieu and Roberts (eds.), *Orientalism's Interlocutors.*

10 See Çelik, "Speaking Back to Orientalist Discourse."

11 Shaw, *Possessors and Possessed*, 18.

12 For an analysis of the impact of such debates on art in South-East Asia see J. Clark, *Modern Asian Art* (Sydney: Craftsman House, 1998), especially the introduction (pp. 11–27).

13 Benjamin, *Orientalist Aesthetics*, 3.

14 T. Barringer, "Imperial Visions: Responses to India and Africa in Victorian Art and Design," in J. Mackenzie (ed.), *The Victorian Vision: Inventing New Britain* (London: V&A Publications, 2001), 315–16. Nineteenth-century monuments to empire are integrally connected to processes of nation-building through civic monuments and memorials, such as the phenomenon of *statuomanie* in France. *Statuomanie* was the term coined to characterize the proliferation of monuments to French artists and other celebrated citizens, which served as "rallying points, binding the individual to the collectivity." N. McWilliam, "*Objets retrouvés*," *Art History*, 10 (1987), 113. See also J. Beaulieu, "'Voice of the People': The Monument to Corot at Ville-d'Avray," *Australian Journal of Art*, 8 (1996), 57–80, and N. Green, "Monuments, Memorials and the Framing of Individualism in Third Republic France," *New Formations*, 1 (1987), 127–43.

15 Z. Çelik, "Colonial/Postcolonial Intersections: *Lieux de mémoire* in Algiers," *Third Text*, 49 (Winter 1999/2000), 63–72.

16 G. C.-L. Low, "White Skins/Black Masks: The Pleasures and Politics of Imperialism," *New Formations*, 9 (Winter 1989), 83–103; D. S. Macleod, "Cross-Cultural Cross-Dressing: Class, Gender and Modernist Sexual Identity," in Codell and Macleod (eds.), *Orientalism Transposed*, 63–85; M. Garber, "The Chic of Araby: Transvestism and the Erotics of Cultural Appropriation," in *Vested Interests: Cross-Dressing and Cultural Anxiety* (New York: Routledge, 1997), 304–52; I. E. Boer, "This Is Not the Orient: Theory and Postcolonial Practice," in M. Bal and I. E. Boer (eds.), *The Point of Theory: Practices of Cultural Analysis* (Amsterdam: Amsterdam University Press, 1994), 211–19.

17 Reid, *Whose Pharaohs?*

18 Ibid. 2.

19 F. Bohrer, *Orientalism and Visual Culture: Imagining Mesopotamia in Nineteenth Century Europe* (Cambridge: Cambridge University Press, 2003), 2.

20 C. A. Bayly and L. T. Fawaz (eds.), *Modernity and Culture: From the Mediterranean to the Indian Ocean* (New York: Columbia University Press, 2002), 1. We are indebted to Zeynep Çelik for introducing us to this term, which so elegantly encapsulates the extended focus of this anthology.

1

Commemorating the Empire: From Algiers to Damascus

Zeynep Çelik

Nineteenth-century empires constructed complex iconographies to define and disseminate an official image. These "invented traditions" extended to architecture, bringing together a range of references charged with meanings. Due to their visual legibility, which made them easily accessible, buildings served as effective devices to communicate notions of imperial power through symbols. Commemorative structures, the most obvious sites for iconographic messages, participated in the broader enterprise to convey the idea of colonial empires, and the interconnectedness of the nineteenth-century world enabled iconography to travel considerable distances, resulting in collages of fragments from unlikely contexts. The story of an unexecuted design by prominent French architect Eugène-Emmanuel Viollet-le-Duc for Napoleon III, its relationship to architectural theory, and its re-emergence and reinterpretation under the very different conditions of the Ottoman empire shed some light on the invention and recycling of visual symbols for political agendas.

By the time of his second visit to Algeria in 1865, Napoleon III had developed his vision of a *royaume arabe* that called for a significant change from the earlier French policies of military imposition and control. Initially revealed in the emperor's first visit to Algeria in 1860, this shift was influenced by the writings and direct advice of Thomas Ismail Urbain, a Saint-Simonian who served as a government officer in Algeria and who advocated a biracially harmonious society for the colony.[1] Taking a stance against the practice of 35 years of French domination, Napoleon III stated his refusal to treat Arabs as "Indians of North America" and expressed his intention of bringing prosperity to "this intelligent, proud, warrior, and agricultural race." Addressing the French settlers, he said: "Treat the Arabs, amidst whom you must live, as compatriots," because, he declared a few days after his return to France, "Algeria is not a colony...but an Arab kingdom...and I am as much the emperor of Arabs as that of the French."[2]

The relationship would be founded on notions of reconciliation, protection, and association, but it was also obvious to the emperor that a hierarchy should be maintained: "We must be the masters," he continued, "because we are more civilized; we must be generous, because we are stronger."[3] He made his message clear to Algerians when he addressed them: "I want to increase your well-being, to make you participate more and more in the administration of your country as well as the blessings of civilization; but, these depend on conditions, from your side, you will respect those who represent my authority. Say to your lost [*égaré*] brothers that to attempt new insurrections will be fatal for them.... Two million Arabs cannot resist forty million Frenchmen.... As your ruler, I am your protector."[4] In a meticulous choreography, the emperor was welcomed by ceremonies that included Muslims throughout Algeria. To disseminate the message, a long poem by an Arab (in Arabic and French) was commissioned to show the enthusiastic response of Algerians to the idea of *royaume arabe*: "The Arabs said to the Emperor: 'May God keep you victorious! We submitted ourselves to your government, and the love we have for you will never be erased from our hearts.' " And, a few pages later, "I want to live in tranquility under his laws, to be under his wings of an eagle."[5]

Napoleon III's Arab kingdom policy hence adhered to the essence of the *mission civilisatrice*, but reframed it according the Saint-Simonian idea of a racial *rapprochement*, albeit an unequal one. If this concept withered away with the end of his reign, an unrealized architectural project infused with the notion enjoyed a long-term legacy, resurfacing in the early twentieth century in disparate places under different guises and with different agendas. This was a monument to the emperor that would celebrate his visit to Algeria in 1865 and would engrave his special engagement with the colony onto the image of Algiers. Viollet-le-Duc's work was to occupy a prominent site on Place Bresson in front of the Renaissance-style Grand Theater, designed by Frédérick Chassériau and completed in 1853.[6] Right at the juncture of old Algiers with the French quarter, the location was particularly symbolic and the institutions that would complement the cultural expression of the French presence (the theater) were loaded with associations. In addition to the monument to the emperor, Viollet-le-Duc placed the administrative headquarters of Algeria (labeled "Palace of the Governor General" on the site plan, but "Imperial Palace" on another drawing) on the square, cleared the latter from impeding structures in order to endow it with a perfect rectangular shape, renamed it "Place Napoléon," and proposed a palace of justice for the site behind the theater.[7] The entire complex, symmetrical and axial toward the Mediterranean, would meet on the waterfront side the arcades of the newly opened Boulevard de l'Impératrice (named in honor of Empress Eugénie, who had accompanied Napoleon III to Algiers), and terminate in the bastion that descended to the harbor level by sculptural stairs – again, the work of Chassériau.

Viollet-le-Duc had wide-ranging interests and his career as an architect and a theorist displayed an open-minded flexibility. Nevertheless, he is best known in the discourse of modernism as a "structural rationalist," who based his theories on his studies of the medieval architecture of France. He has been celebrated for taking the position that architecture had to be "true to methods of construction," and hence "should employ the materials according to their qualities of properties."[8] His influence is widely associated with his proposal for "a method that would theoretically free architecture from the eclectic irrelevancies of historicism."[9] Innumerable reproductions of his unrealized but technologically forward-looking designs, such as the project for a "concert hall" in iron (ca. 1862), helped reinforce his reputation. Viollet-le-Duc's monument to Napoleon III, which translated the emperor's political message into architecture, does not neatly complement his reputation as a modernist. Diverging from his search for experimental structures articulated in the simple language of new materials, the design harked back to eclecticism in an *architecture parlante.* Perhaps because of its idiosyncrasy and problematic relationship to the architect's oeuvre, the extensive literature on Viollet-le-Duc has overlooked this design.

The project was devised in three stages and the more subdued earlier scheme was progressively developed into a complicated amalgam of symbols in a daring composition. The first design proposed a free-standing monument, with a high cylindrical base on which sat statues of three animals deemed to represent Algeria: the horse, the camel, and the ox. Interspersed between them, three pylons symbolized the three provinces of the colony: Algiers, Oran, and Constantine. In the center, the architect placed a much higher column, topped with an eagle on a sphere from where the soaring figure of Marianne rose.[10] The second project revealed a more complicated monument that introduced "Islamic" elements, acknowledging the Arab Kingdom notion of the emperor. An article in *L'Illustration* put it clearly: "This monument... is designed to remind the acts of the government of the Emperor, who gave the Arabs the advantages and rights they did not possess before the conquest."[11]

Not exactly a triumphal arch, but nevertheless composed of three arches that defined an interior space open on three sides on the lower level, the monument rose up to 44 meters.[12] With its soaring height and prominent positioning on the waterfront, it would dominate the image of Algiers. Its various pieces were cluttered with legible symbols that revealed a great deal about the current political climate. The base brought together cylindrical towers in a generic French medieval military mode with North African Islamic lobed arches, conveying an ambiguous message. On the one hand, this coexistence could be read as a dialog between the two cultures and the two peoples and as an architectural expression of Napoleon III's call to treat Arabs as "compatriots." On the other hand, the juxtaposition between the heavy and imposing French military forms and the delicate and ephemeral lobed arches seemed a reminder of a relationship based on force and hierarchy, underlined by the emperor.

The "conquered wild animals" lying tame on the three towers made a reference to the subjugation of the country, whereas the "domestic" animals, carried over from the first scheme and contrasting in their dynamic forms with the pacified ones, pointed to production in the Algerian countryside – activated by the European settlers.[13] The pillars representing the three provinces of the colony were kept from the initial design, but elongated. The central column, also made taller, was ornamented with three projecting prows. The third and final design brought further elaborations. The pillars were now terminated by three identical "mosques" that still celebrated the three capital cities. Ironically, the architectural model chosen to represent Algerian towns, the miniature buildings with central domes with four pencil minarets, were derived from Ottoman monuments and had no precedents in Algiers, Constantine, and Oran. Marianne was deleted, but the eagle with open wings continued to sit on a sphere that in turn was placed on an enormous capital, and crowned the whole structure, signifying the French empire – an uncanny reminder of the emperor's "wings of an eagle" in the poem quoted above. The column, taken in its entirety,

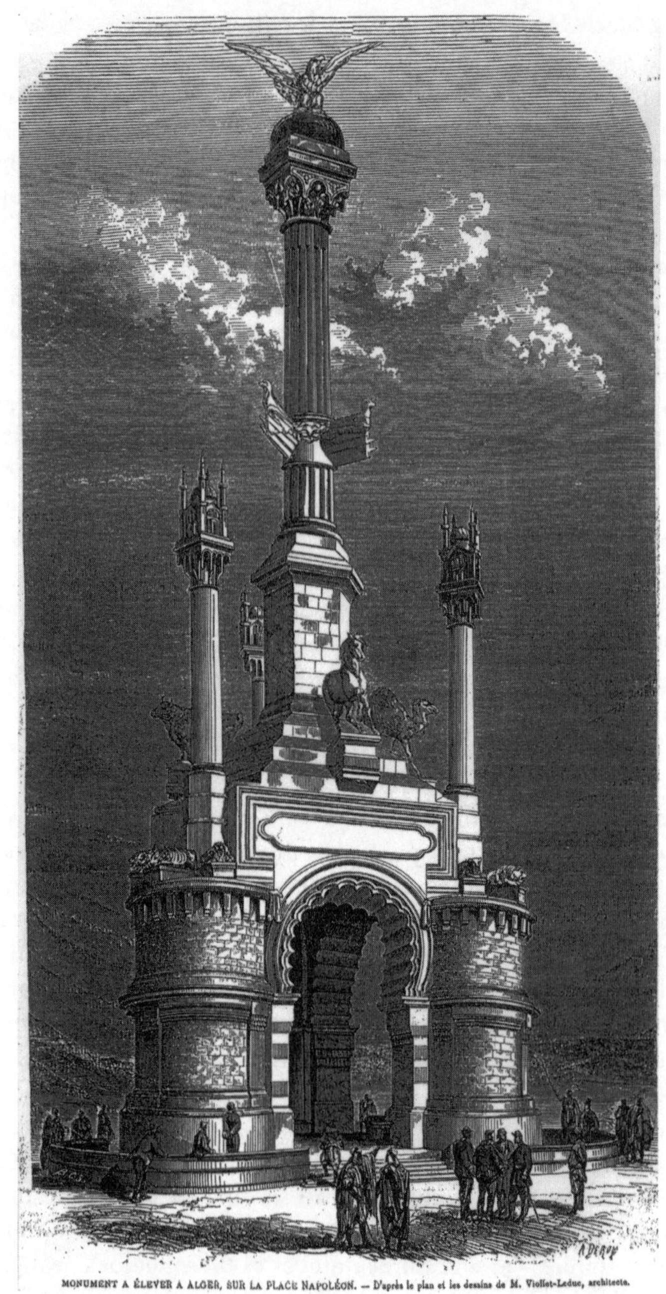

Figure 1.1 Eugène-Emmanuel Viollet-le-Duc, Monument to Napoleon III, Algiers. Drawing (from *L'Illustration*, 1865, 2e semestre)

commemorated "the expedition following which Algeria had become French."[14]

While the "Islamic" character of certain fragments was highly legible, references to local culture were muddled. In accord with the prevailing climate in France and elsewhere in Europe, different historic traditions in areas dominated by Islam were collapsed into a simple kit of forms and combined randomly. The Moorish lobed arches, the Ottoman "mosques," and the hybrid capitals were put together in a most unusual manner, in addition to being integrated into "French" architectural forms in an overall design and a building type that were also decidedly "French." The use of another "typical" element that represented Islam testified further to the uninformed decisions made by the architect: three fountains, placed in the interior space, were intended to be used by Algerians for ablutions before prayer – even though there were no mosques nearby. When hailed in the pages of *L'Illustration*, Viollet-le-Duc's project was described as "a singularly original conception, which owes nothing to Arab architecture, and which nevertheless derives from it a spirit and elegance."[15] The monument to Napoleon III thus epitomized an Orientalist attitude common to various artistic productions, but hitherto not seen in public architecture.[16]

The project had French critics at the time. According to one, the new image for the square was esthetically unbalanced as the immense scale of the palace would dwarf the more delicate theater, and the congested configuration of the site would not allow for informal structures, such as cafés, restaurants, and shops, that give life to any quarter. This would result in a sinister space, a definitive "adieu to the stroller, the curious, the *flâneur* – the true animators of streets." The monument itself was nothing but a "factory chimney flanked by a horse, a camel, an ox and four stovepipes with lion cubs at their feet." Rather than this "ridiculous piece," a kiosk, a fountain, or a simple statue would be preferable for the square intended as the new center of Algiers.[17]

Viollet-le-Duc's hands-on experience with Islamic architecture was through this controversial project. Nevertheless, the architect had an ongoing interest in Islamic architecture and owned a respectable collection of books on the topic.[18] He had expressed his views in his *Entretiens sur l'architecture*, published a year before he designed the monument. The opening paragraph of the book posed the essential question regarding non-European architecture as: "From our modern point of view, is it possible for a people to be barbarian, that is, savage, superstitious, fanatical, unbalanced in action, governed only by imperfect laws, but at the same time possessing very perfect arts?" Arguing that Islamic architecture (North African, Iranian, and Ottoman in this case) was worth studying, he stated that developments in different spheres of life were not necessarily parallel and that they could display discrepancies; hence "barbarians" could produce good art.[19] In a quest for a rational system in Islamic architecture that complemented his broader theoretical approach, Viollet-le-Duc's conflicting and confused ideas on Islamic architecture in *Entretiens* provide a useful framework to his monument to Napoleon III. On the one hand, he saw no originality in Islamic architecture and claimed that "the Semitic races, the Arabs, have no aptitude for the arts, and what has been called Arab Architecture is nothing but a derivation of the architecture of Persians, modified by the Greeks."[20] On the other, he praised the Islamic builders as "masters in decoration," because their decoration "never destroys the effects of the massing." He explained what he considered the rationality of Islamic (in this case Iranian) architecture that was manifest in the unity of composition, structure, program, and decorative elements: "decoration is contemplated in the plan, takes shape in the first conception of the program. It is indicated in the structure... it fits the edifice..."[21]

In the years that followed, Viollet-le-Duc pursued his academic and analytical interest in Islamic architecture even though he never traveled to study the buildings in situ. His direct encounter with them was restricted to the ambitious displays in the 1867 Universal Exposition in Paris and the wealth of literature around them. The Exposition took place at a critical time when certain Muslim rulers were pursuing reforms to modernize their countries while struggling to maintain their national identity. Welcoming the opportunity, they issued orders to represent their cultures in a scholarly and comprehensive way to the world. Sultan Abdülaziz's Ottoman Empire was brought to Paris with three pavilions carefully derived from major Ottoman monuments: a mosque (derived from the Green Mosque in Bursa), a mansion (recalling the Çinili Kiosk in the Topkapı Palace), and a bath (a diminutive version of Sinan's Hürrem Sultan Bath in Istanbul). Ismail Pasha's committees summarized the long history of Egypt by a temple that corresponded to antiquity, a palace that referred to medieval Arab history, and an *okel*, a commercial building similar to the contemporary European department store, that stood for modern Egypt. Khayr al-Din Pasha, the Bey of Tunisia, offered another "palace" that duplicated the Bardo Palace in Tunis.[22] The Islamic pavilions attracted a great deal of attention and were subjected to scholarly analysis, famously illustrated at the time by an extensive essay on the Ottoman pavilions by Anatole de Baudot, a former student of Viollet-le-Duc.[23]

The interest generated by the 1867 exhibition was paralleled by publications on Islamic architecture. Two theoretical works stood out among them: *Les Arts arabes* (1873) by Jules Bourgoin and *Architecture et décoration turques* (1874) by Léon Parvillée, the latter the architect of the 1867 Ottoman pavilions. Viollet-le-Duc wrote introductions to both texts, underlining their original search for principles, and thus taking a stand against Orientalist interpretations. He argued, against the beliefs of the "partisans of fantasy," that when submitted to "scientific" analysis the "charming" and "seductive" character of Ottoman architecture revealed itself to be "very developed and learned [*savant*] . . . in terms of design [*tracé*] and color"; it depended on rules and formulas, rather than instincts.[24] The rules of Islamic architecture and decoration were derived from geometry, and, under the scrutiny of "cold science," the "most fantastic-looking" works dissolved into simple, somber lines – not a surprise given the proficiency of Arabs in mathematics in the Middle Ages. Thus Bourgoin showed that the Cairene ornamental forms were determined by straight lines that intersected at certain angles and Parvillée revealed the use of the straight line and the circle in Ottoman decoration, while Edmond Duthoit highlighted the circles that dominated design in Algeria. Parvillée and Duthoit had arrived at a similar conclusion regarding architectural design principles: triangles assured good proportions.[25]

Viollet-le-Duc went further than Parvillée and Bougoin, expanding their analyses of geometric abstraction in terms of race: "It is especially in Semitic people that these tendencies manifest themselves with energy, at least beginning with Muhammedism. There, where the mixes of races exist, ornamentation undergoes diverse influences and representations borrowed from organic nature mix with purely geometric combinations."[26] Geometric decoration applied to flat surfaces stood out as the main characteristic of Arab architecture, creating a tapestry effect that could be explained historically: "These Arab conquerors lived, from time immemorial, in tents, like the majority of Semitic peoples. They did not have any other luxury than fabrics and arms. For them, just like for the Jews of the primitive period, monuments were nothing but the tent, the hut, covered by a precious fabric."[27] The simple and unchanging way of life, deemed characteristic of "Oriental" people, hence clarified the lack of concern for "program" that resulted in sparse, unspecialized spaces.[28]

This explanation was based on Viollet-le-Duc's broad concept of history that "should take into consideration everything, and even ethnography...[and] conditions of formation, existence, and development of populations in different periods."[29] Its reductive reasoning on a par with the dominant Orientalist discourse of the time, the argument still opened up the possibility of incorporating Islamic art into European practice. If the buildings studied could not inform contemporary architects about program, structure, and construction, they could offer decorative models for woodwork, bronze, and textile designs. Viollet-le-Duc praised Bourgoin and Parvillée for producing "practical treatises" that "discovered a new order of composition."[30]

Viollet-le-Duc's arguments echoed in Ottoman publications on architecture. For example, *Usul-u Mimari-i Osmani*, prepared at imperial command by Montani Efendi and Boghos Efendi Chachian on the occasion of the 1873 Universal Exhibition in Vienna, elaborated the principles of classical Ottoman monuments in order to show their relevance to contemporary practice.[31] In 1907 Celal Esad, the first Ottoman "art historian," revisited Viollet-le Duc's ideas, defended their universality, and attempted to apply them to Ottoman architecture. He maintained that the only way to improve Ottoman architecture was to discover its rules, which could be done by taking careful measurements of major monuments and drawing them with precision. The fundamental principles (*kaide-i esasiye*) of Ottoman architecture would surface only after analyzing these drawings scientifically.[32]

If Viollet-le Duc's theories (in general and on Islamic architecture) enjoyed considerable reception, his monument to Napoleon III was excluded from the discourse. It is noteworthy that the architect himself did not mention it in his writings. He may have been thinking about the details of the monument when he alluded to designing some "Arabic ornaments that are called *entrelacs*,"[33] but the brevity of his reference may indicate that he had possibly reached a critical perspective on his heavy-handed manipulations as his knowledge of Islamic architecture increased. The silence was repeated in historiography. Scholars have recently associated the change in the attitude toward the Islamic culture of Algeria with Napoleon III's *royaume arabe* policies and discussed their impact on architecture in the early twentieth century, but did not make a connection with Viollet-le-Duc's monument. Neither was the latter evaluated in reference to the Islamic pavilions that filled the grounds of the Universal exhibitions from 1867 on and that were seen as influential models on the later appearance of a new type of Beaux-Arts architecture with neo-Islamic fragments several decades later. The *style Jonnart,* coined in reference to Charles-Célestin Jonnart, the governor general of Algeria (1900–1 and 1903–11), resulted in some of the most memorable public buildings in Algiers – among them the Central Post Office by Jules Voinot (1911), the Préfecture by Henri Petit (1906), and the Médersa d'Alger, again by Petit (1905). They adhered to a series of regulations from 1904 to 1907 that mandated the "Oriental style" as the "style of the state," specifically in schools and in administrative and public buildings.[34]

One concept from Viollet-le-Duc's design, a tower topped by a pavilion in the form of a mosque sitting on a capital, enjoyed a special legacy. Given the criss-crossing of ideas on art and architecture between the French and the Ottoman empires, it should not come as a surprise that the design re-emerged in Istanbul on a monumental scale in an unrealized project for a bridge over the Bosphorus by Ferdinand-Joseph Arnodin in 1900 as part of a regional plan; the date corresponded to the twentieth jubilee of Abdülhamid II's ascension to the throne. The three piers that carried the suspended spans were terminated by identical structures with central domes and four symmetrical minarets. Curiously, Arnodin's model for these mosques now came from Mamluk Cairo, adding to the confusion that accompanied the travels of architectural forms across the Mediterranean. Despite the "Islamic" appearance of the bridge, Arnodin's scheme was to bring the new technology to the capital, unifying it with a transportation system and defining a zone for future growth by means of a railway ring road and two bridges across the Bosphorus (the second had more subdued "Islamic" forms).[35]

Elements from Viollet-le-Duc's design were finally incorporated into a real monument a good distance away from Algiers: in a celebration of new technology, a Telegraph Tower in bronze was erected on the Marja Square (also known as Serai Square, taking its name from a series of palaces dating to the sixteenth century; and later as Telegraph Square) in the western extension of Damascus upon the orders of Abdülhamid II in 1904. This symbol, which commemorated the completion of the telegraph line that linked Istanbul through Damascus to Mecca, facilitated communication with the holy city and the pilgrims, and announced the spread of modernization to all corners of the Ottoman empire, was designed by the sultan's chief architect, Raimondo D'Aronco. Like Viollet-le-Duc's monument, it could be easily read in visual terms. The base bore the emblem of the Ottomans, the crescent and the star. The body of the tower was

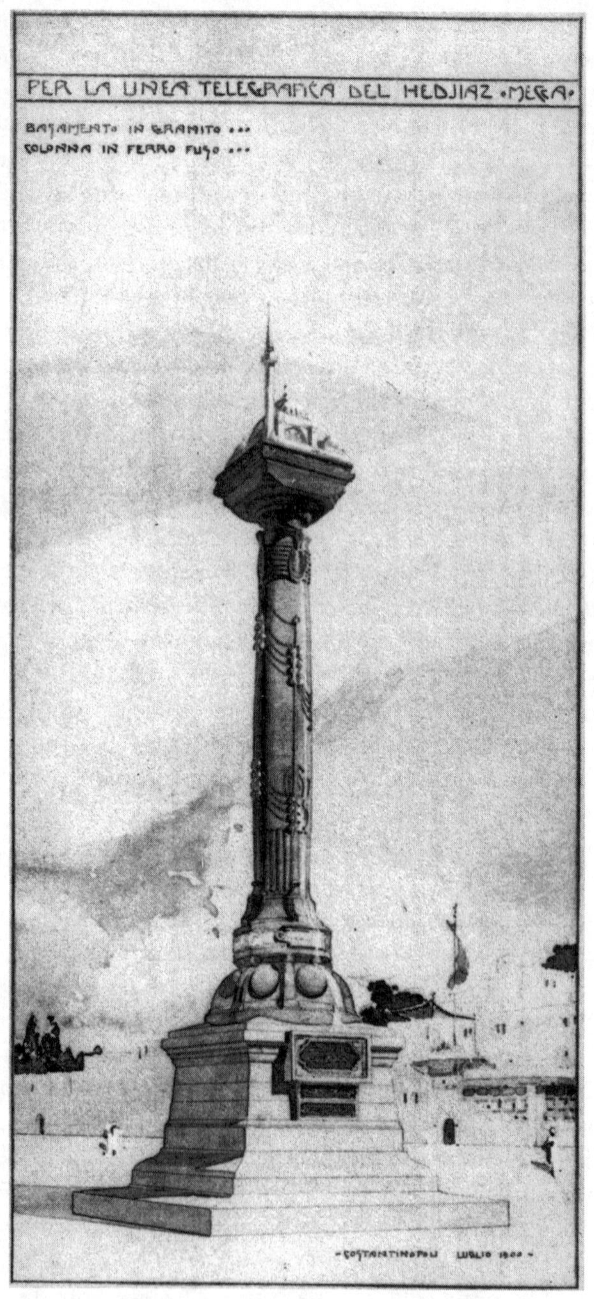

Figure 1.2 Raimondo D'Aronco, Telegraph Tower, Damascus. Architect's drawing (from *D'Aronco Architetto*, Milan: Electra, 1982)

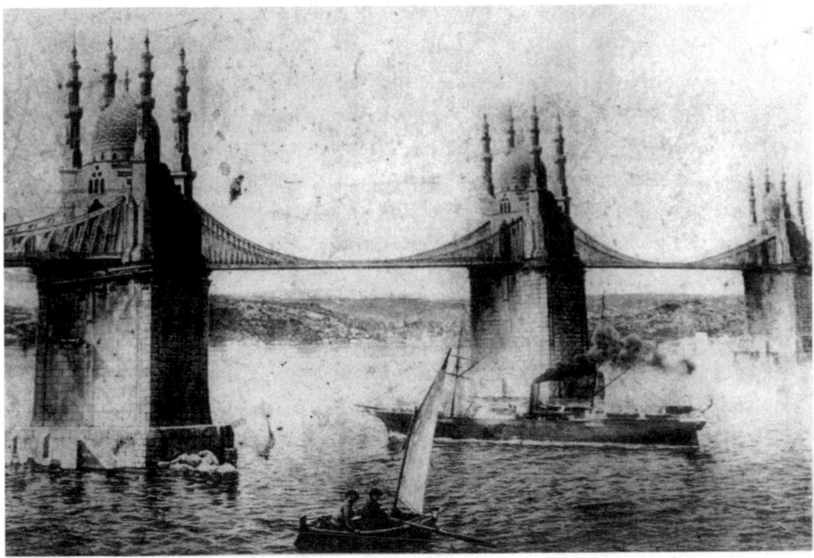

Figure 1.3 Ferdinand-Joseph Arnodin, proposal for a bridge over the Bosphorus. Basbanaklik Arsivi, Istanbul

adorned by bas-reliefs of telegraph towers and lines, stylized according to the conventions of art nouveau. The monument was topped with a huge capital upon which a replica of the Hamidiye Mosque, dating from 1886, was placed. Outside the Yıldız Palace in Istanbul and acting as the site of the elaborate Friday prayer ceremony preceded by a royal procession every week, this mosque had an unmistakable association with the sultan and acknowledged the Hamidian imperial prowess.[36] Furthermore, the concrete image of the mosque represented the pan-Islamist policy of Abdülhamid, which capitalized on Islam to win the loyalty of Arabs in an attempt to rejuvenate the empire, while the telegraph lines announced the adoption of modern technology.[37]

Although facing critical problems on all fronts at the turn of the nineteenth century, the Ottoman empire still maintained considerable power in the world order and clung to imperial ambitions. To compensate for the increasing loss of the European territories, the government turned its attention toward the Arab provinces and Anatolia. The goal was not only economic returns, but also to create social solidarity much needed for the Ottoman state's survival.[38] As Ahmed Cevdet Paşa, a main protagonist of reforms, articulated:

> Because of the devastation of Rumelia, the revenues of the government have become reduced by nearly a half. In order to make up for this loss, the most important issue for us now is to render prosperous and increase the wealth of the Anatolian and Arab provinces... The development of Syria [i.e. Damascus and its environs], Aleppo and Adana would turn this area into an Egypt... This can be accomplished with ease under the aegis of our sovereign.[39]

In concert with the mechanisms deployed by European powers, Abdülhamid II concentrated on the "legitimation" of the Ottoman state in the Arab provinces, but also addressed the exterior world. As Selim Deringil argues convincingly in *The Well-Protected Domains*, to that end an "official [Ottoman] iconography," ranging from coats of arms to commemorative medallions, *salnames* (yearbooks), ceremonies, linguistic codes, and architectural works, was developed.[40] The Telegraph Tower was projected as an appropriate symbol that would legitimize imperial claims on all scales. It pointed not only to the unification of the Ottoman territories by Islam and new technology, but also to the integral part the empire played on the world scene. After all, communication by telegraph from India to London had to pass across the Ottoman empire throughout Abdülhamid's reign.[41] Furthermore, this unusual memorial complemented another type of tower that symbolized modernity and that dotted the cities of the empire: the clock tower, the sign of change in the concept of time and an alternative to its former regulation by calls to prayer from minarets. Placed in public squares, the ultimate nineteenth-century spaces with their geometric plans and axially placed official buildings, the towers thus constituted essential elements in the iconographic program of the empire.

Paralleling Viollet-le-Duc's unexecuted "Place Napoléon," the entire Marja Square served as a metaphor for modern order, represented by the state. The purely symbolic function of the Telegraph Tower was complemented by a series of government buildings on or in the vicinity of the public space in Damascus and sheltered operations that inscribed the presence of the Ottoman imperial control on the urban image. They included the Municipal Building (1892–3), the post and telegraph headquarters (1883), the Palace of Justice (1878–80), the Ottoman Bank (1892), Hamidiye military barracks (1895), and the police headquarters

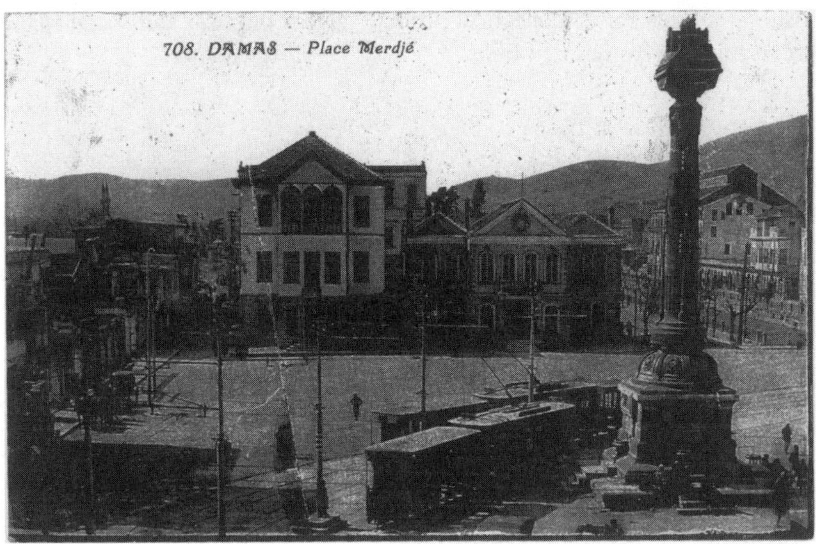

Figure 1.4 Postcard of Marja Square with Telegraph Tower in the foreground, Damascus, ca. 1910 (author's collection)

(1878–80), as well as a number of educational institutions.[42] As theaters, hotels, cafés, and restaurants crowded the square and its surroundings, the neighborhood gradually assumed a "modern" image that contrasted with the walled historic city to the east, recalling the transitional role between the Casbah and the French city in Algiers played by "Place Napoléon."

The emergence of an *architecture parlante* in Damascus similar to Viollet-le-Duc's colonial intervention in Algiers was not a simple act of appropriating French notions, but a reworking of the formal elements of modern public space to convey political messages. This episode testifies to the existence of alternative trends in modernism in architecture and city planning, still commonly identified as a "Western" phenomenon, by underlining the Ottoman participation in the shaping of a universal imperial iconography in the late nineteenth/early twentieth centuries. It also makes a case that historic, economic, social, cultural, and military differences (and inequalities in power relations) did not matter in creating a universal culture that belonged to the "connected world of empires."[43] A comparative analysis of urban forms in Algiers and Damascus thus opens up modernism's conventional associations, pursuing Marshall Berman's "broad and open" definition of the concept that – among other issues – argued for a "dialectical process" across physical and social space to reveal hitherto ignored links.[44]

Notes

1 On Thomas Ismail Urbain, see Edmund Burke III, "Two Critics of French Rule in Algeria: Ismail Urbain and Frantz Fanon," in L. Carl Brown and Matthew S. Gordon (eds.), *Franco-Arab Encounters* (Beirut: American University of Beirut, Lebanon, 1996), 329–44, and Michel Levallois, "Ismayl Urbain: Éléments pour une biographie," in Megali Morsy (ed.), *Les Saint-Simoniens et l'Orient: Vers la modernité* (Aix-en-Provence: Édisud, 1990), 53–82. Literature on Napoleon's notion of "Arab Kingdom" is extensive. For concise discussions, see Charles-Robert Ageron, "Peut-on parler d'une politique des 'royaumes arabes' de Napoléon III?", in Morsy (ed.), *Les Saint-Simoniens et l'Orient*, 83–96, and Benjamin Stora, *Histoire de l'Algérie coloniale (1830–1954)* (Paris: Éditions La Découverte, 1991), 21–2.
2 Stora, *Histoire de l'Algérie coloniale*, 21–2.
3 Octave Teissier, *Napoléon III en Algérie* (Paris: Challame, Ainé; Algiers: Bastide; Toulon: J. Renoux, 1865), 14.
4 Ibid. 19.
5 *Félicitations et Allégresse au sujet de l'entrée de S. M. Napoléon III à Alger: Poème composé par M'hammed el-Ouennas* (Algiers: Imprimerie Typographique Bouyer, 1867), 18, 26. The quotations in French read: "Les Arabes dirent à l'Empereur: Que Dieu vous maintienne victorieux! Nous sommes soumis à votre gouvernement, et l'amour que nous avons pour vous ne s'effaçera jamais de nos cœurs . . . Je désire vivre tranquille sous ses lois, être sous ses ailes d'aigles . . .".
6 On May 10, 1865, Napoleon III watched a performance of *Rigoletto* in this building. See Henri Klein, *Souvenirs de l'ancien et nouvel Alger* (Algiers: Imprimerie Orientale Fontate Frères, 1913), 26.
7 "2e Esquisse d'un monument à élèver à Alger sous le règne de l'empereur" (1864), Monuments Historiques et des Sites (MHS), Fonds Viollet-le-Duc, No. 1444. The document shows a site plan on a scale 1:1000. Another sketch plan on trace paper is of the "palais impérial." The idea for a palace of justice survived from Viollet-le-Duc's project, and a competition was launched in 1867 by the Gouvernement Général de l'Algérie. According to the competition guidelines, the palace would now be situated to the north side of the square; its main façade would be on the Place Napoléon and a secondary entrance on Rue Bab-Azzoun. Following the architecture of the neighboring structures, it would have to incorporate continuous colonnades to its ground level.

See "Concours pour la construction d'un Palais de Justice à Alger," *Revue générale de l'architecture et des travaux publics*, v/XXV (1867), cols. 41 and 42.

8 Eugène-Emmanuel Viollet-le-Duc, *Enretiens sur l'architecture*, quoted in Kenneth Frampton, *Modern Architecture: A Critical History* (New York: Oxford University Press, 1980), 64.

9 Frampton, *Modern Architecture*, 64.

10 "1ère esquisse d'un monument à élèver à Alger sous le règne de l'empereur," MHS, Fonds Viollet-le Duc, No. 1442.

11 Gestère, "Monument à élèver à Alger sur la Place Napoléon," *L'Illustration* (1865) (2e semestre), 189.

12 "2e Esquisse d'un monument à élèver à Alger sous le règne de l'empereur Napoléon III," MHS, Fonds Viollet-le-Duc, No. 1443.

13 For a description of this project, see Gestère, "Monument à élèver à Alger."

14 Ibid.

15 Ibid.

16 Another genre of temporary monument in a similar (if much more subdued) architectural vocabulary had dotted the places that the emperor had visited: celebratory pavilions. For example, in Algiers, a square structure open on four sides by lobed arches and covered by a dome with a crescent on top was placed at the point where Rue Bab-Azzoun met the Place du Gouvernement, not far from the projected location of Viollet-le-Duc's monument.

17 Charles Desprez, *Alger naguère et maintenant* (Algiers: Imprimerie du Maréchal, 1868), 201–5.

18 Viollet-le-Duc's library not only had books on Islamic architecture (among them the monumental oeuvre of Napoleon I's *armée de savants, Description de l'Egypte*, 19 vols. in 21 (Paris: Imprimerie impériale, 1809–28), and Pascal Coste's *Architecture arabe; ou monuments du Kaire* (Paris: Typ. de Firmin Didot Frères et Compagnie, 1839), but also books on Arabic and Persian poetry. See *Catalogue des livres composants la bibliothèque de M. E. Viollet-le-Duc* (Paris, 1880). Viollet-le-Duc argued that the books made available a vast architectural terrain for "analytical and critical work" and Coste's drawings often raised intriguing questions that could lead to "unique" theories. See Viollet-le-Duc, "Préface," in Jules Bourgoin, *Les Arts arabes* (Paris: Ve A Morel et Cie, 1873), n. p.

19 Eugène-Emmanuel Viollet-le-Duc, *Entretiens sur l'architecture*, 2 vols. (Paris: Ve A Morel et Cie, 1863), i. 9–10.

20 Ibid. 431.

21 Ibid. ii. 197, 205.

22 For the pavilions of Islamic countries at the Universal Exposition, see Zeynep Çelik, *Displaying the Orient: Architecture of Islam at Nineteenth-Century World's Fairs* (Berkeley: University of California Press, 1992).

23 Anatole de Baudot, "Exposition Universelle de 1867," *Gazette des architectes et du bâtiment* (special issue) (Paris, 1867).

24 Viollet-le-Duc, "Préface," in Léon Parvillée, *Architecture et décoration turques au XVe siècle* (Paris: Ve A Morel et Cie, 1874). For further discussion on nineteenth-century European texts that deal with Islamic architecture and especially Islamic decoration, see Gülru Necipoğlu, *The Topkapi Scroll: Geometry and Ornament in Islamic Architecture* (Santa Monica, CA: Getty, 1995), ch. 4 (pp. 61–71).

25 Viollet-le-Duc, "Préface," *Les Arts arabes*, and "Préface," *Architecture et décoration turques*. The Egyptian triangle (height = 5/8 base) considered by Viollet-le-Duc as a generator of good proportions in *Entretiens*, emerged in the Ottoman monuments analyzed by Parvillée. For Viollet-le-Duc's discussion of the Egyptian triangle, see Viollet-le-Duc, *Entretiens*, i. 426–31.

26 Viollet-le-Duc, "Préface," *Les Arts arabes.*

27 Ibid.

28 Ibid.

29 Viollet-le-Duc, *Art russe* (Paris: Ve A Morel et Cie, 1877), 260.

30 Viollet-le-Duc, "Préface," *Les Arts arabes*, and "Préface," *Architecture et décoration turques.*

31 For a discussion of this treatise, see Zeynep Çelik, *The Remaking of Istanbul: Portrait of an Ottoman City in the Nineteenth Century* (Seattle: University of Washington Press, 1986; repr. Berkeley: University of California Press, 1993), 148–50.

32 Celal Esad, "Osmanlı Mimarisi," *Ikdam*, January 3, 1907. I discuss this article in *The Remaking of Istanbul*, 151–2.

33 Viollet-le-Duc, "Préface," *Les Arts arabes.*

34 Nabila Oulebsir, "Du politique à l'esthétique: L'Architecture néo-mauresque à Alger," in Jocelyne Dakhlia (ed.), *Urbanité arabe* (Arles: Sindbad/Actes Sud, 1998), 312, 320 n. 21.

35 For a discussion and images of Arnodin's bridge, see Çelik, *The Remaking of Istanbul*, 107–9.

36 Selim Deringil, *The Well-Protected Domains: Ideology and Legitimation of Power in the Ottoman Empire 1876–1909* (New York: I. B. Tauris, 1998), 23–4.

37 For discussions of this tower, see Stefan Weber, "Der Marga-Platz in Damaskus," in *Damaszener Mitteilungen*, 10 (1998), 316–17, and Diana Barillari, *Raimondo D'Aronco* (Rome: Laterza, 1995), 49.

38 Engin D. Akarli, "Abdülhamid II's Attempt to Integrate Arabs into the Ottoman System," in David Kushner (ed.), *Palestine in the Late Ottoman Period: Political, Social, and Economic Transformations* (Jerusalem: Yad Izhak Ben-Zvi; Leiden: E. J. Brill, 1986), 75.

39 Quoted ibid.

40 Deringil, *Well-Protected Domains*, especially 1–43.

41 Roderick H. Davison, *Essays in Ottoman and Turkish History, 1774–1923: The Impact of the West* (Austin: University of Texas Press, 1990), 137–8.

42 For a comprehensive history of the Marja Square and the buildings on and around it, see Weber, "Der Marga-Platz in Damascus."

43 I borrow this term from C. A. Bayly and Leila Tarazi Fawaz. See "Introduction: The Connected World of Empires," in Bayly and Fawaz (eds.), *Modernity and Culture: From the Mediterranean to the Indian Ocean* (New York: Columbia University Press, 2002). The collection of essays in the volume casts a new look at the intellectual and political culture of modernity in the Middle East and South Asia, focusing on the Ottoman and British empires.

44 Marshall Berman, *All That Is Solid Melts Into Air: The Experience of Modernity* (New York: Penguin Books, 1982), 1–2.

2

Out of the Earth: Egypt's Statue of Liberty

Darcy Grimaldo Grigsby

In 1855, at the age of 21, Frédéric-Auguste Bartholdi, most famous for creating the Statue of Liberty in New York City, visited Egypt with the painter Jean-Léon Gérôme, ten years his senior.[1] At the side of the older, facile draftsman, the young sculptor depicted many of the same subjects in drawings which often appear crabbed and clumsy, without either Gérôme's practice or skill (figure 2.1). Bartholdi was incessantly mocked for his efforts; at least this is the claim made in a letter by the French painter Léon Belly. The teasing did not stop an artist whose career attests, if nothing else, to his perseverance. From Egypt, Belly wrote his mother:

> I see you have judged Bartholdi as I have judged him and I believe of all the Egyptian artists [meaning the French artists in Egypt, that is, Gérôme, Narcisse Berchère, Édouard Imer], he is the best. His good character has a certain naive side, in the good sense; his youth, because he is only 20 [*sic*] years old, has made him the butt of all jokes. During the voyage to Upper Egypt his painting and his drawings were continually mocked. Nevertheless, it was he alone who worked; he made a quantity of photographs and a considerable number of studies and drawings, because although a sculptor, he does not lack interest in color, and his studies, a bit unformed like those of a beginner, seem to me much better than those of Gérôme who made so much fun of him.[2]

Belly's letter, as Régis Hueber has noted, betrays a personal animosity towards Gérôme born of rivalry and also resentment of his affluence and the easy confidence which is so often its corollary.[3] Bartholdi shared Gérôme's middle-class privilege, but his youth and relative lack of skill allowed Belly to express towards him a generosity born of condescension.

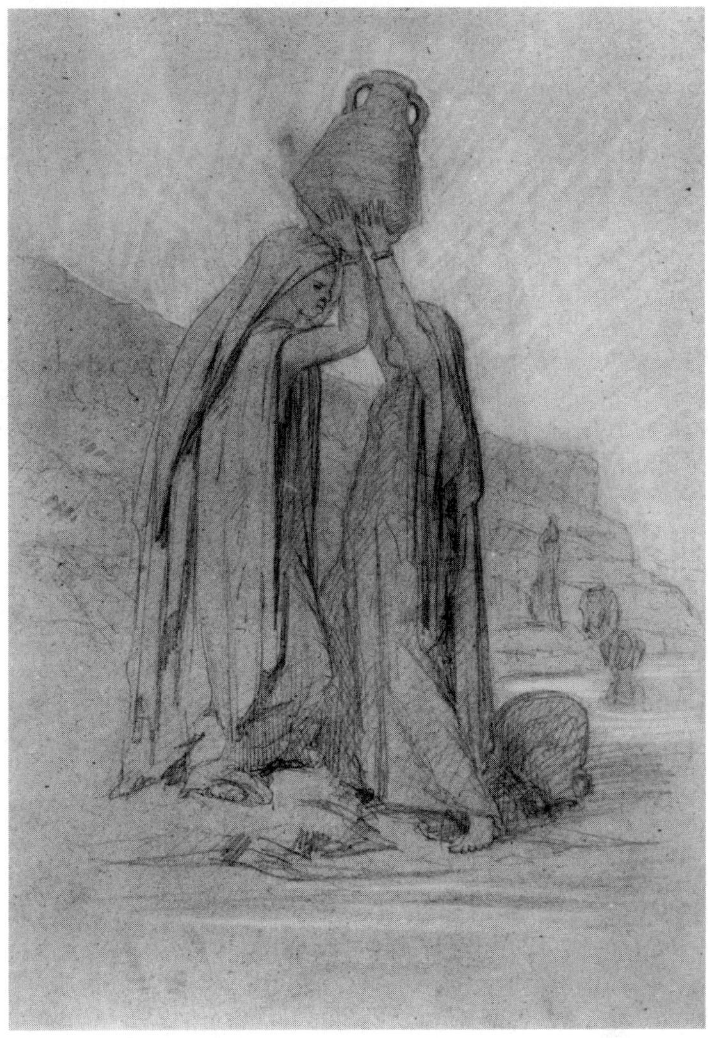

Figure 2.1 Frédéric-Auguste Bartholdi, *Untitled* [*Fellaheen carrying water*], 1855–6. Graphite on paper, Colmar, Musée Bartholdi. Photo: Christian Kempf

Still, Belly was right in one regard. Bartholdi was immensely productive in Egypt, far exceeding Gérôme in output. Not only did he produce 211 drawings and 28 oil studies, but in the very early, taxing days of photography, he made some 103 calotypes.

Besides youth, inexperience, and a lack of facility, the sculptor suffered yet another disadvantage relative to his companions. He was the only one among them to be forced by the circumstances of travel to work in media other than his primary art. He was the only sculptor. While Anne Wagner has taught us how central was *dessin* to a nineteenth-century French sculptor's training, drawing was nonetheless a medium that was ancillary, preparatory, and also radically unlike the three-dimensional products ultimately displayed to an audience.[4] For sculptors of bronzes like Bartholdi, drawing represented but one step in a series of translations from the three-dimensional referent (often a "live model"), through two-dimensional experiments in drawing, to a series of three-dimensional studies, eventually made into a negative mold from which were derived plasters, and finally bronzes. Translation was therefore a problem at the center of the sculptor's art: translation not just between media and thus between two and three dimensions, but between sizes, small and very large, and between materials with unlike effects – clay, plaster, and metal, for example – and also between negative imprints and positive things. To make sculpture thus entailed an appreciation of the provisionality of a series of efforts and the long deferral of an end-product. In this process, the discrete thing, the ultimate fixing of referent and ideas as artistic form, was long delayed and a matter of much sustained work, patience, and postponed gratification. For all the associations of sculpture with mere objecthood, the process of its making was remarkably dispersed. Provisional and discrepant things and ideas were coaxed into a discrete form (which could, of course, be endlessly repeated and modified in scale). By contrast, painters traveled much more quickly to their final figuration. With far greater speed and fewer steps, they arrived at their definitive possession, in art, of their object.

How, then, would a sculptor try to make art during and out of a voyage to Egypt? Voyages are by definition transient and short-term, making the realization of sculpture difficult, and voyages also entail continual acts of translation of the foreign into some legible representation. Provisionality is the situation's precondition, but so too is the shaping of the ephemeral into figuration. From November 1855 to June 1856, Bartholdi exerted great effort to make the foreign into form. With the diligence of a young, ambitious student, he understood such efforts to be his job. He was traveling, after all, with Gérôme, on an official mission to make "the study of the antiquities of these different countries and the photographic reproduction of the principal monuments and the most remarkable types of the diverse races."[5]

* * *

If Bartholdi was immensely productive in Egypt, he was equally determined to turn his voyage's bulging portfolio into art which he could display in Paris. The sculptor exhibited five paintings of Egyptian scenes at Salons between 1857 and 1865.[6] Around 1857–8 he created five Orientalist lithographs, inspired by his on-site drawings and photographs; and he also made some preliminary plans in 1858 for an *Album de dessins orientalistes*, a collection of types which never appeared. Bartholdi appears to have been uncertain as to whether his talents as a draftsman and painter would help or hinder his career as a sculptor. He exhibited his paintings under the astonishing pseudonym Amilcar Hasenfratz, but he signed his lithographs "Aug. Bartholdi." At the Salon of 1857, he exhibited a two-figure sculpture group entitled *The Lyre of the Berbers* under his own name. To this sculpture inspired by his Egyptian trip, we certainly must add his statue of the famous French Egyptologist Champollion standing on the head of a sphinx, exhibited as a plaster in the Egyptian section of the 1867 Universal Exhibition, as well as his most famous sculpture, the Statue of Liberty, the design of which originated in the drawings and clay models of an "Egyptian woman" or "female fellah" executed between 1867 and 1869 (figures 2.2 and 2.3). The names are Bartholdi's, but he would not have agreed with my claim of lineage from fellah to Liberty. This lineage is, however, verified by the visual evidence.[7]

Indeed, the resemblance between Bartholdi's Statue of Liberty and his earlier project for a monumental female lighthouse at the Suez Canal was noted and made public in the 1880s. In print, Bartholdi contested what he took to be an accusation of a clandestine and opportunistic recycling of a failed Egyptian project into an American success.

> At this period I was expecting to execute a statue of Egypt for the Suez Lighthouse. I even laid before Ismaïl Pasha a project. It was this that made an evilly disposed newspaper say, and others repeat, that I had executed a colossal statue for Egypt, which had not been used, and that I had resold it to the Society of the French-American Union in order that from it might be made the Statue of Liberty. Now I never executed anything for the Khedive except a little sketch which has remained in his palace, and represents Egypt under the features of a female Fellah.[8]

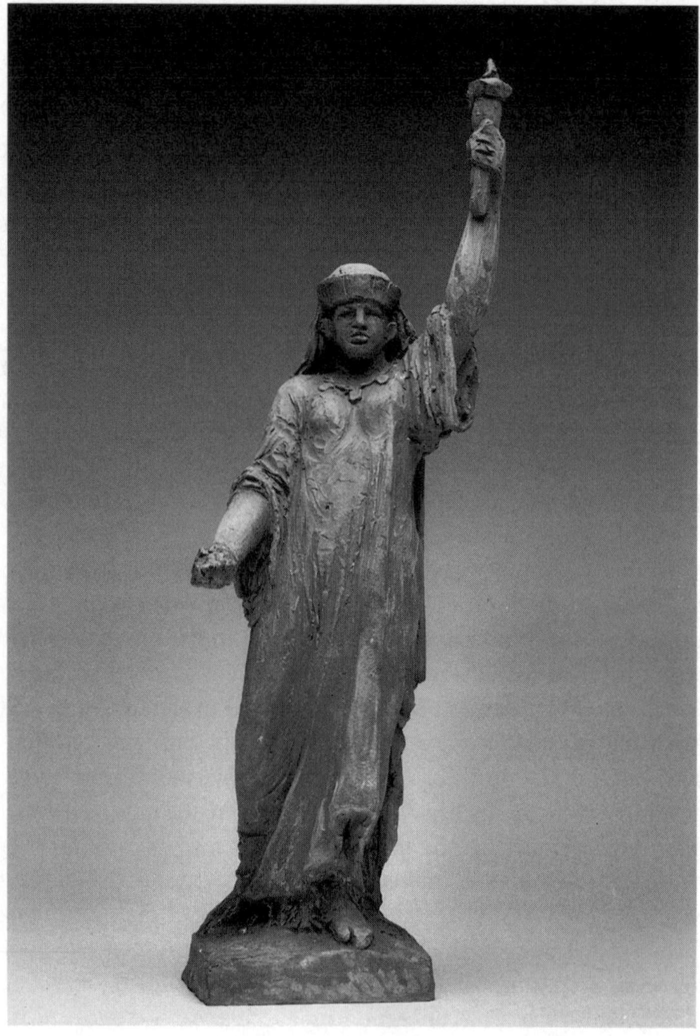

Figure 2.2 Frédéric-Auguste Bartholdi, *Maquette for Egypt Bringing Light to Asia*, 1869. Terracotta, Colmar, Musée Bartholdi. Photo: Christian Kempf

And here he is replying to a journalist concerning charges in the *New York Times*:

> [A] colossal statue of an Egyptian woman holding a light aloft . . . was declined on account of the expense. At the time my Statue of Liberty did not even exist, even in my imagination, and the only resemblance between

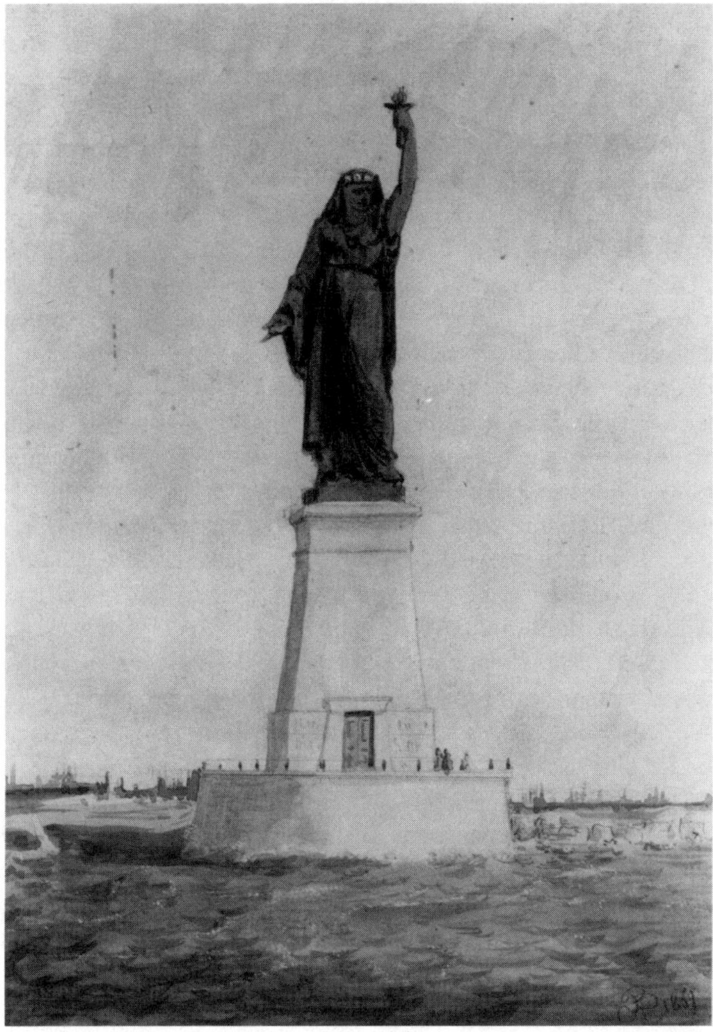

Figure 2.3 Frédéric-Auguste Bartholdi, *Egypt Bringing Light to Asia*, 1869. Watercolour glued on paper, Colmar, Musée Bartholdi. Photo: Christian Kempf

the drawing that I submitted to the Khedive and the statue now in New York's beautiful harbor is that both hold a light aloft. Now, I ask you, sir, how is a sculptor to make a statue which is to serve the purpose of a lighthouse without making it hold the light in the air? My Statue of Liberty was a pure work of love, costing me the sacrifice of ten years and of twenty thousand dollars – little perhaps for Americans, but a great deal for me.

> The Egyptian affair would have been purely a business transaction. I declare most emphatically, and I defy anyone in the world to contradict me, that the Statue of Liberty was ever offered to any other government.[9]

The defensive tone is unmistakable, and so too is the desperate reaching for counterclaims. Bartholdi seems to believe that the issue hinges on what he actually "executed" for Ismaïl Pasha, the ruler of Egypt from 1863 to 1879: not a colossal statue but only a "drawing," "a little sketch." And also why. Differences in motive as well as media and scale are marshaled to prove that the Statue of Liberty, "a pure work of love," was never offered to another government. Bartholdi assumes that Liberty by definition could not be "purely a business transaction," partly because it cost him so much money and time. Yet a fellah could. Liberty is thereby associated with the artist's self-sacrifice, a self-sacrifice that removes the sculpture from economies of money and time, even as the artist draws attention to their expenditure. And the fellah is defined as a matter of money and its exchange (Ismaïl merely failed to meet the necessary costs). Bartholdi's argument is odd and incoherent, but it signals the sculptor's anxiety: here was one translation he wanted to abort. Liberty and fellah were not, he claims, translatable despite their formal and functional resemblances (a colossal woman with hand holding high a torch serving as a lighthouse in a harbor). But, as Bartholdi knew well, the five extant clay models and two watercolor drawings of a female fellah were easily confused with the other small clay models which metamorphosed into the female figure that would become the colossal Statue of Liberty. The translations are apparent. Moreover, all of these clay models began in on-site drawings, three of them to be exact, which included no less than five female fellaheen at the edge of the Nile – as many drawn fellah women as subsequent clay models. The Statue of Liberty, so remote and abstractly chastened and generalized, began in actual encounters with Egyptian peasant women.

* * *

That Bartholdi chose to focus on a fellah in a proposal submitted to Ismaïl Pasha in 1869 is not surprising. Not only did the Viceroy call himself the "prince of fellaheen,"[10] but this was the period when Orientalist art underwent a "georgic mode" wherein peasants replaced warriors.[11] Bartholdi had drawn fellah women during his first voyage and included them repeatedly in his later painted genre scenes, such as *Café on the banks of the Nile* shown at the Salon of 1861. He was not alone; fellaheen proliferated in the sculptures and paintings exhibited by other artists at the official Salons.[12] They also figured prominently at the Universal Exhibition of 1867, both as the subjects of four of Charles Cordier's ten "mannequins" of ethnographic types in the Egyptian pavilion where Ismaïl Pasha himself held court, and also in several French paintings, one by Charles Landelle and another by an unidentified artist which presided over the Suez Canal Company's exhibition (figure 2.4).[13] Moreover, 1869 was the very year that Ismaïl bought and officially took credit for a novel entitled *Le Fellah* by Bartholdi's friend Edmond About.[14] When Bartholdi returned to Egypt specifically to make his proposal to the Viceroy in April 1869, About's novel had already been appearing in serial form in the *Revue des Deux-Mondes* since February. In addition, fellaheen cultivation of cotton had just become newly pivotal to Europe during the American Civil War, much to the (temporary) benefit of Egypt's economy. Ismaïl himself had seized one-fifth of Egypt's cultivated lands, thereby anchoring his family's wealth to its agricultural fertility.[15]

The fellah was, moreover, a key "type" for the French, encountered in ancient Egyptian art, in voyage accounts, and also throughout Egypt, especially its countryside.[16] By the late 1860s, the fellah had come to be identified by Frenchmen with the land of Egypt itself. Here is Théophile Gautier's *Voyage en Egypte* of 1869:

> An observation that arises in the mind of the least attentive traveler, from his first steps in this lower Egypt, is the profound intimacy of the fellah with the earth. The name of autochthone [aboriginal inhabitant] truly suits him; the fellah comes from this clay that he treads; he is molded by it and barely extricates himself from it. As a child nurses its wetnurse, he manipulates it, he presses it in order to make spurt from this brown breast the milk of fecundity... [The fellah] works almost without tools, with his hands... Nowhere is this accord of man and soil more visible; nowhere does the earth have greater importance. It extends its color over all things...[17]

Gautier suggests an identity between fellah and earth so profound as to call into question the distinction between them. Here are people who scarcely attain human status, so "molded" and "barely extricated" are they from the clay out of which they have been made. Yet human they are in a primitive, infantile way, grasping with their hands the great mammary of the Egyptian earth in order to make it give forth without tools.

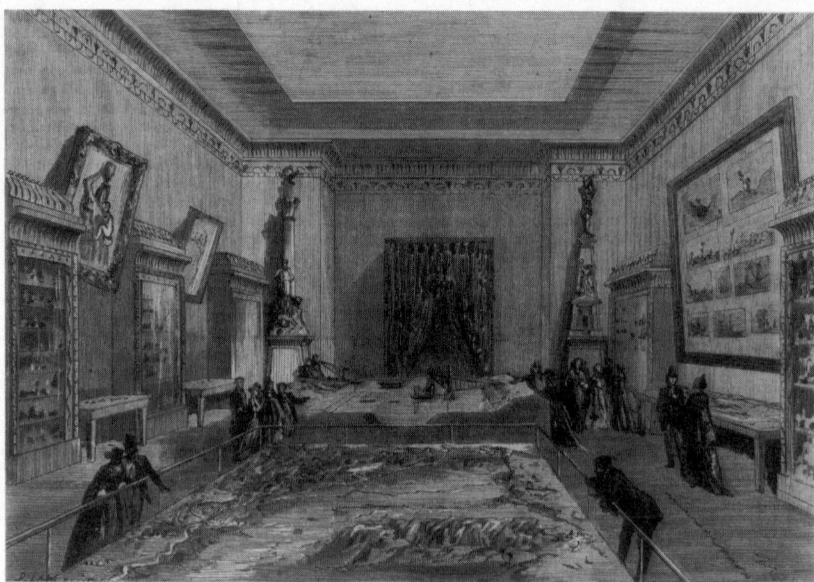

Figure 2.4 Engraving after D. Lancelot, *Relief Plan of the Canal and Model of the Works*, Suez Canal Company Pavilion, 1867. From *L'Exposition Universelle de 1867 illustrée. Publication internationale autorisée par la Commission Impériale*, Paris, 1867, I, 116. Photo: Julie Wolf

Such are the associations also informing an art review by Alfred Assollant of Charles Landelle's *Woman Fellah* at the Universal Exhibition of 1867, a picture whose cloying, pretty elegance would seem far from Gautier's primitive clay dwellers. Yet this art critic also interprets fellaheen as a thoughtless, immobile people. He condemns Gautier, however, for positively evaluating attributes which ultimately destine these Egyptians to extinction:

> One recognizes [in this picture] another race of women, modest and strong at once . . . What is lacking in this woman, otherwise so beautiful, is thought. From this characteristic one recognizes a race which will die.
>
> Certain painters and poets of this century have much admired the fatalistic immobility of the figures of the Orient. This is the typical theme of M. Théophile Gautier. For him, nothing is more beautiful than a dervish, crouching in a contemplative attitude, smoking his pipe and thinking of nothing. But grass also thinks of nothing and yet is not more admirable for it; and rock is not superior to man. To move, even by chance, is to live.

> He who remains immobile is already dead and wants little more. This is why the Orient which nothing disturbs has been for such a long time prey to the first come... An entire destiny of a people is traced in a few brushstrokes on this woman.[18]

Assollant and Gautier share many familiar Orientalist assumptions; they differ primarily in how they evaluate the stasis and immobility they associate with the Orient.[19] Gautier's timeless, even primordial primitivism is cast by Assollant as a frightening, mindless inertness. For him immobility signifies death and the end of a people who in the most fundamental way cannot move with history. This pervasive sense of Egypt's petrification was only compounded by the stasis associated with pharaonic art, by the stone persons apparently frozen in time which littered Egypt's landscape.

In 1856 Bartholdi had also juxtaposed Egypt's stasis to French progress. Gautier's description of Egypt's timelessness was written "while traversing this vast brown plain with the gallop of the locomotive."[20] For Bartholdi too, the machine underscored Egypt's unchanging primitivism. While he was far from sure how to evaluate Egypt's failure to change, he was certain that technological progress was as an index not only of modernity but of "civilization."

> How adorable a thing is Egypt in all regards, for art, for customs, nation and its civilization which I had forgotten. She certainly has her charm.
>
> To write you, for example, I am obliged to confide my letter to couriers who with a bell on their foot will carry it from village to village until Cairo. This is very pretty, but does not offer very much security. Whatever one can say about Mohammed-Ali [the modernizing ruler of Egypt from 1805 to 1848], it was he alone who searched to make something of Egypt. He made Europeans be respected who hardly had been. He organized some administrations, some schools, and a little industry and he bought some machines, etc. Since then, the administrations have tended to return to their original state, as have the schools. Industry goes similarly because the Arabs are too dazed and lazy to occupy themselves with it. The machines bought by Mohammed-Ali were magnificent. They all rust in the Arsenal in a frightening disorder. The cavalry trumpets on top of the weaving looms, the boilers, the cannonballs, the gears, the cannons, the keys of pianos, old windows, astronomical instruments with the butts of rifles...here is the ensemble of the Arsenal. This is a visible metaphor laid bare of the history of all things in Egypt. One has at hand all the perfect instruments to use, but

> one makes gears out of wood. They have all the hydraulic machines to furnish water for miles around; they construct *chadoufs*. They appear to concern themselves with civilization only in order to make clear that they prefer not to make use of it. If Europeans could possess the land, they could probably make something from it but they could not get it except by a feat of skill and then it would be necessary that they were married. You can understand how in these conditions, this would almost be impossible.[21]

Admittedly, esthetic pleasures were to be found in Egypt's charm, but the sculptor ends by championing modernization over the picturesque, whether couriers with bells on their feet or a vast still-life of rusting machinery. If in this 1856 letter, art and modernization wage war for Bartholdi's loyalties, it is clear that the latter ultimately wins out. Indeed Bartholdi speaks as an incipient imperialist (too bad about the problem of wives).

In 1855 Bartholdi had traveled to Egypt on a ship with Ferdinand De Lesseps and his official 15-man International Scientific Commission to design the Suez Canal.[22] From his childhood friend Saïd Pasha, who ruled Egypt from 1854 to 1863, De Lesseps had won the rights to a project that had long preoccupied Napoleon I and also the Saint-Simonians. The building of the canal required more than ten years of continual digging; its inauguration occurred in November 1869 although it was not yet finished. Thus to discuss Egypt as a space outside time, change, and modernization, especially in the late 1860s, was to hark back to earlier Orientalist rhetoric and to ignore the present: the locomotive on which Gautier rode was only a glimpse of a key moment in technological modernization, and it happened in Egypt. In fact, Gautier was traveling to the canal's inauguration even as he conjured a people "petrified" by the "clay" out of which they had been "molded." When the 21-year-old Bartholdi traveled in Egypt from 1855 to 1856, he visited a country on the verge of immense change. When he returned in 1869 to sell his lighthouse he could appreciate how profound had been its transformation: the canal almost completed; Cairo, in his words, "Haussmannized" and "Europeanized" beyond recognition.[23]

Like so many Frenchmen, Bartholdi had already been partly prepared for what he would find in Egypt in 1869 by the Universal Exhibition of 1867, where Ismaïl Pasha had sat and held court for Napoleon III and the Empress Eugénie, and where De Lesseps himself had delivered educational lectures on the Suez Canal in the company pavilion next door (figure 2.4).[24]

In that gallery, the painting of a female fellah with child and urn looked down from its elevated position onto two relief maps which celebrated modern man's capacity materially to transform Egypt's very geography, to cut an isthmus, and to do so with the assistance of newly designed French machines. But the presence in painting of a fellah woman managed at once to celebrate and to mask traditional Egyptian labor: the way fellaheen moved earth in baskets as well as water in vessels on their heads.

Indeed, the company pavilion effaced the forced labor of as many as 40,000 male fellaheen, infrequently accompanied by wives, who dug the Suez Canal until 1863. The machinery that served as the company exhibition's centerpiece had only been devised after Ismaïl Pasha's abolition in 1863 of the *corvée*, that is, the forced labor that Egypt had agreed to provide De Lesseps in his original contract. The abolition of the *corvée* was what made the machines signify so powerfully in the company's pavilion. Without machines, the Suez Canal would have come to a halt in 1863.[25] Here, for example, is a reviewer discussing the models of machines at the far end of the room:

> It is known that at the beginning, the Company counted on the labor of the indigenous to remove this enormous quantity of earth. The unskilled Egyptian roadworker is an expeditious laborer. He has almost no need of tools. With his hands he digs out the earth; he [then] fills pans that he carries on his head...This process of extraction is only as rapid as the workers are numerous, and in all other countries the expense would be exorbitant. But in the ancient land of the pharaohs where the custom is immemorial to make populations pay part of their taxes in labor, the employment of men in grand public works has nothing that can wound sincere philanthropy...[Suddenly, after the abolition of the *corvée*] it was necessary to improvise new means of execution; to substitute the machine for man.[26]

Thus fellaheen were agriculture workers, nursing the "brown breast" of Egypt's soil, but they were also indentured laborers who had executed public works from time "immemorial." "Poor devils, subject at will to exploitation and *corvées* since the invention of the pyramids."[27] That is how Narcisse Berchère described them and most others as well. Here, according to Europeans, were the very people who had built colossal ancient Egypt, its pyramids, its monuments, its canals.[28] Gautier described fellaheen as "molded" and barely "extricated" from the earth, but their work also included the soil's transport, its removal with a minimum of tools. Writing before the replacement of men by machines, Berchère conjured the spectacle of the sheer number of Egyptian peasants moving earth in the most primitive way at the Suez Canal:

> At the bottom of this large ditch which is amplified and enlarged every day... men are occupied removing earth with a pick and pickax, moving it with shovels and putting it in baskets which must be transported to the top of the excavation... Certainly, a man with a shovel in hand or carrying a basket on his back would hold no interest in himself, but multiply this unity, increase it to the number of 20,000, look at the profile of one of these trenches which we can follow to the horizon, this human hive of activity which changes and tosses; thus El-Gisr, this worksite number 4, in which a mass of small black points in movement indicate to us their occupation; and you have before your eyes a spectacle made to strike the coldest and most prejudiced minds. What here gives the measure of the work is the grandeur of the means employed to realize it; and this army of workers, this multitude, creates a truly grandiose and most moving scene.[29]

Far from being immobile, fellaheen endlessly toiled. Far from being molded by the earth, they were molding it. But together the ceaseless repetitiveness of their labor and their absorption within a multitude conjured an inextricable binding of persons and soil and also an activity that was paradoxically unchanging, like bees at a hive.

When Ismaïl Pasha abolished the *corvée* partly under English pressure to end what they called "slavery," machines emptied the isthmus's landscape of men. A few (heroic) French protagonists moved center-stage, replacing the anonymous collectivity. In his 1869 novel *Le Fellah*, Bartholdi's friend Edmond About has an Englishman concede the brilliance of France's engineers:

> The edict which forbade *corvées* constrained the genius of men to make miracles. The large dredge and the conveyor of Mr. Lavalley and Mr. Borel are the highest expressions of modern industry. You will see machines as grandiose as cathedrals and as precise as Greenwich marine watches. I visited one which did the work of 300 workers with only fifteen men; it extracted 80,000 cubic meters of earth in a month.[30]

After 1863, the spectacle no longer resided in the unimaginable number of dirt-cheap men, men whose numbers and subjection conjured the building of the pyramids by slaves. Instead, the marvel of man's prowess was signified by French monuments of modernization: those precision machines the size of cathedrals. The female fellah who supports both child and clay water vessel on the wall of the Suez Canal Company pavilion thus sublimates the labor of her 40,000 male counterparts, those men who had been forced to leave wives and children in order to work for five years altering Egypt's geography, dredging those straight-edge, modern lines of transport with their hands, picks, and baskets.

Modernization had exploited fellaheen labor but it had also moved beyond it. To be fully realized technologically, the remapping of Egypt required the loss of its "slaves" and the return of the fellaheen to their "timeless" role as agricultural workers. After extricating the soil, they needed to be returned to it in order that machines designed by French engineers take their place. And Ismaïl also hoped to profit from cotton. "Egypt is destined to become the salvation of Europe, sometimes for its wheat, sometimes for its cotton and soon for its transit. He who rules the confluence of three worlds, in such a position and with such resources, will always be a powerful and everywhere well-cherished prince."[31] Here was an Egypt that Assollant had entirely denied, and both he and this critic responded to the same Universal Exhibition of 1867. Was Egypt a land of a dying race or Europe's salvation, or both? Was the fellah a sign of Egypt's past or a necessary maker of its future? Were Egypt's people petrified by their land or were they the mobile authors of its reinvention? Was it possible to imagine Egypt without the endlessly exploited labor of its poorest class? In the late 1860s, these questions remained undecided, but how one interpreted the relationship among fellaheen, machines, and Egypt's land determined whatever provisional answers were on offer.

* * *

Listen to Photography
Who speaks and demands its turn:
"I defy all pencils!
My only master is the light of day!
The most difficult outlines,
Drawings a man would not attempt
Are, for me, always docile;
I need but look upon them.
With you I will travel,
Stopping at every moment

I will gather landscapes,
Cities and monuments;
I come as an aid to painting!
Painters who travel the roads,
I will master nature
and place it in your hands!"

(Maxime Du Camp, "Songs of Matters," 1855)[32]

Bartholdi's statement in 1885 that his earlier project represented "Egypt under the features of a female Fellah" suggests that he believed somatic, even racial, differences distinguished the Suez statue from its American counterpart. Such a suggestion returns us to his original mission, which emphasized the "study," an ambiguous term connoting drawing, and also the photography of "monuments and types." During his voyage of 1855–6, Bartholdi's efforts to turn "monuments and types" into representation were tentative, experimental, and also unlike one another. Like his draftsman's hand, the photographic machine Bartholdi wielded in Egypt had its profound limitations. One of the more famous and striking of his photographs, the *Colossi of Memnos*, introduces the problem (figure 2.5). The gravity, majesty, and silent immobility Bartholdi would later celebrate repeatedly in textual manifestos on colossal ancient Egyptian art are here beautifully conjured.[33] The photograph's vertical composition, tight cropping, extremely low horizon, and formal severity successfully exploit the eerie doubling and syncopated rhythm of difference in the two colossi, the far statue more eroded than the other, the two bluntly, blindly, gravely staring off stage left.

But early photography returns all things to the hand-held. Indeed this was considered one of its wondrous achievements: in 1849 David Brewster underscored that the sculptor now "may virtually carry in his portfolio . . . the gigantic sphinxes of Egypt."[34] Among photography's many losses was scale. Like printmakers and photographers before him, including most famously Maxime Du Camp, Bartholdi resorted to the inclusion of human beings to signal the colossal size which he so admired. At the lower left corner of the foreground statue of Memnos appear two standing, presumably Egyptian, men but they are barely visible. Not only are they diminutive (and, of course, this is what they were intended to be), they are subject to the same lighting as the statue itself. They precisely repeat in tone the corner's harsh divide between light and shadow: one man is bleached into the whiteness of light; the other darkened into the shade's obscurity. Photography seems to absorb the men into a black and white

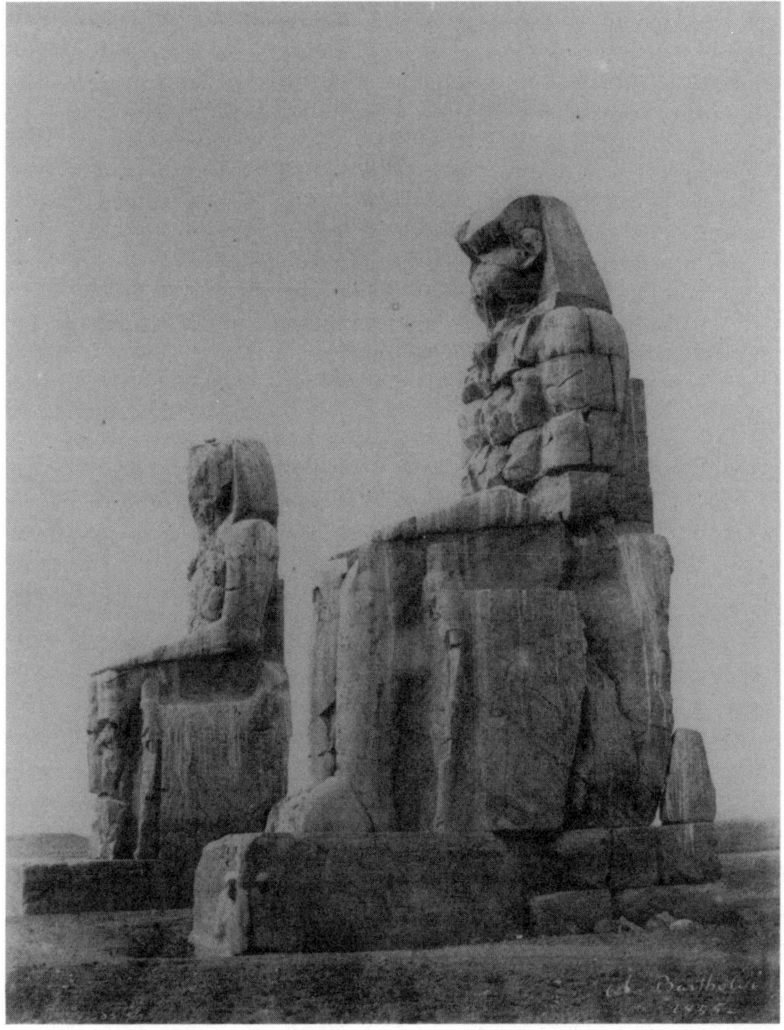

Figure 2.5 Frédéric-Auguste Bartholdi, *The Colossi of Memnos*, 1855. Salt print, Colmar, Musée Bartholdi. Photo: Christian Kempf

system that swallows their difference from their environment; it assimilates them. To focus on the monument is to lose the type.

Yes, but not quite. In one of his unpublished letters written in Egypt in 1856, Bartholdi himself further elucidates the challenge: "As for the types, I am working on them . . . Everything is fine except that people do not want to let themselves be molded [*mouler*], in photography some are afraid, the others move without stop."[35] The photograph of the Colossi of Memnos may seem to turn men into stone but in fact the medium struggles to do so, because men, unlike stone, may refuse to be photographed or they may move. The minimum two-minute exposure required for calotypes in the 1850s demanded that people mimic stone's stillness, but they seldom were able to do so. Looking again at Bartholdi's photograph, the doubling of men appears ambiguous: did the two men really look so alike or does the photograph register the occupation by one person of two different positions? Is the blurred figure at right swallowed by the shadow or by a temporal incommensurability with a self at left? Is it darkness or time or failed self-discipline that makes the man at right a ghost compared to his double at left?

Bartholdi's phrase, "people do not want to let themselves be molded," is unusual. He imagines photography's action as that of the sculptor, as a matter of molding or casting. And he ascribes volition to the people who do not allow themselves to be fixed. The term *mouler* is inherently ambiguous, connoting both "mold" and "molded," but it is clear that Bartholdi wanted the Egyptian people to fix themselves, to become statues in order to become types.[36] We are reminded of Roland Barthes's oft-cited resistance to the imperatives of photography in *Camera Lucida*: "Now, once I feel myself in the process of 'posing,' I instantaneously make another body for myself, I transform myself in advance into an image. This transformation is an active one: I feel that the Photograph creates my body or mortifies it . . ."[37] But Barthes imagines posing to entail a fixing of the self as "image" while Bartholdi imagines it as the fixing (of an other) as sculpture. The sculptor focuses, that is, not on the photographic product, but on the earlier step in which the models emulate three-dimensional sculpture in order to be made into two-dimensional representations. Thus he shifts the emphasis from photography's indexicality as an imprint of light to a prior molding of the three-dimensional world into the stillness which is photography's precondition.[38] To be photographed, the world first must be made static – impressed – but people, annoyingly, must do this themselves. While Barthes leaves undecided whether he or photography mortifies his body, Bartholdi believes the photographer cannot mortify; only models can enact their own mortification. Relative to sculpture and drawing then, photography was for Bartholdi peculiarly vulnerable to the agency of other persons. They needed to acquiesce in the making of themselves into art.

As a draftsman, the incessant movement of models was also annoying. Bartholdi said as much in another letter from his trip to fellow artists:

> I work as much as I can; as you told me, the models are not easy to make pose . . . What is absurd is that all these people when they pose, do not pose; this is even more absurd because: when individuals (especially of the female sex) decide to pose for you, they laugh and do not remain for an instant in the same pose.[39]

"When they pose, [they] do not pose": surely Bartholdi was comparing these foreign persons to paid Parisian working-class models like a man named Galali who modeled for his colossal sculpture of General Rapp in 1854 and whose self-disciplining capacity for stillness was proven in one of Bartholdi's earliest photographs. Unlike the blurred figure of Bartholdi, he performs the tour de force of holding himself in a dynamic position long enough to come into photographic clarity. Here was a man who knew how to turn himself into a statue. Sculpture and drawing and painting could compensate for the movement of the model as photography could not. The movement of sitters in photography led to invisibility. The movement of models in the other arts led to repeated sessions or to exercises of memory or to improvisations, often to anatomical inaccuracies or deformations; in short, to drawings sometimes like Bartholdi's (not blurring but another kind of uncertainty). Significantly, the painter Léon Belly wrote at length about the challenge of drawing fellah women at the river. Like Bartholdi, he admitted in a letter: "I can hardly make them pose and it is necessary entirely to remember them. Once I am sure of a *living movement,* I use models for the arms and hands, but for the movement, one no longer has it truthfully once it is posed. A figure drawn thus and found is worth a hundred made in the studio."[40] Movement thus represented a difficulty that the draftsman and painter needed to overcome through the exercise of his art (and memory). Not so for the photographer, according to Bartholdi. In this medium models, not camera operators, decided the outcome.

No surprise then that most of Bartholdi's calotypes are entirely empty of people. With some notable exceptions, often involving himself, fellow artists, and the sailing crew with whom he long lived (people whom he could apparently influence), the few photographs to include figures show them "half-consumed in blurs of emulsion."[41] The most modern of European representational technologies returned the world to the stasis associated with the primitive in Orientalist rhetoric, but it also evacuated it. The only way to capture the ethnographic type, that is, to depict people's characteristic look and dress, was to wield the rudimentary pencil just as they wielded urns, baskets, and picks. In his "Song of Matter," Du Camp had told a lie. Photography was not equivalent to seeing; it was not able to capture more than the draftsman's hand. People were not docile: it is no coincidence that Du Camp's list of subjects does not include persons. Early photography in Egypt disproved the stereotype. The Egyptian fellah was animated, not inanimate. Fellaheen were sometimes afraid, but they also moved continually, and, most vividly and most disruptively, women laughed (how powerful is that detail in Bartholdi's letter).

If Bartholdi wanted to fix Egypt's timeless primitivism in photography, he needed to point the machine at the inert. Instead of fellah women getting water, represented in the artist's drawings and later paintings, Bartholdi's calotypes – at least three – depicted ancient Egyptian water machines like the wooden *chadoufs* he denounced in his writing for their inefficiency relative to the hydraulic machines rusting at the Arsenal. Inert (water) machine may have better suited inert (photographic) machine, but many photographs, while formally quite satisfying, prove far less legible than oil paintings. For example, a calotype of a row of three *chadoufs* is uninformative relative to Bartholdi's landscape painting of the same subject exhibited at the Salon of 1864. Bartholdi's proximate, narrow view in the photograph includes neither the river from which water is being extracted nor the farmland which is being irrigated nor the persons who make the machines work. The calotype does not narrate as does his painting; instead we are offered the unpredictable arrangement of bright light and deep shadows across an irregular rocky bank and its rubble, punctuated by three vertical lines spiking a white sky; a boat at left orients us but also occludes our view. As viewers, we feel ourselves to be blocked; prevented by clumsy, irrelevant things from acquiring the information needed to situate what we see. Nor does this series of *chadoufs* look ancient as it does in the painting; rather, we see a technology which remains opaque, even trivial, to those who do not already know its mechanism, its purpose, and its centrality since antiquity to Egyptian life.

In Egypt, Bartholdi was forced to contend with the technical limitations of his media and his skills. Despite his mission to make "the photographic reproduction of the principal monuments and the most remarkable types of the diverse races," he could not fix people in photography. "Types" could only be "molded" provisionally in the (iconic) medium of drawing.

And doggedly Bartholdi made drawing after drawing that attempted to do just that, many of persons simply standing against a blank ground, either seen from the front or back – standing, that is, like statues. His later paintings would often rely on photographs for settings and on drawings for the figures, collaging the two together. But Bartholdi's drawings of fellah women stand out for their persistent interest in their activity of moving water (figure 2.1). One woman awkwardly bends down to fill an urn at the river; another crouches resting meditatively at a riverbank; one passes a vessel to another's head; another walks away from us with an urn balanced on her head. We see, in the five figures, the operation, we might say the mechanism, of their labor. We see how they lift and move things (their song of matter). The photograph of the *chadouf* tells us no such thing. Rodin was right when he later denounced photographs for arresting the body's movement while sculpture and painting could seek to evoke its progressive movement within a single figure.[42] In Egypt, Bartholdi had not yet summarized motion within a single body; during his voyage, his drawings were serial – they captured a sequence of frozen moments. Against all likelihood, he was trying again and again, in both drawing and photography, to still action and to mold persons. When he returned home, he would need to decide how to make sculpture out of them.

* * *

Twelve years after his first voyage to Egypt, Bartholdi devised a way to integrate the two objects of his official commission. Finally (colossal) monument became type and type became (colossal) monument. In so doing, he returned the female fellah to the timeless immobility that the peasant women themselves had resisted: laughing, moving, refusing, running away, working. Between 1867 and 1869, Bartholdi molded them as he had not been able to in Egypt. And he did so in the consummate material for such molding, *terre*, that is, clay but also literally "earth." Out of the earth, he would fix her. The clay models show that Bartholdi wanted a figure that was broad, stable, and simple, just the qualities he praised in ancient Egyptian sculpture like the Colossi of Memnos. He experimented with the incorporation of some movement, relying on the convention of animation so central to the European (and ancient Graeco-Roman) tradition: contrapposto, a shift in weight onto one leg, the slight asymmetry of hips. And he threw her arm up to hold a torch rather than an urn. In profile, some of the clay models closely follow Bartholdi's drawing of a fellah lifting a vessel onto her companion's head (as well as an 1863 painting by Belly devoted to the subject). But his proposed statue was intended to be some 86 feet tall on a 46-foot-high pedestal. Such a colossus could afford only so much asymmetry. Bartholdi well appreciated that the stability and majesty of Egyptian monumental sculpture resided in its grave simplicity, symmetry, and immobility. He was therefore trying to create a compromise: a sculpture that emulated and rivaled immobile Egyptian colossi and that also made clear his skill as a French sculptor. Movement, even if subtle, signaled the difference of his Frenchness.

"Egypt enlightening Asia," he grandiosely called his statue, and imagined it punctuating the Suez Canal's harbor, a sculptural monument to welcome ships to an engineering monument. His fellah thus resembled the painting of a fellah woman standing guard, or perhaps acting as hostess, high on the left wall of the Suez Canal Company pavilion at the 1867 Universal Exhibition: a timeless Egyptian water-carrier sanctioning the machine-made water-carrier that was the canal. And similarly, Bartholdi's colossal fellah woman would connote a past and a present that suppressed the recent history of fellah labor on the canal itself. Or, more accurately, this is the question. Would she conjure or erase traditional labor put to new purposes? And which of the two would appeal to the man who needed to commission the lighthouse: not De Lesseps, not Napoleon III, but Ismaïl Pasha, Viceroy of Egypt, landowner, "prince of fellaheen" but also Europeanizer, Haussmannizer, and fluent speaker of French and English?

Bartholdi's correspondence and journal reveal that he had invested great hope and effort in the project but that he also knew it was a gamble. Before returning to Egypt in April 1869, he wrote his mother from Paris:

> I am going to devote myself entirely to my Egypt business; it has the advantage of frankly showing its impossible side; but at least . . . I am seizing all means of possible support. I have excellent ones but with this, there is an aspect of the lottery and a play of luck is needed. I will do all that I can to seize the occasion . . . and if I fail, it is because there will not be a ghost of a chance.
>
> I showed my project to the Emperor and Empress. It seemed that all the world was enchanted, but they limited themselves to making wishes for my success . . . As little as this is, it permits me to say that there are [such] wishes without having to lie.
>
> I will equally have the support of Mr. Nieuwerkerke [French Superintendent of the Arts]. By the end of the week, I will have collected all [the support] that I can get. After that, I will seize the bull by the horns.[43]

Bartholdi's letters suggest that he believed De Lesseps's lack of support for his Suez lighthouse was decisive. He was probably right. Well positioned to influence both Empress Eugénie and Ismaïl Pasha, De Lesseps clearly chose not to exercise that power on Bartholdi's behalf. He was not present when the sculptor presented his idea to the emperor and empress. In Egypt, when Bartholdi joined him in his train compartment, De Lesseps slept all the way to Cairo; in Bartholdi's words, "he made [only] a diplomatic welcome to my project"; he "dampened my enthusiasm"; he continually offered an "amiable but superficial welcome." De Lesseps was again pointedly absent when Bartholdi was finally able to make his proposal to Ismaïl himself.[44] On April 11, 1869, the sculptor wrote an especially revealing letter:

> At this moment I am with M. De Lesseps at Isamaïlia in the middle of the isthmus. I acted as if he was devoted to my projects; he is very amiable to me; his hospitality is very gracious. I can only reproach him for one thing, that is for hardly supporting me in my enterprise. I pardon him although generally one prefers one's affairs to those of others; still one needs to consider how much he is occupied by his great work. My project being only a very accessory detail, he does not wish to exert himself on its behalf. Nevertheless he shows me much amiability and sympathy like someone who says: Try to succeed and I will be enchanted by it.[45]

The diplomat of Herculean ambition was damn good at what he did. Even when offering no support whatsoever, De Lesseps seemed irreproachable, even well-wishing. And Bartholdi, now 35 years old, also had the makings of a courtier: "I acted as if he was devoted to my projects."

De Lesseps may have been an instrumental, even a necessary, ally, but the man Bartholdi knew he had to convince was Ismaïl Pasha. Here is Bartholdi's account of their long-awaited encounter, arranged with some strategic behind-the-scenes effort.

> After having waited two hours the Viceroy's doctor arrives and he introduces me. I enter apartments with an entirely European aspect; the only particular characteristic being the divan which extends the circumference of half the chamber. In the salon were M. Mariette, the doctor Burguières and some servants. After some generalities, I present my drawings and statuette to the Viceroy. He looks with interest, I give him explanations, he says to me that he would prefer to see the light apparatus held on her head in the manner of fellah women. I respond to him that this would be easier, in

> order not to contradict him (although this would be less good). I ask him permission to leave him my drawings and to see him during his voyage [to France] in a month, and with a small salute I retire.
>
> This is the result of my enterprises. It is not much as you see, yet it is something. Moreover in the works being done in Cairo, I see many things to do and I will attempt to procure a little work. Thus my voyage will not remain without some fruits. For the moment it is finished. During the afternoon I made some visits . . . to the Cabinet of the Viceroy. I found no one there . . .[46]

Our limited evidence thus suggests that Ismaïl was not inclined to dislike Bartholdi's choice to represent Egypt as a female fellah. Indeed, he wanted the statue to be *more*, not less, characteristic of that "type." Sitting in his European apartments in a Cairo in the midst of being Haussmannized in time for the spectacular November inauguration of the Suez Canal, he looked favorably on the idea of art's representation of a traditional Egyptian peasant woman. The problem may have been that Bartholdi's watercolor drawing and clay statuette did not look artful enough to him. It is likely that Bartholdi intended the statue to be made out of cast metal and its light to be electric like the electrified, tall, metal lighthouse celebrated in the French section of the Universal Exhibition of 1867. But to Ismaïl, Bartholdi's monument may have appeared neither a modern engineering machine like the canal itself nor a valuable French artwork. I conjecture here. Certainly financial reasons may have played a decisive role: Ismaïl and De Lesseps were struggling to finance the completion of the canal as well as the urban transformations of Cairo. Yet, during his reign, Ismaïl paid for both lighthouses and sculptures.[47] Despite antique precedents like the Colossus of Rhodes, Ismaïl may not have liked Bartholdi's combination of these functions.

The Viceroy also may have been responding negatively to *how* Bartholdi designed his sculpture, how he imagined the female fellah. The key piece of evidence to support such a hypothesis is Ismaïl's sustained patronage of Charles Cordier. The latter sculptor, most famous for his capacity to fix ethnographic types in naturalistic, lush, often polychrome statues, had met Ismaïl and his father Ibrahim Pasha through his brother, a captain. He thus had a personal family connection to Ismaïl as had had De Lesseps to Ismaïl's predecessor, Saïd Pasha, who had granted him the rights to build the Suez Canal.[48] In 1865 Cordier had received a commission to travel to Egypt and was there from February to June 1866. He thereafter produced plasters which may also have served as seven of the ten mannequins in the Egyptian pavilion of the Universal Exhibition of 1867. According to the specialist Jeanine Durand-Révillon, Ismaïl gave Cordier as a token of gratitude his Egyptian palace at the Universal Exhibition of 1867, which Cordier moved and rebuilt in Orsay between 1868 and 1870.[49] Nor did Muslim injunctions against figural art impinge on Ismaïl's support of Cordier. He did not hesitate, for instance, to commission the sculptor to make an equestrian statue of his father Ibrahim Pasha to embellish Cairo.[50] Cordier exhibited that statue at the Salon of 1872 and it still stands outside Cairo's Opera House. (Here was a sculpture that Ismaïl was willing to commission in the late 1860s; note that Ismaïl quite conventionally chose to erect a statue honoring his familial lineage and right to rule rather than an allegorical personification.)

Ismaïl favored a sculptor other than Bartholdi. Knowing this, look at one of Cordier's several sculptures of a fellah woman which may bear a relation to the mannequins shown at the 1867 Exhibition (figure 2.6). The words "ornament" and "facility" come immediately to mind, as do "erotic," "sensual," "serpentine," "young," and "relaxed." What do not come to mind are labor or the land. This woman reaches up not to hold her vessel but as a pretext to display her body in a swelling curve. Her arms do not hold weight or move water; instead they enhance her supple elegance and suggest her receptivity to pleasure. She lifts her arms to permit us to glimpse not only her breasts beneath the low-cut opening of her robe but also the contours of her hips and the swell of her belly and abdomen highlighted by the lapping waves of her clinging drapery. If this was what Ismaïl wanted in a sculpture of a woman – and why not? It was also what Napoleon III wanted – Bartholdi's game of chance had no chance.[51]

How sympathetically does one now return to the placid sturdiness of Bartholdi's clay figures. Their heaviness and androgyny, once so banal and ordinary, now appear a not insignificant achievement. Colossal scale and an admiration of sculptures like the Colossi of Memnos; a relative lack of facility and a reliance on improvised clumsy drawing; a return to clay but an imagining of stone's immensity; even perhaps a heightened awareness of the play of light across architectural mass because of his photographic practice: these ambitions, sensitivities, and limitations had made Bartholdi produce small clay figures with a gravity and monumentality that better resembled the sheer effort and strength of women bearing water in Egypt.[52] Clumsiness can resemble effort. Yet Bartholdi also sought to

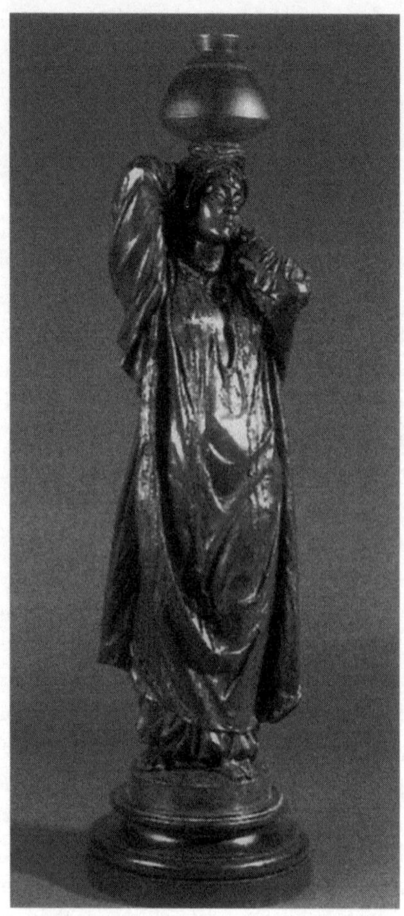

Figure 2.6 Charles-Henri-Joseph Cordier, *Woman Fellah, taking water from the Nile,* 1866. Bronze. Location unknown

immobilize those women who laughed and would not be molded. Whether we interpret the never realized, serial nature of his efforts as an index of his success or of his failure to fix the female fellah remains a question. Ultimately, however, he would immobilize the fellaheen he encountered in Egypt as the Statue of Liberty, that colossus who stands petrified in the harbor of New York City (despite her name and the chains of slavery lying broken at her feet).

Turning the living into the inanimate was not, after all, solely the purview of photography. Gautier had described not only the fellah as petrified. Some 30 years earlier he had called sculpture "a dead art . . . Nothing is more dismal to look upon than this kind of sculptural morgue, where under one pale damp ray of light are laid out the marble cadavers of former gods which their heavenly relatives have failed to collect."[53] For Gautier, moreover, the death knell of sculpture was modernization: "In our industrial and civilized world, who gives a thought to the purity and whiteness of marble? In this age of hydrogen gas and steam engines, who is still thinking of the day when Venus came naked from the sea?"[54]

This was the longstanding nineteenth-century anxiety and also the trap from which Bartholdi tried to free himself but into which he fell. As a 21-year-old, Bartholdi had shared all the arrogance and commitment to technological innovation of contemporaries such as De Lesseps. He had condemned rusting metal machinery and a reliance on traditional methods and materials like wood. He had drawn picturesque types and photographed picturesque machines in order to make art out of them, but he had been certain that Egypt's future necessarily lay in modernization and technological progress. In 1869 he expressed greater ambivalence because suddenly not only Egyptian artisanal traditions seemed to be at risk but so too did their French counterparts, including art. In 1869, Bartholdi admitted that his sculpture would have been only "a very accessory detail" to the Suez Canal. And a few days later he lamented: "It is unfortunate that with modern ideas, art and poetry seem superfluities; because truly I believe that few works of art presented in these conditions are more striking than this one. We will see; one need not despair about it yet."[55] Bartholdi believed his lighthouse was a "work of art" and yet, like so many entrepreneurs of the period, he wanted to exploit the opportunity of Egypt's modernization. In order to do so, he felt he needed, like Egypt, to update his product: to modernize sculpture by enlarging and functionalizing it in order to make it less of an "accessory detail," less of a "superfluity." But to compete with engineering on its own terms was to lose. By contrast, Cordier's elegant ornamentation claimed a traditional function for French art and, for this, Ismaïl Pasha was willing to pay.

* * *

"It was he alone who worked": so spoke Belly about Bartholdi. And work hard Bartholdi did, twice in Egypt and also throughout much of his career in France and the United States. The sculptor's work was both manual and social, a matter of making and also of continual negotiation as he sought and attempted to control commissions and also the production by artisans of his work. He acted, that is, not only as a manual laborer but also as a diplomat, businessman, foreman, and engineer. His primary identification was, however, as an artist who, with his hands, made his art. Yet his particular specialty, sculpture, especially colossal sculpture, as well as his moment in history, were so betwixt and between: between the hand-made and the engineered, between clay and the machine, between the primitive and the modern. So too was Egypt. And the French, perhaps especially the artists, were undecided about what they hoped for there.

In Egypt Bartholdi wielded both the rudimentary pencil and the modern photographic machine. And although it is true that only the primitive tool could represent the primitive fellah who carried urns and picks, while the camera could record machines like *chadoufs*, the difference between what a pencil could do and what a machine could do hinges on other distinctions: not primitive versus modern, not simple tool versus advanced technology (*chadoufs* after all were ancient and simple machines), but animate versus inanimate, active versus static, living versus inert. The camera returned man to an immobile world of stone things and also prophesied an engineered future in which machines evacuated people from the landscape: it pointed in both directions. The draftsman, by contrast, participated in the same (present-day) economy of human effort as the fellah and only Bartholdi the draftsman and sculptor of clay was able to create that effort's analog, that effort's representation. When, however, Bartholdi turned the female fellah into a lighthouse he projected turning her not merely into a cast (rather than hand-molded) sculpture but also into a hollow, inert, and static machine, a machine which inverted the camera's absorption of light and sent light out from its empty core.

Valued "a little less than an animal and a little more than a plant," the fellah, according to Maxime Du Camp writing in 1854, was no more than a mechanism of labor: the fellah was "something which is born, lives and dies like a man, but is not one... [the fellah] is not even a slave because a slave represents capital, this is an animated machine."[56] Fundamentally, the question in nineteenth-century France was whether the fellah, or to be more specific the fellah's labor, was deemed human or not. Inertness, after all, describes both the clay fellah conjured by Gautier and the machine fellah denigrated by Du Camp, both the molded and the mold, both the primordial, earthen past and the industrial future. The dehumanized fellah could be identified with either. In Egypt, the laughing, restless, hardworking women had proven that fellaheen were animate, human, and resistant to the machine's propensity to render the world inanimate and inert. Bartholdi's colossal Suez statue began in the frustrating encounter of draftsman and photographer with these animate persons. Nevertheless, the fellah as lighthouse seems to me characteristically undecided, conjuring a stone past and an industrial future but entirely uncertain about Egypt's living present.

Notes

This essay stems from a book in progress entitled *Colossal Engineering (Reconnecting the Suez Canal, Statue of Liberty, Eiffel Tower and Panama Canal).* Another aspect of this work has been published as "Geometry/Labor = Volume/Mass?", *October*, 106 (Fall 2003), 3–34. Both essays were funded by an Andrew W. Mellon New Directions Fellowship and a UC Berkeley Townsend Center Initiative Grant for Associate Professors. I am indebted to my invaluable graduate research assistant Amy Freund, whose industriousness both in Paris and Colmar made this essay possible. I also would like to thank Bartholdi expert Régis Hueber, curator at the Musée Bartholdi, for providing access to his archives, and Christian Kempf for his professional generosity. As always discussion with Todd Olson importantly enriched my thinking. All translations are mine unless otherwise indicated.

1 On Bartholdi's voyage of 1855–6, see the catalogs to three key exhibitions curated by Régis Hueber at the Musée Bartholdi, Colmar: *D'un album de voyage: Auguste Bartholdi en Egypte (1855–1856)* (1990); *Au Yemen en 1856: Photographies et dessins d'Auguste Bartholdi* (1994); and *Dahabieh, Almées et Palmiers: 52 Dessins du premier voyage en Orient 1855–56 d'Auguste Bartholdi* (1998). Also see Régis Hueber, "Les Salons d'Amilcar: Notes sur les dessins et tableaux orientalistes d'Auguste Bartholdi," *Annuaire de la Société d'Histoire et d'Archéologie de Colmar* (1993), 75–137. On Bartholdi's photography in Egypt, see the fine essays by Christian Kempf, "Bartholdi et le Calotype," in *D'un album de voyage*, 15–23, and Claire Bustarret, "Du Nil au Yémen: Bartholdi Photographe," *Histoire de l'art*, 7 (October 1989), 35–52. See also Pierre Provoyeur, "Artistic Problems," in *Liberty: The French-American Statue in Art and History*, New York Public Library, exhibition catalog (New York: Harper & Row, 1986), 78–99. The latter catalog is an excellent resource concerning Bartholdi.

2 Léon Belly, to his mother, Cairo, July 7, 1856, Archives Municipales de Saint-Omer, MS 1159, cited in Hueber, *Dahabieh, Almées et Palmiers*, 7. On Belly, see Conrad de Mandach, "Léon Belly (1827–1877)," *Gazette des Beaux-Arts*, I (1913), 73–84, and 143–57.

3 Régis Hueber, "A Thousand Miles up the Nile," in *D'un album de voyage*, 25–47.

4 Anne Middleton Wagner, *Jean Baptiste-Carpeaux: Sculptor of the Second Empire* (New Haven: Yale University Press, 1986).

5 Cited in Kempf, "Bartholdi et le Calotype," in *D'un album de voyage*, 19.

6 Salon of 1857, *View of Monfalout on the banks of the Nile*; Salon of 1861, *Café on the banks of the Nile*; Salon of 1864, *Children are everywhere the same*; and *Chadoufs: Irrigation Machines on the banks of the Nile*; Salon of 1865, *Mosque of Djirdjeh.*

7 Other scholars have recounted this fact; see, for example, Provoyeur, "Artistic Problems," 92, who states that the watercolors and maquettes for the two projects "provide visible proof of a line of descent." See also Pierre Vidal, *Frédéric-Auguste Bartholdi: Par la main. Par l'esprit* (Paris: Les Créations du Pélican, 2000), 47. The term *fellah* was current in France from the seventeenth century and generally connotes an Egyptian peasant; it derives from the Arabic word *fāllăh* (Maghrebian Arabic: *fęllăh*), meaning cultivator.

8 See also Frédéric-Auguste Bartholdi, *The Statue of Liberty Enlightening the World* (1885; New York: N.Y. Bound, 1984), 37.

9 Provoyeur, "Artistic Problems," 92.

10 Edmond About [Charles-Edmond Chojecki], *Le Fellah: Souvenirs d'Egypte* (Paris: Hachette, 1870), 154.

11 Christine Peltre, *Orientalism in Art*, trans. John Goodman (New York: Abbeville Press, 1998), 158.

12 See, for example, statues by Louis Kley, *Egyptian Woman Getting Water* (Salon of 1861), and by Didier Debut, *Small Girl Fellah* (Salon of 1868). See paintings, for example, by Léon Belly, *Female Fellaheen on the Banks of the Nile* (Salon of 1863); Léon Bonnat, *A Female Fellah and her Infant Son* (Salon of 1870); Gérôme, *Fellah Women Getting Water* (Salon of 1870).

13 On Cordier's "mannequins" and statues of female fellaheen, see *Charles Cordier, 1827–1905: L'autre et l'ailleurs*, Musée d'Orsay, exhibition catalog (Paris: Éditions de La Martinière, 2004), 72–7, 166–8, 214–16; Georges Douin, *Histoire du règne du Khédive Ismaïl: L'Apogée 1867–1873* (Rome: Stampata nell' Istituto Poligrafico, 1934), ii. 16; Charles Edmond, *L'Egypte à l'Exposition Universelle de 1867* (Paris: Dentu, 1867), 238.

14 Jean-Marie Carré, *Voyageurs et écrivains français en Egypte* (Cairo: Institut français d'archéologie orientale, 1956), ii. 267.

15 Alexander Schölch, *Egypt for Egyptians! The Socio-Political Crisis in Egypt 1878–1882* (London: Ithaca Press, 1981), 18–20.

16 In 1787 Volney argued that the original Arab conquerors, the first of Egypt's four races, were perpetuated in the fellaheen who conserved their original physiognomy. *Voyage en Syrie et en Egypte* (1787; repr. Paris: Fayard, 1998), 62.

17 Théophile Gautier, *Voyage en Egypte*, ed. Paolo Tortonese (1869; Paris: La Boîte à Documents, 1991), 47–9.

18 Alfred Assollant, "La Femme fellah de M. Landelle," *L'Exposition Universelle de 1867 Illustrée: Publication Internationale autorisée par la Commission Impériale* (Paris: 106 Rue Richelieu, 1867), ii, 115–16.

19 Edward Said, *Orientalism* (New York: Random House, 1978), 108–9.

20 Gautier, *Voyage en Egypte*, 47.

21 Colmar, Musée Bartholdi, letter to Emile Jacob, January 26, 1856, partially cited in Hueber, "A Thousand Miles up the Nile," 44.

22 Hueber, "A Thousand Miles Up the Nile," 25. On the Suez Canal, see Tom F. Peters, *Building the Nineteenth Century* (Cambridge, MA: MIT Press, 1996), 178–202; J. Charles-Roux, *L'Isthme et le Canal de Suez*, 2 vols. (Paris: Hachette, 1901).

23 Colmar, Musée Bartholdi, journal entry for April 11, 1869; letter of April 15, 1869.

24 On De Lesseps's lectures see Frédéric Le Play, *Commission impériale. Rapport sur l'Exposition Universelle de 1867 à Paris. Précis des opérations et liste des collaborateurs avec un appendice sur l'avenir des expositions* (Paris: Imprimerie impériale, 1869), 113. On the Egyptian pavilions, see Edmond, *L'Egypte à l'Exposition Universelle de 1867*, and Zeynep Çelik, *Displaying the Orient* (Berkeley: University of California Press, 1992), 57–63, 111–16.

25 Peters, *Building the Nineteenth Century.*

26 *L'Exposition Universelle de 1867 Illustrée*, i. 116.

27 Narcisse Berchère, *Le Désert de Suez: Cinq mois dans l'isthme* (Paris: Hetzel, 1863), 115.

28 See, for example, Edwin de Leon, *The Khedive's Egypt, or The Old House of Bondage under New Masters* (New York: Harper & Brothers, 1878), 225–8.

29 Berchère, *Le Désert de Suez*, 196–8.

30 About, *Le Fellah*, 302.

31 F. Ducuing (ed.), "Les Visites souveraines: Ismaïl Pacha," in *L'Exposition Universelle de 1867 Illustrée*, i. 374.

32 Maxime Du Camp, "Songs of Matter," in *Modern Songs* (1855). Cited in Julia Ballerini, "Photography Conscripted: Horace Vernet, Gerard de Nerval and Maxime Du Camp in Egypt," Ph.D. dissertation, New York, CUNY, 1987, 209.

33 Bartholdi, *The Statue of Liberty Enlightening the World*, 35–7.

34 Geraldine A. Johnson (ed.), *Sculpture and Photography: Envisioning the Third Dimension* (Cambridge: Cambridge University Press, 1998), 4.

35 Colmar, Musée Bartholdi, letter to Emile Jacob, January 26, 1856.

36 *La Sculpture française au XIXe siècle*, Paris, Grand Palais, exhibition catalog (Paris: Réunion des Musées Nationaux, 1986), 67.

37 Roland Barthes, *Camera Lucida: Reflections on Photography*, trans. Richard Howard (New York: Hill & Wang, 1981), 10–11.

38 Bartholdi's description of photography as a form of casting was certainly informed by scientists' prevalent linking of the two as different means to document specimens, specifically racial types. See Christine Barthe, "Des modèles et des normes, allers-retours entre photographies, et sculptures ethnographiques," 93–113, and Edouard Papet, "Le Moulage sur nature ethnographique au XIXe siècle," in *Charles Cordier, 1827–1905*, 127–8; see also Christine Barthe, "'Les Éléments de l'observation': Des daguerréotypes pour l'anthropologie," in *Le Daguerréotype français: Un objet photographique*, Musée d'Orsay, exhibition catalog (Paris: Réunion des Musées Nationaux, 2003), 73–86, and Edouard Papet, "Le Moulage sur nature au service de la science," in *A fleur de peau: Le Moulage sur nature au XIXe siècle*, Musée d'Orsay, exhibition catalog (Paris: Réunion des Musées Nationaux, 2002), 88–95.

39 Colmar, Musée Bartholdi, letter of April 10, 1856.

40 Mandach, "Léon Belly," 150 (Belly's emphasis).

41 Ballerini, "Photography Conscripted," 281.

42 See Jane R. Becker, "Auguste Rodin and Photography: Extending the Sculptural Idiom," in Dorothy Kosinski (ed.), *The Artist and the Camera: Degas to Picasso* (Dallas: Dallas Museum of Art, 1999), 92.

43 Colmar, Musée Bartholdi, letter of March 23, 1869. Partially cited in *Dessins*, 41.

44 Colmar, Musée Bartholdi, letters or entries of April 5 and April 15, 1869.

45 Colmar, Musée Bartholdi, letter of April 11, 1869.

46 Colmar, Musée Bartholdi, letter of April 8, 1869. Partially cited in *Dessins*, 42.

47 According to De Leon, *The Khedive's Egypt*, 366, Ismaïl Pasha spent £200,000 on lighthouses on the Red Sea and the Mediterranean during his regime.

48 Jeanine Durand-Révillon, "La Galerie anthropologique du Muséum national d'histoire naturelle et Charles-Henri-Joseph Cordier," in *La Sculpture ethnographique: De la Vénus Hottentote à la Tehura de Gauguin* (Paris: Réunion des Musées Nationaux, 1994), 62.

49 Ibid.

50 Ibid. See also Jean-Jacques Luthi, *La Vie quotidienne en Egypte au temps des Khédives* (Paris: L'Harmattan, 1998), 66, who also points out that, contrary to common assumptions, there were no major objections to such sculptures on the part of Muslims, as "they had come to distinguish an idol from a work of art."

51 Add to this Ismaïl's interest in the equally slick, flirtatious art of Gérôme, as evidenced in an 1868 letter to the artist by his secretary; see Hélène Lafont-Couturier, "Mr. Gérôme works for Goupil," in *Gérôme and Goupil: Art and Enterprise* (Paris: Éditions de la Réunion des Musées Nationaux, 2000), 28–9.

52 The thesis about photography is Bustarret's in "Du Nil au Yémen."

53 "Salon of 1841," *Revue de Paris*, 3/28, 155, cited in Wagner, *Jean Baptiste-Carpeaux*, 18.

54 Ibid.

55 Colmar, Musée Bartholdi, letter of April 17, 1869.

56 Maxime Du Camp, *Le Nil, Egypte et Nubie* (1854; Paris: Hachette, 1877), 148, cited in Véronique Magri, *Le Discours sur l'autre: À travers quatre récits de voyage en Orient* (Paris: Honoré Champion Éditeur, 1995), 89.

3

Cultural Crossings: Sartorial Adventures, Satiric Narratives, and the Question of Indigenous Agency in Nineteenth-Century Europe and the Near East

Mary Roberts

> *Travesty.* 1. A burlesque or ludicrous imitation of a serious work, literary composition of this kind; hence, a grotesque or debased image or likeness. 2. An alteration of dress or appearance; a disguise.[1]

Humor, play, transformation, and transgression: such are the pleasures of cultural cross-dressing and the source of its longstanding appeal within Western culture. As an artifact of cultural contact, cultural cross-dressing often expresses a desire to court the exotic and at times threatening, possibilities of cultural difference. Yet, as Low has argued, cultural cross-dressing is also an eloquent distillation of the Western Orientalist's desire for power over the Orient.[2] This expression of power and desire through sartorial metamorphosis engages us with the exploits of many of the most notorious Western travelers. When Ottoman culture is the focus for such sartorial imaginings the myth of the harem is never far from view.

In recent years cultural cross-dressing has been central to the critical reassessment of Orientalist visual culture because of its entanglement with the self-fashioning of the Orientalist.[3] With its emphasis on performance in the construction of identity, cultural cross-dressing remains of particular interest because it challenges us to consider the mutability of identity across the boundaries of culture and gender. For the West, as Garber contends, the East has been not only a site for the affirmation of an authoritative Western subject, but has also been a liminal space in which to articulate a transvestic subject positioning that throws the fixity of gender categories into crisis.[4]

Despite this emphasis on "category crisis," in the recent literature on cultural cross-dressing the focus has remained solely on the identity of the Westerner. An impasse has been reached on the issue of indigenous agency. As Low argues, where the indigene adopts the dress of the West, there is consistently an errant detail that betrays the attempt to pass as a Westerner. This effort by the indigene which suffers from being "almost the same but not quite" marks a failure to accede to the "flexible positional superiority" of the Westerner.[5] While acknowledging the persistence of this disabling trope of the indigene as mimic within Western discourse, it is my contention that the phenomenon of Western cultural cross-dressing also engendered a parodic response within Ottoman culture in the nineteenth century. Through the examples that I analyze in this essay, I will argue that a counter-play emerges in which gendered cross-dressing is engaged by Ottomans to travesty Western cultural cross-dressing. As a consequence of this travesty the Western stereotype of the Ottoman harem is dislodged from its fixity. In order to understand the efficacy of this parody it is important to examine more closely the parameters of the dominant Western myth. The mythology of the British artist John Frederick Lewis, as the "languid lotus eater," addresses the power of this myth within art-historical analysis and functions in this essay as an exemplar of the dominant masculine model and thus a counterpoint to my later examples of Ottoman travesties. What it shares with them is an investment in the power of masquerade that reveals itself as disguise.

Very little is known about the decade John Frederick Lewis spent in Cairo in the 1840s, despite the profound impact of this journey upon his art. In lieu of a first-person narrative, a mythology of the artist's "going native" has developed around William Makepeace Thackeray's laconic account published in his *Notes on a Journey from Cornhill to Grand Cairo*.[6] This mythology of the artist was traditionally assimilated into art-historical accounts, enhancing the authority of Lewis's realist Orientalism.[7] The particular appeal of Thackeray's account lies in its vivid construction of Lewis's Oriental masquerade and its masterful performance of the artist's cultural assimilation.

In Cairo, Thackeray discovered the artist living in the "Arab quarter" away from the expatriate community, transformed from the dandy of the London club into "a languid lotus-eater" living "a hazy, lazy, tobaccofied life" in the "most complete Oriental fashion." Setting the scene, Thackeray characterized Lewis's courtyard and house as picturesque and quintessentially oriental:

> we made J.'s quarters; and, in the first place, entered a broad covered court or porch, where a swarthy, tawny attendant, dressed in blue, with white turban, keeps a perpetual watch. Servants in the East lie about all the doors, it appears; and you clap your hands, as they do in the dear old "Arabian Nights," to summon them. This servant disappeared through a narrow wicket, which he closed after him; and went into the inner chambers to ask if his lord [J. F. Lewis] would receive us.[8]

A slippage between fantasy and realist observation in this text ensures that contemporary Cairo becomes synonymous with the Arabian Nights fantasy, a device through which Thackeray imagines himself as a visitor to Lewis as Eastern "lord." The erotic possibilities of this identification are augmented by Thackeray's description of a woman inside Lewis's house observing the writer through the lattice screens: "There were wooden lattices to those arched windows, through the diamonds of one of which I saw two of the most beautiful, enormous, ogling, black eyes in the world, looking down upon the interesting stranger... Why the deuce was Zuleika there, with the beautiful black eyes!"[9] The entire narrative entertains an image of Lewis as harem master with slaves at his beck and call, and this allusion to his serving girl encourages the reader to imagine what transpires in the private quarters of Lewis's house, which seem veiled in all the mystery of the Oriental harem.

The emphasis on transformation is further enhanced when Lewis emerges to greet him. Thackeray suggests that Lewis looks like and lives as an Orientalized gentleman. The writer gives us a vivid picture of his first encounter:

> J—— appeared. Could it be the exquisite of the "Europa" and the "Trois Frères?" A man – in a long yellow gown, with a long beard somewhat tinged

> with gray, with his head shaved, and wearing on it first a white wadded cotton nightcap, second, a red tarboosh – made his appearance and welcomed me cordially. It was some time, as the Americans say, before I could "realise" the *semillant* J. of old times. He shuffled off his outer slippers before he curled up on the divan beside me. He clapped his hands, and languidly called "Mustapha". Mustapha came with more lights, pipes, and coffee; and then we fell to talking about London, and I gave him the last news of the comrades in that dear city. As we talked, his Oriental coolness and languor gave way to British cordiality; he was the most amusing companion of the —— club once more. He has adopted himself outwardly, however, to the Oriental life. When he goes abroad he rides a gray horse with red housings, and has two servants to walk beside him. He wears a very handsome, grave costume of dark blue, consisting of an embroidered jacket and gaiters, and a pair of trousers, which would make a set of dresses for an English family. His beard curls nobly over his chest, his Damascus scimitar on his thigh. His red cap gives him a venerable and Bey-like appearance. There is no gewgaw or parade about him as in some of your dandified young Agas. I should say that he is a Major-General of Engineers, or a grave officer of State. We and the Turkified European, who found us at dinner, sat smoking in solemn divan.[10]

Thackeray designates a particular social positioning for Lewis, conveying the artist's intimacy with Cairene society and construing him as an expert at the Orientalist's game of semblance. So convincing is Lewis's charade (even down to the precision of his mannerisms) that it is some time before Thackeray can unmask the disguise and identify Lewis's "British cordiality." Although it is unlikely that Lewis's costume worked as camouflage, Thackeray entertained this notion and was particularly impressed by its success in the public sphere, enabling Lewis to blend into his environment as "venerable" and "Bey-like." The descriptive emphasis on Lewis's clothing in this text reinforces the assertion of his assimilation and thereby his capacity to avail himself of exotic pleasures. Thackeray's account of Lewis's Eastern masquerade combines artistic practicality and erotic fascination, because Lewis's clothing facilitates his intimate knowledge of his subject matter.

For Thackeray, Lewis's masquerade signals his transformation from dandy to Oriental. He prefaces his description by entreating his reader to recall Lewis's previous life in London: "You remember J——, and what a dandy he was, the faultlessness of his boots and cravats, the brilliancy of his waistcoats and kid gloves; we have seen his splendour in Regent Street, in the Tuileries, or on the Toledo."[11] This description of Lewis's precision in dress has its parallel in Rochford's portrait of the young Lewis (figure 3.1). In this fashionable portrait, Lewis is self-styled as the immaculately groomed dandy. Each element of dress is carefully considered and worn with self-conscious precision – from the starched dress shirt, the carefully folded black silk stock around his neck, the neatly tailored black coat with patterned vest to the jaunty watch-chain – together they convey an image of a fashionable gentleman of urban refinement.[12] The theatricality of this self-presentation is further emphasized by the staged conceit of the backdrop and the dramatically withdrawn curtain. This representation of the young Lewis as man about town forms a vivid contrast to Thackeray's word-portrait of Lewis as the reclusive "languid lotus-eater" in Cairo and its appealing image of the artist's exotic refuge from modernity. And yet there are some significant similarities in approach to dress in Rochford's young dandy and Lewis's Oriental masquerade. Both are premised upon a notion of dress as artifice, and a theatrical performance of the self is paramount. Indeed the dandy, whose sartorial mode is characterized by a meticulous attention to detail, seems particularly suited to the practice of cross-cultural disguise.[13] The performative aspect of dandyism enables Lewis to assume his Oriental guise. I would argue that Lewis's Eastern costume operates as a supplementary layer in the dandy's cultivation of artifice, and Lewis, as the dandy masquerading in Eastern dress, became a surrogate for Thackeray and other British men in his intimate experience of domestic life in Cairo.

An extract from a short monographic article on Lewis published in *The Portfolio* of 1892 succinctly articulates the enchantment of Thackeray's account for Lewis's subsequent biographers and the power of this myth of cultural cross-dressing: "Lewis here stands before us as a living figure, in his strange metamorphosis from the Western dandy into the bearded, grave, and reverend Oriental, taking his part *au grand sérieux*, and both dressing and playing it to perfection, without the slightest tinge of the amateur ill at ease in his unwonted trappings."[14] In this account replaying Lewis's sartorial metamorphosis, the Occidental writer and reader become complicit with the artist: they have a shared insight into his masterful performance of cultural assimilation. Similarly Lewis's harem paintings offer the viewer an imaginary identification with the artist's privileged vantage point, so that Lewis becomes a proxy for Western men's fictitious access to the harem.

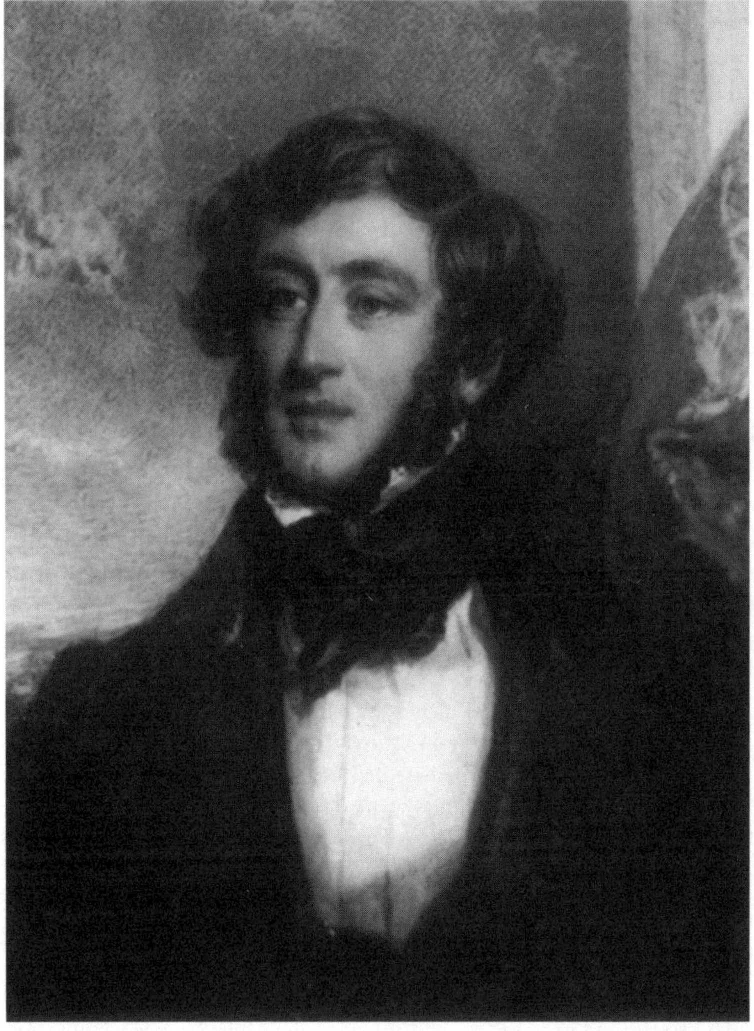

Figure 3.1 Jacques Rochford, *Portrait of J. F. Lewis, R.A*, ca. 1826. Miniature on ivory. Private collection

By the time Lewis exhibited his first Orientalist painting *The Hhareem* to great acclaim in the Old Watercolour Society of 1850, Thackeray's account was well known to the British public. Exhibiting this painting heralded a new phase in Lewis's career, marking his emergence as an Orientalist, a designation that was later given greater authority because of Lewis's decade of isolation from Britain and immersion in Cairene culture.[15] Thackeray's exaggerated, playful account of the artist as a "languid lotus-eater" has been invested with veridical status by subsequent art historians, as proof of the artist's authority in relation to his favored subject matter, the harem, and (following the familiar circular logic of realist Orientalism) his paintings are seen to confirm this.[16] One effect of this myth is to obscure the fact that Lewis would have been unable to enter respectable Ottoman harems in Cairo, and that in all likelihood he relied upon contemporary women travelers, who were able to gain entrance, for his knowledge of this domestic realm. Nonetheless, back in England such constraints were overlooked as Lewis's magnificent painting initiated his particular preoccupation with the ethnographic harem, characterized by the combined traits of exoticism and veracity.

There are parallels between Lewis's masquerade and the spectatorial position implied by his harem paintings. In both, the viewer/reader secures imaginary access to the harem women via identification with the artist's view. In Thackeray's account, Lewis becomes the surrogate through his assumption of the position of harem master, and a similar notion is articulated in the *Illustrated London News*'s appraisal of *The Hhareem*:

> This is a marvellous picture; such as men love to linger around, but such as women, we observed, pass rapidly by. There is nothing in the picture, indeed, to offend the finest female delicacy: it is all purity of appearance; but, at the same time, it exhibits woman, to a woman's mind, in her least attractive qualities. A female slave, of exquisite symmetry, and of beauty too (in the Eastern notion of the term), is brought into the hhareem, and the heavy drapery in which she was wrapped has just been removed by a female attendant. What a scene is now before her! The lord of the seraglio is seen seated, and surrounded by his women, who lie in Eastern repose at his feet. Wherever the eye rests all is Oriental luxury and ease: flowers and fruit and rich dresses lend fresh variety and colour to the scene. How gracefully, how modestly she stands, while surveyed by the lord and ladies of the hhareem; and how unconscious she is of the laughter of the black attendants of the palace. The rich, full lazy eyes of the ladies are exquisitely caught.[17]

In this passage the critic distinguishes several gazes: the surveying gaze of the lord of the seraglio, whose judgment of the new slave is the fulcrum of the painting's narrative; the lazy eyes of the harem wives, who scrutinize the new slave as a potential rival for their master's attentions; the modest recoil and downcast look of the vulnerable new slave, who is not fully conscious of the dynamics within the harem she has entered. It is the gaze of the male viewer, however, which oversees and is pre-eminent in this passage, it is he who interprets all others (even the female gallery visitor). His eye enters and wanders through the harem, lingering on the pleasures of "Oriental luxury and ease" that are so masterfully evoked through Lewis's watercolor technique.[18] Within the narrative logic of the work, the scene of unveiling is offered for the pleasure of the harem master, and his position of visual mastery over the harem is adopted by the male viewer, who enumerates the pleasures of this scene while also maintaining the distance of an authoritative interpreter. The dual capabilities of the masquerade (of identification and distancing) have their parallels in this process of spectatorship. What operates is a double maneuver that functions, like cultural cross-dressing, to enable the viewer (insistently masculine) to take on the imaginary guise of the master and yet also to distance himself from this Eastern lord, casting a "disinterested" gaze, laying claim to veracity and objectivity. In contrast, the gaze of the British woman is nowhere to be located in this image; the critic for the *Illustrated London News* insists that she passes by rapidly, disengaged but not offended. In this passage there is an implicit denial of the British woman's privileged access and sustained interest in Ottoman harems. Such interest is evident in the numerous harem accounts published in women's travelogs throughout the nineteenth century.

Emmeline Lott is one such female traveler whose numerous stories of harem life in Egypt and Turkey were published in her diaries of 1866, 1867, and 1869.[19] One of these tales, in her diary of 1867, provides a fascinating counterpoint to Lewis because this text inverts and displaces the privilege of the European male traveler through a story that enlists cross-dressing for the purposes of parody. Whereas Thackeray's account of Lewis's masquerade implied the artist's access to harem life and authority as an intermediary for his Western audience, the tale recounted by Emmeline Lott satirizes the Western male traveler's desire to enter the Ottoman harem. This English harem governess retold a story recounted to her by the itinerant storyteller, the Mohaddetyn Yusef, inside the harem of Ismaïl Pasha, the Viceroy of Egypt. The story is at least third-hand. Yusef had been told it in the Ottoman court by Hassan Ali, the sultan's grand eunuch, who himself heard it from the story's central protagonist, Kaleb, one of the eunuchs in his charge.[20] Although the story bears some remarkable similarities to Adolphus Slade's travelog, its truth is difficult to ascertain.[21] I am, however, less interested in ascertaining the veracity of this account than in exploring it as a form of mythic recasting of the power relations in the harem fantasy through the strategy of cross-dressing.

The tale involves two travelers, the Duke of Oporto and Sir Robert Cotton, whose desire to enter the Ottoman sultan's harem was exploited by the harem eunuchs. These two "renowned adventurers" approached Kaleb, requesting access to the harem women in his charge in exchange for a vast sum of money. Capitalizing on the gullibility of these English travelers, Kaleb colluded with the young eunuchs in his charge and Barbab Ali to stage an elaborate harem charade. The eunuchs masqueraded as odalisques to "entertain" their Western guests. Those who masterminded this theater conceived it not only as a way of profiting from the fools, but also as retaliation against Western men who had transgressed Islamic religious sanctions through cultural cross-dressing. Their retributive sentiment was focused on Richard Burton, who had paraded as a Pathan doctor in 1853 in order to enter the sacred cities of Mecca and Medina.[22]

We are told that Kaleb thought long and hard about how to carry out his deception and thereby "clutch the *paras* [money] of the *Frenks* [Europeans], and then laugh in their beards, without committing any real indiscretion, or bringing himself within the pale of the Moslem law."[23] In order to negotiate these considerations, a clear distinction was made between the site of the real harem of the reigning sultan and the sham. The chosen venue was the Rococo Kiosk "in the now wild and neglected grounds of the old Seraglio," well away from the Sultan's harem it purported to represent. To further secure the distance between the sultan's harem and its simulation, the reader is informed that at the time the deception was enacted the sultan and his harem were at his summer kiosk in Ismid.[24]

The exuberant descriptions of the rehearsals of this performance evince the anticipatory pleasures for the participants, and our narrators (Yusef and Lott) also enjoy rehearsing it for their respective audiences. Costume and make-up were crucial, so they procured "all the most magnificent dresses, shawls, and kerchiefs, all the most costly jewels, all the prettiest embroidered slippers, all the gaudiest artificial flowers, and all the choicest cosmetics."[25] Much time and effort were expended transforming the young, mostly dark-skinned eunuchs into fair and feminine odalisques. The alchemy of this transformation is described as follows:

> [They used] marvellous cosmetics, by the power of which it was possible to make black, white. Eastern washes and dyes, however, are truly wonder-

> ful . . . the countenances of the dusky eunuchs became as white as alabaster; the tint of roses rested on their cheeks, their lips were ruby bright, and their hands and arms were suffused with a pink shade as beautiful as that which adorns the loveliest damsels of the icy-cold West.[26]

The rituals which conformed to the Western stereotype of the harem were enacted, the smoking of the chibouque, the indulgence in confectionery, and coffee served in exquisite jeweled *findjans* and filligree *zarfs*. The crowning glory of the charade was the presentation of bouquets of flowers by Sorab Ali and Yaneh to the two "duped Englishmen." This action received great praise as evidence of the thespian skills of the "improvised ladies," and the reader is assured that there is no trace of caricature in the elegant performance of these eunuchs. Here we find a satiric counterpart to the finesse that Burton stressed in his narrative of cultural cross-dressing which functioned as evidence of his cultural immersion, just one example of the way in which Burton's prose, as Edward Said has argued, "radiates a sense of assertion and domination over all the complexities of Oriental life."[27] In contrast to the assertion of Orientalist mastery in Burton's account, Lott's reader is encouraged to enjoy the lampoon at the expense of the Western men. Throughout the rehearsals, the hilarity of the charade and its enjoyment by the participants are repeatedly emphasized. The room was decorated to perfection, and the spectacle is described as follows:

> The whole scene was, indeed, one to charm the eyes and stimulate the senses of the infatuated intruders on the sacred precincts. No enchanted palace of the Peris could have more enraptured the gazers . . . The masquerading houris had been so admirably got up, that the delusion was complete.[28]

An important feature of this room was a trap door, on which the two Englishmen were seated, giving Kaleb the power to facilitate their speedy departure. On commencement of the rendezvous the Duke of Oporto and Sir Robert Cotton apprehended the scene before them "in a paroxysm of delight." Refreshments were duly served and the planned entertainments proceeded without difficulties until the two "simulated stars of loveliness" presented their posies of flowers.

> As fate would have it, as they were in the very act of making their last salutation, their headdresses became unfastened, fell, and displayed to view

> two shaven skulls. The two Giaours [foreigners] who were on the point of taking the proffered flowers with outstretched hands, rose from their *kursis* in evident amazement and bewilderment at this unexpected sight.[29]

At this point the trap door was activated and the foreigners were disposed of down its chute into the Bosphorus while the performers dissolved into fits of laughter, shouting: "*Mashallah, Mashallah! Janum! Janum!* We now can laugh in the beards of the *Franks*."[30] The men who retrieved the Englishmen from the Bosphorus reported their response:

> Gradually they called to mind, that, a short time before, they had been feasting their eyes on a bevy of lovely Peris. Then the strange incident of the falling head-dresses crossed their minds, and began to excite grave doubts as to the nature of the spectacle for which they had paid so dearly. Whether they really comprehended thoroughly how far the Moslems had laughed in their beards must ever remain a mystery. At the time, they felt only too thankful at having escaped a fearful death, or a disaster almost more fearful still.[31]

The tale is concluded with an account of their speedy departure from port.

Like the masculine spectator of Lewis's *The Hhareem*, in Lott's story the harem is staged for the British men, organized around their vantage point; it is enticingly close and pleasurably excites all their senses. This tale also, however, places the reader behind the scenes to witness the delight of those who are performing this harem theater. The British gentlemen have the illusion of control, but it is the eunuch Kaleb who orchestrates the show, terminating it at whim. When the charade reaches a climactic point where the illusion is unsustainable, the men are jettisoned from their central position into the Bosphorus, replaying what had been reputedly the sultan's means of disposing of odalisques. What remains is doubt and uncertainty for these men; the prospect of having escaped death or castration is their only consolation. In contrast to the confirmation of identity offered by the harem paintings, this story profoundly disturbs the positioning of the European male subject.

This tale is effectively deployed by Emmeline Lott to imply authority over her countrymen in relation to the Ottoman harem. Indeed she articulates her task in writing her memoirs as "uplifting that impenetrable veil, to accomplish which had hitherto baffled all the exertions of... travellers."[32] In effect Lott also unveils masculine fantasy by making untenable the claim that it was possible to combine ethnography and fantasy in their harem representations. This dislocation is achieved by revealing the impossibility of an eyewitness experience. Lott emphasizes her privileged insider status in the striking portrait that is the frontispiece to her diary of 1866 (figure 3.2). In this unusual portrait, Lott's body is completely encased in the *habarah* and her head entirely obscured by the veil, except for her eyes, which stare out resolutely.[33] There is no telltale hint of the crinoline beneath; instead a swath of luxurious embroidered fabric peeps out through the split in her heavy cloak – her transformation is complete. Lott has so effectively disguised herself that were it not for the fact that her name appears beneath the illustration in the frontispiece we would take her for one of her many harem acquaintances. The effect of this concealment is a confronting intensification of Lott's gaze, which underscores her power to see from behind the veil. As such this cultural cross-dressing is a succinct metaphor for her privileged insight into the forbidden harems.

That said, there is no hint of Lott's identification with the Khedive's harem women in her text. She remains resolutely (often indignantly) English when her narrative voice is that of the eyewitness to the elite harems in Cairo.[34] The solitary pleasures of writing her diary become a refuge from (and compensation for) the rigors of life as a harem governess.[35] Lott explicitly maintains her status as an English lady: her difference is demonstrated in her text through the rituals associated with her dress and is further underscored by the harem women's curiosity about the differences of her clothing. When she turns to storytelling, however, we find another, surprising point of identification for the author – with the position of the Mohaddetyn, the eunuch.[36] Elsewhere in her extensive writings, her attitude to the senior harem eunuchs vacillates between disgust and awe at their power as intermediaries between the harem women in their charge and the world beyond the harem's confines. Their power is counterpointed with her own constrained position within a domain in which she is the newcomer. Yet the process of publishing her diary gave her a position of power as an intermediary, analogous to that of the eunuch who is intimate with the community of women inside the harem while not being of their number. In sum, what we witness in Lott's text is an extremely mobile subject positioning as she capriciously stages her power and privilege over both harem women and Western men.

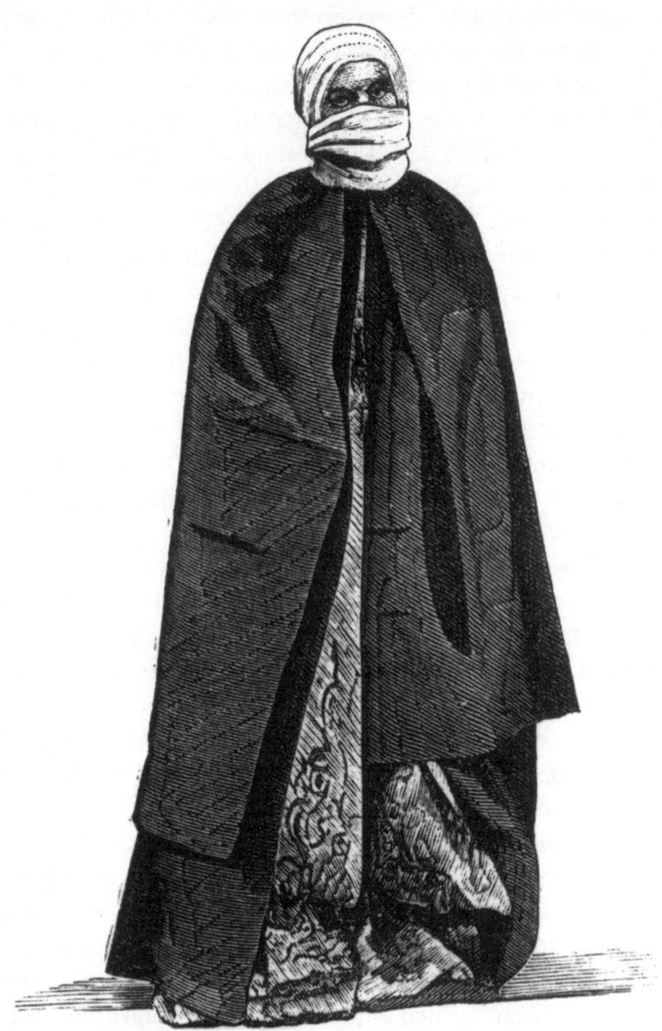

Figure 3.2 *Emmeline Lott*, frontispiece, *The English Governess in Egypt. Harem Life in Egypt and Constantinople*, 1866. R. Bentley, London

There are, however, other subject positions to consider, other storytellers. Lott's tale of the harem masquerade is Kaleb's and Yusef's tale as well. Before its retelling in Lott's travelog, published in London, the story circulated within the elite harems of Istanbul and Cairo. In this context it is placed within a tradition of storytelling in Ottoman culture, where tales were circulated, reiterated, and modified. In this context its retelling enhances the symbolic triumph of the Ottomans over the arrogant and intrusive Western men. Perhaps this Ottoman storyteller was capitalizing on Lott's interest to ensure that this satire of Western cultural intrusion upon Islamic mores would reach a British audience. The reader is made aware of the Ottoman's sophisticated knowledge of Western culture, including recent travel literature and social trends. The tale not only satirizes the ignorance of the British gentlemen through the sham harem performance but also dissimulates the tale from the "real" harem, enabling a number of stereotypes of Ottoman culture to be revised. The story presents an alternative image of the sultan as a learned man and worthy inheritor of a noble lineage. Before entering the sham harem, the two travelers are shown the sultan's magnificent library, a genealogical tree of sultans' portraits, and the magnificent throne room.[37] For the reader the Ottoman palace emerges as a place of both learning and religious reverence, "in full keeping with that exalted sanctity investing the great Deity of Islam."[38]

Yet another Ottoman response to the Western fantasy of the harem is evident in an extraordinary pair of photographs of another member of the Egyptian Khedival dynasty, Princess Nazli Hanım. This time an Ottoman harem woman is both the instigator and the subject of revisionary images in which cross-dressing and cultural cross-dressing are played off against one another. These two photographs commissioned by Nazli sit next to one another on the page of an anonymous album in the Sutherland papers (figure 3.3). Against the same studio backdrop of pyramid and palm trees, the Egyptian princess has choreographed two distinct representations: on the left, an honorific portrait in contemporary European dress, and on the right, a cross-dressed parody of the Western harem stereotype.

The photograph on the left conforms to familiar codes of honorific portraiture. This is cultural cross-dressing from the other side. Its meanings are vastly different to the Western traveler "going native" such as Lewis, whose sartorial transformation signified an escape to a mythical realm of timelessness and langor. In this instance, "going European" signals Nazli's social position as the member of an Ottoman elite, who embraced elements of Western dress as a sign of her modernity. The cut of Nazli's bodice and skirt is in the fashionable European bustle style which Ottoman women of Nazli's elevated social position were readily able to acquire in Cairo or Istanbul by importing directly from Europe or by commissioning from a local dressmaker.[39] Nazli's erect posture and the

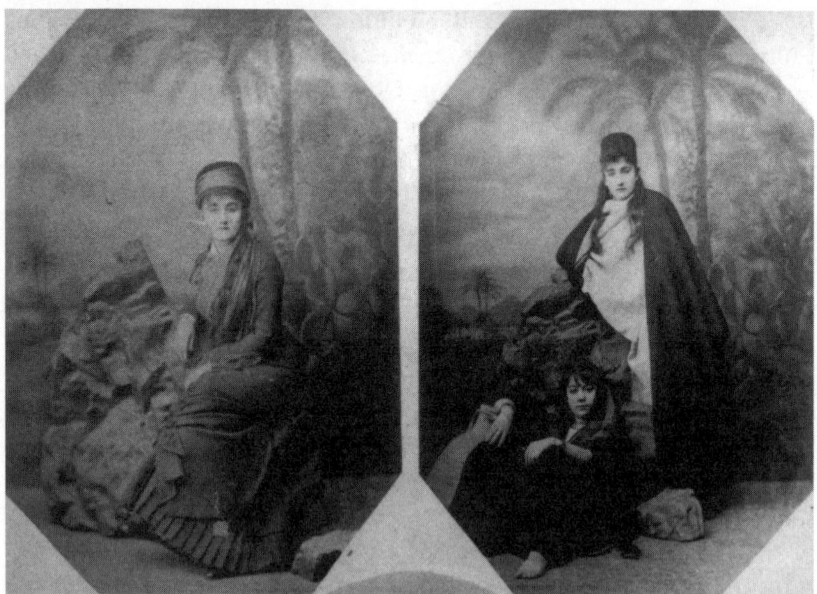

Figure 3.3 *Princess Nazli Hanım*, undated photographs, Sutherland Papers, Staffordshire Record Office

contours of her tight-waisted figure are formed by the corset, a notable contrast to the soft lines of traditional Ottoman dress which facilitated greater ease of movement. Decoration of her skirt is achieved through draping, pleating, and a fabric bow (in line with the current fashions in Britain and France), rather than the profuse embroidery that was conventional in Ottoman dress. Nazli's crossed legs lift the edge of her skirt, revealing the tips of her leather shoes, which she wears in place of the more traditional Ottoman slippers. Her hairstyle, however, represents a departure from European convention. While a respectable European woman of Nazli's age would tie up and pin back her hair, Nazli's long hair sweeps loosely around her neck, following the contours of her headscarf, wrapped tightly around her head, and falls gently across her chest. Nazli's hybrid European dress is clearly not a temporary masquerade for she is completely at ease in this clothing.

No doubt this confidence came from her privileged upbringing and lifelong engagement with European culture. She was an extremely well educated woman, fluent in English and French as well as Ottoman and Arabic. In Istanbul, a combination of her family's wealth and the liberal attitudes of her father, Mustafa Fazil Paşa, ensured she had an unusual degree of liberty for an Ottoman woman of her generation. Her father's social position ensured that she met with the most notable European women visitors to Istanbul, including Princess Alexandra (the Princess of Wales) and Empress Eugénie of France.[40] Later, after she relocated to Cairo following the death of her husband in 1879 (the renowned Ottoman diplomat and statesman Halil Şerif Paşa), she was noted for her salons, where Cairo's elite would congregate to socialize and exchange ideas.[41] Evidence suggests that Princess Nazli, like a number of other Ottoman women of her social standing, was in the habit of presenting her photographic portrait as a gift to European women who visited her. An earlier *carte de visite* of Nazli is known to have been presented to the painter Elizabeth Jerichau-Baumann, and this time the portrait photograph was authorized by Nazli's signature.[42] The role of these *cartes de visite* as part of harem visiting etiquette, bespeaks a form of exchange in which Nazli addresses her European visitors as social equals. Perhaps the Sutherland Papers' photograph was another such gift. Nazli's upright bearing and direct look in this photograph convey an ease and confidence indicating that she has taken command of the sitting; it is as if she is opening up in conversation with the viewer. Here is a self-assured woman addressing her viewer as an equal.

While photographic portraiture became an instrument for the expression of bourgeois subjectivity in Britain and France in the nineteenth century, in the same period it was enthusiastically embraced by Ottoman elites as a means of self-fashioning and of expressing a modernized self-image. Even in the earliest years of photography's advent, the Egyptian rulers were fascinated by the medium.[43] Photography was quickly harnessed by the Ottoman elites as a medium for presenting a revised collective self-image to Europe (the most notable expressions of this sentiment are Osman Hamdy Bey's costume book and the Adbülhamid II albums[44]). This state-sponsored redefinition of the collectivity emerged in tandem with changed concepts of individual identity. Individual members of the Ottoman elite embraced the new technology of photography, having their portraits taken in local photographic studios such as Sébah, Abdullah Frères, and Kargopoulo.[45] While extant honorific portraits from these studios are more often of men, there are a number of portraits of Ottoman women still remaining. For these women, their honorific portraits had an inverse representation – the anonymous clichéd "harem" scenes where non-Islamic women and women on the fringes of respectable Islamic society were co-opted to perform in the production of photographs for the Western tourist.[46] Here these stagings of the timeless, closed world of the "harem" are counterpointed with the experience of Ottoman domestic life for urban women of the Ottoman elite. This, like so many other aspects of life in the Tanzimat era of modernizing reform, was undergoing profound change. The portrait of Princess Nazli participates in this revisionary self-imaging, as she entreats her viewer to acknowledge a complex view of harem life in this period of significant change.[47]

Nazli's honorific portrait expresses this desire to communicate with her viewer; however, her companion portrait is a photograph of a different order. The same studio backdrop has been deployed, but the photographer has drawn back slightly to admit a second figure within the frame. This is a confronting photograph of Nazli cross-dressed as an Ottoman gentleman, her companion dressed as an Egyptian pottery seller, posed as though part of Nazli's imaginary harem in a parodic restaging of the tourist photograph. The context for production of both photographs remains a mystery; however, they invite us to speculate. Perhaps Nazli visited the photographer's studio to commission the honorific portrait on the left and decided to play with the props that she found there. I imagine her playfully cross-dressing, posing with mock solemnity while the photographer registered this second image. Here she plays her role as harem master against the painted backdrop, and the theatricality of these two figures burlesques the staginess of the Orientalist postcard. Her impassive look promises no insights into her psychological interiority; rather, our attention is focused on the theatrical staging of a performance. This irreverent performativity is a powerful testament to the agency of Princess Nazli and profoundly challenges a notion of the silence or passivity of Ottoman women.

The illusion of Nazli's transformation is incomplete: no effort has been made to disguise her long hair, and the heavy cloth underneath has been hastily drawn across the front of her body (one assumes this was done to cover the dress which we see her wearing in the photograph on the left). The effect is to play up the theatricality of the performance and to remind us that underneath she remains the modern Ottoman woman, the sophisticated instigator of this parody. As well as insistently reminding us of Nazli's agency, by emphasizing the process of dressing up, this photograph underscores the notion of identity as a performance.

In contrast to Nazli's openness to the viewer in the photograph on the left, on the right the two masquerading women appear to rally in defiance of the spectator. Nazli has an imposing presence because of her commanding, upright stance; her costume closes her body from the viewer and her look is impassive, withdrawing rather than actively engaging. The lower edge of her cloak encompasses the rock against which the pottery seller rests, emphasizing a unity of the two that is echoed by the implied narrative of harem master and his possession. Their gazes confront the viewer, further allying the two in their separation from us. This photograph implies an erotic subtext between the two women in which we, the viewers, are resolutely refused participation.

Nazli's adoption of the costume of an Ottoman gentleman is a crossing of gender, not culture, as she assumes his powerful position, but metaphorically this can also be construed as a cultural crossing. By dressing to perform the clichéd harem, Nazli inhabits a Western stereotype, both performing that stereotype and exceeding it. Perhaps she is parodying the other "harem" photographs produced in the studio in which this photograph was taken. Through this gift, Nazli sent a satiric missive to England parodying the seemingly limitless Western fascination with the idea of the seraglio. In this way she emerges as a figure of resistance to a dominant scopic regime; she presents herself as a sophisticated, visually literate instigator of the clichéd codes of Orientalist visual culture who rewrites these codes as satire. As in Lott's tale, the object of the joke are those Westerners who desire the fantasy seraglio. With whom did she share this joke? Certainly with her collaborator and, in all likelihood, with other elite Ottoman women who would have enjoyed her travesty. Was it shared with the Englishwoman to whom the photos were gifted, thereby forging an alliance between the two? Or was she poking fun at British women's propensity to subscribe to the fantasy of the harem?[48]

Between left and right photographs there is a shift from earnest self-presentation to parody, from honorific portraiture to travesty. While the photograph on the left is an implicit revision of Orientalist stereotypes of the odalisque, the one on the right is a direct assault on such degrading tropes. Together these two photographs embody a vacillation, on the left, an opening out to dialog, on the right a closing off. Here the optimism and enthusiasm to communicate with her European female audience that characterize her earlier portrait photographs is tempered by experience. Perhaps this experience is the recognition of the persistent imperative of an exoticizing, Orientalizing gaze despite efforts to communicate otherwise. This photograph bespeaks an impatience with a Western attitude that returns dialog to monolog and in which the Egyptian princess is reified as an "odalisque" of Western fantasy.

Next to one another on the album page, these two portraits of Princess Nazli are like an uncanny stereoscopic plate, a popular device for armchair Orientalists that promised possession of the object. As Jonathan Crary argues, through the viewing process, these "mass-produced and monotonous cards are transubstantiated into a . . . seductive vision of the 'real'."[49] Nazli's stereoscopic pairing references this visual technology but doesn't offer resolution into the desired illusionistic effect. The spectator's certainty about the object of vision is disrupted, and their position is called into question.

The disruptive implications for the Western spectator of Nazli's masquerade could not be further from the affirmation of Western mastery promised by Lewis's cultural cross-dressing, and yet both representations are premised upon self-consciously cultivated artifice. With Lewis the cultivated artifice of the dandy provided a model of masculine sartorial display that was suited to the artifice of his Eastern masquerade. In this instance, the gap between the British performer and his performance as Eastern Bey establishes his authoritative position. Lewis's exomorphic transformation facilitated this crossing of cultural boundaries (and the assumption of an imagined position as harem master) while sustaining his intrinsic identity as British interpreter. The reiteration of this performance of the self established Lewis's authority in art-historical literature and also provided an identificatory model for masculine spectatorship.

By contrast, in Lott's tale, identity is articulated on both sides of the cultural divide through a parodic response to this Western masculine fantasy of the seraglio. Lott's travelog establishes her authority as an intermediary for her British readers, proposing a flexible subject position for the English woman that has numerous points of identification. Her cultural cross-dressing is evidently extremely mutable. At one point the eunuch's power as the go-between is transmuted into the authoritative position of the travel writer as storyteller and ethnographer. At another point, Lott adopts the veil of the Ottoman woman in an assertion of her privileged insider status, but this text also restages the eunuch's symbolic revenge, shared with his harem audience. Again the gap between performer and performance is crucial. In Kaleb's tale, great pleasure is derived from the effectiveness of the disguise in deceiving the unsuspecting Englishmen, and from the conspiratorial knowledge of a distinction between the eunuchs and their cross-gender masquerade. The revelation of this discrepancy at the moment of narrative climax, when the eunuchs' wigs slip revealing their bald heads, ensures an appropriately humiliating revenge for the two Englishmen as they are ejected from their fantasy of mastery and disposed down the notorious chute into the Bosphorus – thus suffering the fate of the degraded odalisque. All the while the Ottoman harem is dissociated from this sham performance. Nazli's photographs bring together the strategies of both cultural and gendered cross-dressing to establish the authority of this Ottoman princess. The gap between the two photographs of Nazli (as modern Ottoman woman and parodic harem master) sustains the humor of the image by making clear its author and target. The humor here is premised on a recognition that this is an elite, culturally sophisticated Ottoman woman occupying the position of the harem master in this travesty of Western fantasy.

In both cases indigenous agency is articulated through cross-dressing and inhabiting a Western stereotype. The strategy for Princess Nazli and the harem eunuchs is not to didactically refute myth but to defuse its power by inhabiting and displacing its effect and thereby usurping the position of mastery. The stereotype *becomes* masquerade. The result is a parody that is "almost the same but not quite." In neither case is there a seamless adoption of the stereotype – in the Rococo Kiosk the wigs of the masquerading eunuchs slip, and Nazli's paired photographs don't cohere stereoscopically. In these cases the "not quite" is the hinge around which symbolic Ottoman retribution takes place, rather than being the element that betrays the indigene's failure to accede to a position of mastery reserved for the Westerner. The power of the joke is premised on that gap between the stereotype and its knowing performance by the indigenous subject. In both cases the Western stereotype is inhabited and exceeded through gendered cross-dressing. What better demonstration of mastery of another culture than to parody that culture's stereotypes of one's own? To joke in a foreign tongue displays a sophisticated grasp of that language – in Nazli's case it is the degrading language of the harem stereotype that she returns as a joke.

Let us contrast the notion of pleasure in each of these masquerades. The pleasure for Lewis and his viewers is derived from an imagined identification with the harem master; for Lott the pleasure comes from empowerment in respect of her countrymen; for Kaleb and Nazli Hanım the pleasure is that of stepping into a Western stereotype of their culture, of playing to and disrupting expectations. And let's not forget the profits. The payoff is financial for Kaleb and his co-conspirators, but it is also symbolic, because revenge is exacted for the cultural transgressions of Richard Burton and others. In these case studies the practice of cultural cross-dressing emerges not only as a powerful Orientalist strategy that has been critiqued from a post-colonial perspective, but one that was strategically engaged by Ottomans in the nineteenth century. Sartorial transformation emerges as both a Western and an Eastern strategy for engagement across cultures.

Notes

I would like to express my sincere thanks to Jos Hackforth-Jones and Hannah Williams for their astute feedback on earlier drafts of this essay. Part of this essay is developed from an article on Emmeline Lott and John Frederick Lewis that I published in *The Olive Pink Bulletin, Anthropology, Race, Gender*, 5/1 (1993). The further research for "Cultural Crossings" was funded through the Australian Research Council's Discovery Grant Scheme.

1 *The Shorter Oxford English Dictionary.*

2 Gail Ching-Liang Low argues that "the visual and imaginative pleasure of stepping into another's clothes forms one of the central legacies of orientalism. Needless to say, much of the fantasy of native costume is reserved for the dominant White Man; as one of my colleagues puts it, it is the white man who dresses up and the native who reveals his body for consumption by dressing down. Hence, unlike the theorization of cross-dressing which sees a deliberate reversal of gendered costume as calling into question the artificiality of such stereotypes, the act of donning another's clothing, I would argue, is seldom indicative of the disruption of power hierarchies. Instead, it works – however problematically – towards reinforcing them." Low, "White Skins/Black Masks: The Pleasures and Politics of Imperialism," *New Formations*, 9 (Winter 1989), 83–103: 83.

3 Key contributors to this reassessment of the practice of cultural cross-dressing include Low, "White Skins/Black Masks"; M. Garber, "The Chic of Araby: Transvestism and the Erotics of Cultural Appropriation," in *Vested Interests: Cross-Dressing and Cultural Anxiety* (New York: Routledge, 1997), 304–52; D. S. Macleod, "Cross-Cultural Cross-Dressing: Class, Gender and Modernist Sexual Identity," in J. F. Codell and D. S. Macleod (eds.), *Orientalism Transposed: The Impact of the Colonies on British Culture* (Aldershot: Ashgate, 1998), 63–85.

4 Garber, "The Chic of Araby."

5 Here Low is using Homi Bhabha's well-known phrase, coined in a discussion of mimicry. Low, "White Skins/Black Masks," 90. On this issue see Inge E. Boer, "This Is Not the Orient: Theory and Postcolonial Practice," in Mieke Bal and Inge E. Boer (eds.), *The Point of Theory: Practices of Cultural Analysis* (Amsterdam: Amsterdam University Press, 1994), 211–19.

6 William Makepeace Thackeray, *Notes on a Journey from Cornhill to Grand Cairo* (London: Smith Elder, 1869). This text was written in 1844; quotations below are from the 1869 edition.

7 For example, in 1929 Hugh Stokes wrote: "Thackeray's vivid story of his life in Cairo explains largely how Lewis absorbed the spirit of the East and was able to reproduce it with such actuality in his work." H. Stokes, "John Frederick Lewis R.A. (1805–1876)," *Walker's Quarterly*, 28 (1929), 22.

8 Thackeray, *Notes on a Journey*, 504.

9 Ibid. 504–5.

10 Ibid. 506–7.

11 Ibid. 504.

12 For an analysis of costume of this period see Nevil Truman, "Empire and the Dandies," in *Historic Costuming* (London: Sir Isaac Pitman & Sons, 1962), 87–92.

13 The literature on the dandy is extensive. See in particular E. Wilson, "Oppositional Dress," in *Adorned in Dreams: Fashion and Modernity* (London: Virago, 1985), 179–206; L. C. Black, "Baudelaire as Dandy: Artifice and the Search for Beauty," *Nineteenth-Century French Studies*, 17/1–2 (Fall/Winter 1988/9), 186–95.

14 *Portfolio* (1892), 94.

15 "Other painters had been eastwards and returned with a respectable tan; but Lewis lived there and the sunshine was in his bones. In Spain he had for years been warming himself up, so that when he settled in Cairo he was fairly acclimatized, and during his long sojourn there so completely absorbed the atmosphere of the place that he was able to give it off on his return like a fire of coals... Thackeray happened to visit Egypt, and in his account... has told us something about Lewis that we should never have known from other sources; and the interest of it is that the change he describes in Lewis's manner of living is in entire accordance with the change in his work." R. Davies, "John Frederick Lewis, R.A. (1805–1876)," *The Old Watercolour Society's Club*, 3rd annual volume (1925/6), 36–7. And: "The novelty of the first drawings in this style was emphasized by the new spirit in which his subjects were treated – the spirit, not of a traveller in search of the picturesque, but one who by a long sojourn in a strange country had become intimate with the character of the inhabitants and familiar with their mode of life" (a critic of *The Hhareem*) quoted in Stokes, "John Frederick Lewis R.A.," 32.

16 For instance, this tendency is evident in M. A. Stevens (ed.), *The Orientalists: Delacroix to Matisse. European Painters in North Africa and the Near East* (London: Royal Academy of Arts, 1984), 202–8; M. Lewis, *John Frederick Lewis R.A. 1805–1876* (Leigh-on-Sea: F. Lewis, 1978), 23; and R. Green, *John Frederick Lewis R.A. 1805–1876* (Newcastle-upon-Tyne: Laing Art Gallery, 1971), 7.

17 *The Illustrated London News*, May 4, 1850, 300.

18 I have explored this more fully in my doctoral dissertation on Lewis's harem paintings, "Travel, Transgression and the Colonial Harem: The Paintings of J. F. Lewis and the Diaries of British Women Travellers," University of Melbourne, 1995, and also in my entry on the painting in R. Benjamin (ed.), *Orientalism: Delacroix to Klee* (Sydney: Art Gallery of New South Wales, 1998), 79–80.

19 Emmeline Lott was employed as governess to Ibrahim, son of Ismaïl Pasha by his second wife. She entered into a contract with the Khedive Ismaïl's agents in 1861. "She was probably employed for one year only and may have been forced to leave her post": B. Melman, *Women's Orients: English Women and the Middle East, 1718–1918. Sexuality, Religion and Work* (Basingstoke: Macmillan, 1992), 150. For further biographical information about Emmeline Lott, see J. Robinson, *Wayward Women: A Guide to Women Travellers* (Oxford: Oxford University Press, 1990), 141–2. Lott published the following memoirs of her time in Egypt: *The English Governess in Egypt: Harem Life in Egypt and Constantinople* (London: R. Bentley, 1866, repr. 1867); *Nights in the Harem, or, The Mohaddeyn in the Palace of the Ghezire*, 2 vols. (London: Chapman & Hall, 1867); and *The Grand Pasha's Cruise on the Nile in the Viceroy of Egypt's Yacht*, 2 vols. (London: T. Cautley Newby, 1869).

20 Yusef was in Istanbul having accompanied Princess Fatimah Hanım, who was spending Ramadan at the Ottoman court. Lott, *Nights in the Harem*, i. 103.

21 Captain Adolphus Slade, RN, FRAS, Admiral of the Turkish Fleet (Muchaver Pacha), *Records of Travels in Turkey, Greece etc. and of a Cruise in the Black Sea with the Captain Pacha* (London: Saunders & Otley, 1854).

22 R. Burton, *Personal Narrative of a Pilgrimage to Al-Madinah and Meccah, 1855–56*, 2 vols. (New York: Dover Publications, 1855).

23 Lott, *Nights in the Harem*, i. 113.

24 Ibid. 106.

25 Ibid. 117–18.

26 Ibid. 121.

27 Edward Said, *Orientalism* (Harmondsworth: Penguin, 1978), 196. See also Low, "White Skins/Black Masks," 90.

28 Lott, *Nights in the Harem*, i. 140–1.

29 Ibid. 142.

30 Ibid.

31 Ibid. 145–6.

32 Lott, *The English Governess in Egypt*, p. xxiii.

33 Lott describes this outdoor dress: see ibid. 147.

34 In the mid- to late nineteenth century, British women claimed for themselves a role (albeit marginalized) in the emergent disciplines of ethnography and anthropology by writing about Eastern harems. Despite the purported "ob-

jectivity" of their texts they were normalizing harems in the image of the bourgeois home. However, in order to do so they rejected notions of the fantasies perpetuated in the nineteenth century by male artists and poets. It is within this context that we can understand Lott's story and the reasons why it exhibits such great delight in destabilizing the position of the masculine voyeur. See Melman, *Women's Orients.*

35 Lott notes that, despite the conspicuous wealth of her employer, she endured conditions worse than those of a governess in Europe: *The English Governess in Egypt*, 255.

36 Indeed the complex interactions between the two storytellers appear in Lott's account: she interjects with asides to the reader, elaborating on points made to educate those readers who are less familiar with particular customary practices in the harem.

37 It is noted that "at one time [the library was] the favourite resort of the Sheik-el-Islam (the Moslem patriarch)": Lott, *Nights in the Harem*, i. 137.

38 Ibid. 138.

39 J. Scarce, *Women's Costume of the Near and Middle East* (London: Unwin Hyman, 1987), 81.

40 For information on Princess Nazli's father, Mustafa Fazil Paşa, and their life in Istanbul, see Mehmed Süreyya, *Sicill-i Osmanî* (Istanbul: Kültür Bakanliği ile, 1996), ii. 511; İsmet Özel, "Tanzimatin Getirdiği "Aydin"," *Tanzimat'tan Cumhuriyet'e Türkiye Ansiklopedisi* (Istanbul: İletişim Yayınları, 1985), i. 65; Emine Foat Tugay, *Three Centuries: Family Chronicles of Turkey and Egypt* (Oxford: Oxford University Press, 1963), 109–11; Mithat Cemal Kuntay, *Namık Kemal Devrinin İnsanları ve Olayları Arasında* (Istanbul: Maarif Mataasi, 1944), i. 311–39; Roderic H. Davison, "Halil Şerif Paşa: The Influence of Paris and the West on an Ottoman Diplomat," *Osmanlı Araştırmaları (The Journal of Ottoman Studies)* (Istanbul), 6 (1986), 59.

41 Afaf Lutfi al-Sayyid notes that Princess Nazli's salon was one of the three famous salons in late nineteenth-century Cairo in which there were signs of political activity. A. L. al-Sayyid, "Rumblings of Opposition," in *Egypt and Cromer: A Study in Anglo-Egyptian Relations* (London: John Murray, 1968), 95.

42 For further information on the relationship between Princess Nazli Hanım and Elisabeth Jerichau-Baumann, including the portraits that this Danish Polish artist painted of Nazli, see M. Roberts, "Harem Portraiture: Elisabeth Jerichau-Baumann and the Egyptian Princess Nazli Hanım," in D. Cherry and J. Helland (eds.), *Local/Global: New Narratives of Women's Art in the Nineteenth Century* (Aldershot: Ashgate, forthcoming).

43 Mehemet Ali is rumored to have experimented with photography inside his harem. Nissan N. Perez (ed.), *Focus East: Early Photography in the Near East (1839–1885)* (New York: Harry N. Abrams, 1988), 196.

44 O. Hamdy Bey and M. de Launay, *Les Costumes populaires de la Turquie en 1873: Ouvrage publié sous le patronage de la Commission Impériale Ottomane pour l'Exposition Universelle de 1873 à Vienne*, phototypie par P. Sébah (Constantinople: Imprimerie du *Levant Times & Shipping Gazette*, 1873). For an analysis of the Abdülhamid II albums see Z. Çelik, "Speaking Back to Orientalist Discourse at the World's Columbian Exposition," in H. Edwards (ed.), *Noble Dreams, Wicked Pleasures: Orientalism in America, 1870–1930* (Princeton, NJ: Princeton University Press, 2000), 77–95.

45 E. Özendes, *From Sébah and Joaillier to Foto Sabah: Orientalism in Photography* (Istanbul: Yapı Kredi Yayınları, 1999), and B. Öztuncay, *Vassilaki Kargopoulo: Photographer to his Majesty the Sultan* (Istanbul: Birieşik Oksijen Sanayi A. Ş., 2000).

46 As Sekula has astutely noted, the photographic portrait as an expression of bourgeois subjectivity in British culture in this period had its inverse in the instrumentalist use of photography for disciplinary purposes: as a record of the criminal, the insane, and the colonized subject. I am intrigued by the cross-cultural counterpart to this of Ottoman portraits and harem photographs. A. Sekula, "The Body and the Archive," *October*, 39 (Winter 1986), 3–64. On harem photographs see M. Alloula, *The Colonial Harem*, trans. M. Godzich and W. Godzich, Theory and History of Literature 21 (Manchester: Manchester University Press, 1986).

47 The Tanzimat era was the period in which the Ottomans responded to European economic and military supremacy by embracing a series of Westernizing reforms. At every level this was a negotiated response in which modernizing reforms were balanced with respect for Islamic cultural traditions.

48 For an analysis of British women's harem fantasies see M. Roberts, "Contested Terrains: Women Orientalists and the Colonial Harem," in J. Beaulieu and M. Roberts (eds.), *Orientalism's Interlocutors: Painting, Architecture, Photography* (Durham, NC: Duke University Press), 179–203.

49 J. Crary, *Techniques of the Observer: On Vision and Modernity in the Nineteenth Century* (Cambridge, MA: MIT Press, 1990), 132.

4

"Oriental" Femininity as Cultural Commodity: Authorship, Authority, and Authenticity

Reina Lewis

This essay is something of a detective story, structured by the twists and turns of fiction and "fact" that characterize the selling of harem literature. Having written elsewhere about the development of Western women's harem narratives and the emergence of accounts by women who had themselves been raised in segregating societies,[1] I want here to look at examples of harem writing that trouble the authorial identities so central to the field. I am focusing on authors and the author function[2] because the reliability of the female author as witness to the harem's forbidden domains was indispensable to the successful production, distribution, and reception of all harem accounts. From Lady Mary Wortley Montagu onwards,[3] this reality effect was established as the unique selling point of Western women's harem literature. Women's writing emanating from within the harem's secluded domains could claim an even higher truth status, and women coded as Oriental knew they had something very particular to sell.

But in a field characterized by disputes about veracity their accounts were often challenged by attempts to discredit the authenticity of the "Oriental" author herself. My approach to this is both to offer historical material about the life of the writer which might refute accusations of inauthenticity (while always problematizing the terms on which that authenticity is based) and to evaluate how these disputes functioned as part of the citational nature of Orientalist discourse.

In the pages that follow, my exploration of harem literature begins with books of apparently known provenance that were nonetheless subject to sustained attacks on their authenticity, before proceeding to examine a corpus of works whose point of origin seems impossible to define. In these works the authenticity of the author – as "Oriental" and even as female – is harder or impossible to establish. Unsettling historiographical methodologies and hovering at the junction of different literary genres, these limit cases delineate the field of harem literature and enhance the understanding of how Orientalized female authenticity came to be codified as a cultural commodity.

The Emergence of Ottoman Women Writers in Harem Literature

For too long seen as hapless sex slaves or conniving savages,[4] it was not until the late nineteenth century that women from Islamic cultures began to present the West with their own accounts of segregated life. In English-language publications spanning the end of the Ottoman empire and the beginning of the Turkish Republic, Ottoman women re-presented harem life for a Western audience, at the same time as they sought to contribute to local debates about modernization and emancipation. Operating as a counter-discourse, these accounts contested Orientalist knowledges through an adept manipulation of Western cultural codes not normally attributed to the presumed to be silenced Orientalized woman. But for all these authors – educated, elite, traveled, modernized – the ability to reach Western audiences relied on a complicated negotiation of the very Orientalist stereotypes they sought to undermine.

Though Billie Melman identifies the turn of the nineteenth century as the period in which harem literature began to wane, there was still sufficient demand to fuel a market for publications by Ottoman women.[5] The late arrival of written accounts in English by Ottoman women, starting at the end of the 1870s,[6] can be explained by a number of local reasons. Firstly, even elite women were often not literate in sufficient numbers to produce writing for publication until the mid-nineteenth century, when Ottoman reforms increased education opportunities for the entire population. Secondly, women who wanted to intervene in how the West saw them needed to be literate in European languages, something also on the increase in the mid-nineteenth century. With the introduction of Western governesses into elite Ottoman harems, women learned French and English and encountered foreign literature in greater amounts. Though often receiving an indifferent education from these (frequently not very well qualified) governesses, Ottoman women, like their male counterparts, who were receiving instruction in Western literature, science, and ideas at the new state education institutions, became *au fait* with Enlightenment concepts and Western cultural forms.[7] The image of the harem as a space segregated not only from men but from ideas, politics, and progress was as unrealistic as the vision of the Ottoman state as resolutely superstitious and isolationist. Although Ottomans on all sides of the political divide were often wary of what they saw as Western immorality, Ottoman state and society were engaged in a process of selective adaptation of Western commodities, ideas, and behaviors that had a wide-ranging impact on all aspects of domestic and public life.

Thirdly, once the literacy and linguistic conditions needed for the emergence of women's writing were met, they had also to be prepared to break Islamic conventions about the privacy of family life. As literacy within the Ottoman empire grew so did the periodical press, and women were contributing to their own newspapers and magazines in increasing numbers, writing about everything from marital relations to fashion.[8] But, fourthly, the Ottoman women who published books in English were not writing only for a local readership. They were deliberately targeting a Western audience that they knew regarded them through the lens of Orientalist stereotypes. Writing for the West transgressed boundaries of politics as well as propriety: the Ottoman state had for some time been concerned with how it was seen by the West, convinced, rightly, that Orientalist stereotypes played no small part in the direction of Western foreign policy. Locked into an often unequal struggle with the Western powers, the Sublime Porte took an active part in trying to control Western perceptions and depictions of the Ottomans in particular and of Islam in general. By the time of Sultan Abdülhamid II (1876–1909), the state was using its envoys abroad to try to stop or remedy negative representations in newspapers, visual culture, and public performance. In their political dealings with the West, the Ottomans monitored matters of precedence and protocol, determined to propound the status of the Ottoman empire as an equal among other imperial nations.[9] As part of their official self-display on the world stage, the contribution of Ottoman pavilions to the international exhibitions was an important aspect.[10]

But the publication of women's grievances was not officially sanctioned. Indeed, under Abdülhamid, the communication of any Ottomans with foreigners was strictly regulated – mainly to prevent foreign support for internal dissidents, but also to control the interaction of, in particular Muslim, subjects with the potentially morally corrupting *giaours.*

Yet this was never an absolute or totally enforceable separation. Ottoman society was by the last quarter of the nineteenth century accustomed to Western ideas and engaged in a critical appropriation of Western technologies and behaviors. For women, seeking emancipation in specifically Ottoman and/or Muslim terms, the benefits of Western so-called liberation were critically evaluated. This was done not just through their consumption of Western literature – though French novels were often held to be the cause of their discontent – but also through interaction with Western women. Meeting through correspondence and visits, Ottoman women of the modernizing elite were increasingly in contact with their Western counterparts, and this played another part in the emergence of their writing.[11]

It is in this context that the identifiable Ottoman writers I am discussing here emerged onto the world stage as authors. All hailing from Istanbul, they chose English as their medium of communication and set store by the power of literature to alter perceptions of women from the harem. Halide Adivar Edib was the most prominent and the only one still well known today. The daughter of a high-level palace bureaucrat, Edib was given a Western-style education by her progressive father and, unusually for a Muslim girl, attended the American College for Girls in Istanbul, graduating in 1901. Marrying one of her teachers, a friend of her father's, she came to fame after the Young Turk revolution of 1908, writing for the Constitutionalist newspaper *Tanin* and publishing novels concerned with women's lives. Her public role continued, and increased when the Allies occupied Turkey after its defeat in World War I. Breaking boundaries of segregation, Edib delivered famous public speeches at nationalist rallies in Istanbul and moved to Ankara to work with the nationalists and Mustafa Kemal (Atatürk).[12] However, she and her second husband,[13] Adnan Adıvar, fled into exile in Britain in 1926 after their faction was outlawed by the increasingly autocratic Mustafa Kemal. It was at this point that her memoirs were written, long planned to appear in English, "a language far better fitted to reach the world than my own."[14] The first *Memoirs of Halidé Edib* appeared in 1926 published by John Murray and were followed two years later in 1928 by *The Turkish Ordeal: Being the Further*

Memoirs of Halidé Edib, with the same publisher. Though the first volume details her early life and includes a heartfelt criticism of polygamy (unsuccessfully entered into by her otherwise progressive father), the second volume concentrates on nationalist and international politics, seeking to counteract the version of events put forward by Kemal's own account, *Nutuk*, published in 1927.

In the West, Edib's two volumes were well received: her authenticity was not disputed. The *Times Literary Supplement* hailed *The Turkish Ordeal* as "history written by the novelist who helped to make it happen,"[15] and Edib was feted as visiting professor at Columbia in 1931–2. But in Turkey, out of favor with Kemal, she appeared in *Nutuk* as a dangerous Westernizer, castigated for her support for an American mandate after the war.[16] By the time her memoirs appeared, Edib was already internationally known, her image familiar from newspaper reports and her name familiar from her letters to London periodicals. But her identity was also familiar to Westerners due to her prominence in accounts by Western women who featured her among the group of progressive women they reported on in Istanbul at the turn of the century.

Two women whose names were not known to the West before they appeared in publication, and whose authenticity was challenged from the start, were the authors known as Zeyneb Hanım and Melek Hanım. These two sisters did not take the public stage in political campaigns but emerged on the pages of fiction to become notorious as the heroines of Pierre Loti's *Les Désenchantées*. Raised like Halide Edib with a Western education by a prominent and progressive father, the two sisters (whose real names were Hadidjé Zennour and Nouryé Neyr-el-Nissa) were unhappy with their projected future. Expected to make arranged marriages and live a conventional life of elite seclusion, they determined to enlist the aging French Orientalist author to their cause. They, like most Turks, already valued Loti for his famous romance *Aziyadé* (1879), in which the protagonist, his loosely disguised alter ego, visits Istanbul and falls in love with a beautiful Circassian woman. Based on his actual liaison with an Ottoman woman (Hadidjé), the book kills her off in stereotypical tragedy when the naval officer is posted home. Loti's love for Turkey endeared him to many in Istanbul, and when he was posted back to the city in 1901 the sisters determined to make contact.

This is where the issue of authenticity becomes murky and reveals its status as a contested commodity in the depiction of the harem. The two sisters wrote to Loti, asking him to help publicize the plight of educated

Ottoman Muslim women who were fated to live by the harem's restrictions.[17] But they knew that, though their educated state was part of their novelty, it was with the old-style *hanım* (elite lady) that the novelist was obsessed. So, with the assistance of a French journalist named Marie Léra (who wrote under the pseudonym Marc Hélys), they conspired to present Loti with a suitably exotic picture. Orientalizing themselves, they met him thickly veiled in cafés and parks, on the Bosphorus, and "at home" – though these premises were in fact the old-fashioned apartments of a friend which they had scene-set with a mishmash of antiquated goods, not their modern apartments full of Western furniture. The author was delighted with the Oriental spectacle they contrived, and used their letters to produce the narrative that became *Les Désenchantées.*

Loti knew that it was dangerous for Ottoman subjects to converse with foreigners (the young Edib had once been chased off an American's yacht by palace spies for fear that she was about to defect),[18] and changed their names for publication. Hadidjé Zennour became Zeyneb, Nouryé Neyr-el-Nissa became Melek, and the third woman became Djénane. It was she, the character played by the French woman, who was cast as the protagonist's love interest (his alter ego this time disguised as a successful French novelist André Lhéry), dying from a broken heart. The other two also die in *Les Désenchantées*, Zeyneb from a chest infection allowed to run its course to avoid an unwanted marriage, and Melek from brain fever. Of course, very much alive, the two sisters realized that the name change would not be enough to protect their identities and fled to Europe in disguise to avoid imperial reprisals. Once they arrived there, their father had officially to disown them (though he managed surreptitiously to pay them an allowance until he died, of a broken heart they maintained).[19]

The sisters did not only exist on the page as characters for Loti. They both wrote their own books, with the editorial assistance of the British feminist and Turkophile Grace Ellison. Using their fictional names, they published in English. Zeyneb Hanım's *A Turkish Woman's European Impressions* appeared, edited by Ellison, from Seeley Service Co., in February 1913, and later the same year Melek Hanım brought out *Abdul Hamid's Daughter*, with an introduction by Ellison, published in October by Methuen. I have discussed Zeyneb Hanım's book in detail elsewhere;[20] here I want only to note that this epistolary volume, addressed to her respondent Ellison, offers accounts of life in Istanbul mixed with critical observations of Europe, culminating in her disenchantment with the difficulties and lack of grace in the apparently liberated West. Zeyneb

Hanım returned to Turkey at the start of World War I, though her sister (by now married to a Polish aristocrat) remained in France.

Though Zeyneb Hanım's book offered to tell the truth about the harem, her authenticity was disputed from the start. This was often because her grandfather had been French: the Marquis de Blosset de Chateauneuf had converted to Islam when in the service of the sultan and had married a Circassian, living thereafter as an Ottoman and Muslim under the name Reschid Bey. For some, this European heritage invalidated the sisters' claim to authenticity: "she is no typical Turkish lady, but the granddaughter of a Frenchman who, to use Mr Pickthall's coinage 'islamed' and her upbringing and the political unrest encouraged her inherited disposition to revolt."[21] The sisters' claim to have provided Loti with his material was also disputed by Hélys, who, in her account published in French in 1923, downgraded their role.[22] This charge was specifically refuted by Melek Hanım in her 1923 article in the *Strand Magazine*, where she dismissed Hélys as merely some "French lady we took into our confidence" who helped with their English. The part of Djénane was, she insisted, "no one in particular... one day it was one cousin; one day another."[23]

But whatever the divisions between the three women about the primacy of their role with Loti, the sisters' identity as authentically Ottoman and Muslim would not have been disputed by the society in which they grew up, where a different concept of identity prevailed. Raised in the years prior to the advent of the Turkish nationalism that was to come to the fore with the Young Turks after 1908, the sisters would have seen themselves as Ottoman subjects – part of a supra-national empire based on the ideal of inclusivism rather than the exclusivism of the nation-state model by then prevalent in Europe. Divisions within the Ottoman empire were those of faith, not nationality or race. In the late Ottoman empire, even and until World War I, most people would have regarded themselves as subjects of the sultan, mediated by their allegiance to a millet (the loosely faith-based units of community organization) or, if Muslim, by their loyalty to the sultan as caliph (leader of the world community of the faithful).[24] Within the multi-ethnic empire birth did not necessarily determine social status: the sisters' European ancestry would not have invalidated their Ottoman subjecthood, and their grandfather's conversion would not have raised questions about their religious identity. For Muslims, conversion was a secure change of identity and one that was not uncommon, especially among individuals in high service to the sultan. Neither would their grandmother's origin have been an issue: elite families were frequently populated by women from the central Caucasian region of Circassia (famed for their pale beauty), many of whom might have arrived as slaves or concubines and subsequently risen to positions of considerable status and influence. For members of the palace elite there was nothing particularly unusual about Zeyneb Hanım's and Melek Hanım's background. What was unusual was that they left the country and wrote for publication.

Like Zeyneb Hanım and Melek Hanım, Demetra Vaka (later Brown) also found that her complex Ottoman identity was difficult to explain to the West. From a Greek Christian family, raised in Istanbul, Vaka Brown had grown up an Ottoman subject. Living within a community that harbored hopes of overthrowing the "Asiatic yoke" that had conquered Byzantium, she nonetheless spent her childhood and youth with Muslim girls. When she emigrated to the USA in 1895, to escape the restricted opportunities available to a young woman within her own Greek community,[25] she discovered that the Turks were denigrated as "despicable, their women as miserable creatures, living in practical slavery for the base desires of men."[26] Realizing that this also besmirched her own Ottoman identity, something that was very hard to make the Americans understand, she set out to tell the Turks' side of things. In her three volumes about Muslim Turkish women, she offered a mix of exoticism, criticism, and support that aimed to establish the terms of her nuanced Ottoman (not Muslim, not Turkish, but also not mainland Athenian) Greek identification. For her, the struggle for authenticity was not in Turkey, where her respondents recognized her as a kindred Ottoman regardless of her ethnicity (and even during the war with Greece after 1918), but in the West, where the blunt force of Orientalism threatened to disallow a heritage that remained important to the diaspora writer.

For Ottomans seeking dialog with the West, this clash over markers of identity was one of the many tensions they encountered in crossing cultures. For Ottoman women, seeking specifically to intervene in Orientalist discourse via a cultural form like harem literature that relied emphatically on the establishment of a gendered and racialized female authenticity, the ways in which regional markers of identity failed to transculturate were particularly acute and threatened to invalidate totally the authority of their accounts.

The Price of Provenance: Non-Attributable Books

However much the authenticity and authority of authors such as Demetra Vaka Brown or Zeyneb Hanım was challenged, at home and in the West, and however much I have been concerned to analyze their Ottoman identity as performative rather than natural or innate,[27] it is nonetheless possible to match historical personages to the names on the spines of their books. Though it has been my business to problematize the classificatory terms "Oriental," "Turkish," and "woman" that made their books saleable, the works circulated under the authorial names of Demetra Vaka Brown, Melek Hanım, Zeyneb Hanım, and Halide Edib are relatively easy to deal with. But if these sources are fairly easy to categorize, how does one deal with texts whose provenance is more uncertain: books where the gender and/or nationality or ethnicity of the author are unverifiable?

How, for example, should one respond to the two books published under the anonymous but gender- and ethnic-specific authorial index of "Une Circassienne" (Circassian woman)? Both the *Romance of a Harem* (1901) and *The Woman of the Hill* (1902) exhibit the signature of an anonymous female author: they come to us "translated from the French" by a named Englishman, Clarence Forestier-Walker. These Oriental tales, narrated in the first person, do not fit into generic classifications. Part autobiography, part confessional novel, part historical romance, their generic confusion is not uncommon in publications by Ottoman women who were, after all, trying to accommodate themselves to alien cultural conventions. But whereas other publications can be more securely located, the ambiguous point of origin of books by "Une Circassienne" complicates the picture.

Romance of a Harem is at first glance an account of historical events. It covers the revolt against Sultan Abdülaziz in 1876, which culminated in his deposition in favor of his nephew Mourad. The palace coup is presented through the eyes of a young woman, Ela, who, herself of uncertain parentage, has been living in the household of Prince Halim, the nephew of Khedive Ismail, the ruler of Egypt.[28] The events of the coup and the mysterious death of the deposed Abdülaziz (depicted here as murder but at the time initially promoted as suicide) are presented through the eyes of Ela, who is given a prominent role in political events. Her ability to access the harems of the sultan's court and those of key plotters, such as the minister of war Hussein Avni, makes her an important conduit for passing messages and for advising the key male players. In this, her uncertain social origin is presented as crucial: abandoned as a child she was adopted into Prince Halim's entourage where, despite the passionate love that grew between them, he determined that she should be raised as a Christian woman, able to make her own choice as an adult if she wished to take the Muslim faith (at which point he would marry her as his second wife). Familiar with the practices of Islam and emotionally attached to the Muslim world, Ela is nonetheless able to move between households and to speak to non-familial men with an ease that would have been impossible for a woman born Muslim. After the coup, the Valide Sultan (Abdülaziz's mother) plots against those who destroyed her son. She manipulates one of Abdülaziz's aides-de-camp, a young Circassian named Hassan, who she knows to be in love with one of the dead sultan's widows, to murder the minister of war, Hussein. Though Hassan dies in the struggle, it subsequently emerges that the young princess with whom he had been in love was in fact one of his two missing sisters, whose whereabouts had been unknown since they were stolen from the garden of their country house. Her identity is revealed when it is discovered that she bears the identifying mark of a small tattoo under the left breast. At this, Ela faints – she too has such a mark on her chest! Rushing to the Çırağan Palace where Abdülaziz's harem are living in imprisonment, she is reunited with her sister.[29] But Ela's story does not end happily: the Valide Sultan takes revenge on Ela for her part in the coup, causing the Prince to believe that she has been unfaithful and is pregnant by another. Ruined in his disbelieving eyes, Ela elects to leave his home and to live alone, closing the narrative with a cautious welcome for the new Sultan Abdülhamid, who within a few months had replaced the mentally unstable Mourad.

So far, so good: though sensationalist and self-promoting there is no reason why this should not be a retrospective account of palace events by one who had lived through them. The next publication in this sequence was, however, more clearly a historical romance. *The Woman of the Hill* (published the next year with the same cover and also "translated" by Forestier-Walker) is a love story in an elite provincial household, telling of the struggle for recognition by a courtesan whose illicit but tolerated role in local society is displaced by the coming of the Europeans. The establishment of a Christian factory puts local sexual politics under new observation and the courtesan, hopelessly and self-sacrificingly in love with a great military leader, can no longer be accommodated. Like *Romance of a Harem*, *Woman of the Hill* presents a narratorial voice that implies itself to be part of, rather than spectator to, its Oriental location.

Both books offer a geographical and ethnic correlation between narrator and author similar to that activated by the codes of autobiography.

In the memoirs and autobiographies written by Vaka Brown and Halide Edib, the reliability of their accounts lies in the correspondence between the events described by their first-person narrator and the actual historic subjects of their authors, whose life pattern broadly accords with the events in the books. But this conventionally autobiographical truth-effect cannot be produced in the books sold under the name "Une Circassienne," even though the construction of an Orientalized narratorial voice "owned" by an author function coded as Oriental activates a claim to authenticity similar to the authority established by the habits of autobiography.

I do think that signature matters – not least as a sign of points of production whose specificity determined in part both the words on the page and their reception.[30] But I am prepared to see signature as often as much a part of the fiction as the narrative it allegedly authorizes. The externally verifiable historical personages that can be correlated to the signatures Halide Edib and Demetra Vaka Brown do not guarantee that their writings are a true, unbiased account of Ottoman female life. Like "Une Circassienne," part of their importance lies in the authenticity with which those authorial labels endow the pages inside. But where Vaka Brown and Halide Edib, as author functions, do not bring their Orientalness and their womanness into serious dispute, the same cannot be said for the much vaguer "Une Circassienne." Anyone working on women's fiction or autobiography will recognize in "Une Circassienne" a possible variant on the convention of female anonymity usually signaled by "A Lady." The geographical location suggested by Circassian has specific meanings within Orientalist discourse, and – even for a wide and nonspecialist audience – would have located the putative author securely in the realm of the eroticized Orient. But the claim to have "discovered" or translated documents is also a well-worn ruse for disguising or pretending to disguise authorship.

The Orient was perhaps a particularly fertile zone for "fake" authors and the loss of the author function. In contrast to the historical signatures Demetra Vaka Brown and Halide Edib, everyone connected to *Les Désenchantées* has one or more literary alter ego. As Roland Barthes points out in his discussion of *Aziyadé*, the identity "Loti" is

> false twice over; the Pierre Loti who guarantees *Aziyadé* is not at all the Loti who is its hero; and this guarantor (*auctor, author*) is himself fabricated, the

> author is not Loti but Viaud: it is all played out between a homonym and pseudonym; what is missing, what is passed over in silence, what is wide open, is the proper name, the propriety of the name (the name which specifies and the name which appropriates). Where is the scriptor?[31]

The scriptor, the historical personage who manipulates paper and ink to produce the book, was, in the case of Loti, the esteemed French author Louis Marie Julien Viaud who, by the time he encountered Hadidjé Zennour and Nouryé Neyr-el-Nissa, was an aging and successful writer. In *Les Désenchantées* he retains the fictional authorship of Loti (by now a recognizable and reputable brand, with a particular currency in Turkey where his pseudonymous comings and goings were followed with great interest). But he creates a new hero, Lhéry, whose life history (as the successful author of international romances) appropriates the intertextual corroborations made possible by the Loti association. This is perfect for a contribution to the literature of the harem, where truth, identity, and romance operate in a heady mix alongside the ethnographic rationale of classified local information.

That Zeyneb Hanım and Melek Hanım come to us through a similar veil of fictional identities and missing scriptors seems perfectly appropriate. The difference is in terms of genre: though Loti's books were novels they were read as what would now be called "faction," that mix of fictionalized truth that evocatively appears to reveal more than mere documentary. For the two sisters producing books under different gender and ethnic circumstances, their personal history was particularly valuable as the guarantor of content within the conventions of harem literature. Where Loti had "given to himself, the author, the name of his hero,"[32] a reversal of the diary writer who gives to his character the proper name of the scriptor, the sisters gave to themselves the names of their Lotiesque characters. Relying on the Loti connection to sell their books, and moved around the world by the fear of exposure in Turkey, the sisters inhabited an intertextual zone in which they and their publications were invariably comprehended in relation to the type of the *désenchantée.* The author function ascribed to Melek Hanım and Zeyneb Hanım was always linked to their fictional existence in the writings of a French man, yet though their evocative noms de plume might have tied them too closely to fiction, their assertion that they were in many ways the originators of the famous fiction of *Les Désenchantées* went some way to ameliorating the shadowiness of their existence. Retaining their fictional names may well have served (in addition to continuing to protect their family) to emphasize their claim to have been instrumental in the composition of Loti's novel. In this, the validation of their status as the *désenchantées* by Grace Ellison in her prefaces to both their books simultaneously emphasizes their reality as Ottoman women and their celebrity status as Loti's heroines.

But when I tried to track the author of *Romance of a Harem* things became more complicated at every level. In the first edition of *Romance of a Harem* (1901), there is no author given on the title page at all – only the name of the "translator," Clarence Forestier-Walker. But a year later *The Woman of the Hill* does appear with "Une Circassienne" as the author, "done into English by C. Forestier-Walker," himself identified as author of *The Silver Gate* (also published by Greening & Co.). By the second edition of *Romance of a Harem* in 1904 (by which time "her" second book was already published), the book is sold under Forestier-Walker's name as translator, and the pseudonymous "Une Circassienne" has disappeared. The absence is explained in Forestier-Walker's preface to the second edition where, in response to "innumerable letters from known and unknown correspondents," he confirms, on the advice of the publishers, that "it is an absolutely true story." The authoress, he tells us, is a French woman who moved to Constantinople as a small child when her father was sent on a "mission to the Sultan" by the French government. The sultan (he does not specify which) "received him and his family on terms of the greatest intimacy, and...had a profound respect for the distinguished French gentleman":

> It was with her father and mother that the authoress learnt the Turkish language, and visited during her youth, before marriage, all the leading Turkish families, and thus gained what is so rare among Europeans, an intimate knowledge of the little-known private life of great harems.
>
> This true story, as given to the public, was known and approved of by the children of Prince Halim, who plays so large a part in the romance.[33]

It would appear that the Circassian woman does not exist, that her anonymous but evocative identity is the pseudonym of an unnamed French woman writer. Where does this leave the reader? The possibilities are endless: Forestier-Walker could himself be the originator of the script; there could be an unnamed French woman author; the French author could be a man who lived in the East during his childhood; the French man or woman writer may never have visited the Orient at all; there may even be a real Circassian woman who wrote anonymously and concocted a French alter ego in order to protect her identity for fear of imperial reprisals (in which case the note in the second edition of *Romance of the Harem* that the book was approved by Prince Halim may be a way of rescuing her good name at home for those in the know). But even if there were a real Circassian woman, the story of the authoress attested to by the preface does not accord with the life story attributed to "Ela" the first-person narrator. Clearly, the apparently reputable female author is not the abducted Circassian heroine of the palace coup, and, with the timing of the French family's emigration to Istanbul unspecified, may have been too young to have been present at those events. The book, now paired with the other first-person story of *The Woman of the Hill*, emerges as historical romance, or a romanticized history – itself a common method for the telling of dynastic dramas.

Can we tell from the text itself if it is "authentic"? The content and style of the two books by "Une Circassienne"/Forestier-Walker bear many of the hallmarks that I see in other writings by "verifiably" Ottoman women: references to palace intrigue, details of male and female dress including commentary on the incorporation of Western fashions, summaries of female education, explanations of the social structure of the imperial harem and how this fitted into the workings of the Ottoman state apparatus, details of the characters and shifting reputations of leading politicians and military men, character sketches and evaluations of elite and imperial women, attention to the power available to palace servants, slaves, and eunuchs, and so on. And all this rendered with a dash of whimsy and a clear understanding of the preoccupations of the Western reader, whose assumptions are reinforced and challenged in turn. So, yes, it could derive from the pen of an Ottoman subject, but the evidence provided by content and style is not conclusive.

Can we tell from the books as commodities if they are "authentic"? Tragically for my purposes, there are no publisher's records of any transactions concerned with these books, or others by Forestier-Walker published by Greening. But the books that remain give a few clues to their status at the time. The reference to Forestier-Walker as author of another novel in the first edition of *Romance of a Harem* links the book extra-textually to what were presumably felt to be the benefits of his status as successful middlebrow writer (though no trace of him remains in literary or biographical dictionaries). And *Romance of a Harem* did get considerable press coverage. In the first edition of *The Woman of the Hill* in 1902

"Une Circassienne" is identified as "authoress of Romance of a Harem" and the fly leaf proudly quotes reviews for the prior publication, most of which dwell on its authenticity: the *Morning Leader* called it "a really interesting and realistic work," echoed by the *Court Circular*, which reckoned it "well told, and bear[ing] the evident imprint of veracity," while *The Lady* found it "undeniably a clever and interesting piece of work." "Interesting" was the description most often used, featuring also in plaudits reproduced from the *Irish Times*, the *Topical Times*, and the *Dundee Advertiser*, indicating that the book was read on a register of fact, rather than only one of fiction. The truth status of the account was signaled by *The Onlooker*, which gleefully proclaimed, "we can safely prophesy a *succès de scandale*."[34] In contrast Forestier-Walker's novels, similarly puffed on the fly sheet, were evaluated as fiction; hailed variously as "finely conceived, cleverly contrived, and well carried out" "tales" and "stories" with "well-expressed characters" and "artistically worked out" plots. Where "reality" is brought in, it is clear that the term refers to his skills at achieving verisimilitude in fiction writing: the *Literary World* noting that "the story has a frank directness and reality that make it thoroughly readable... The story is well expressed and the characters have vitality. Altogether a satisfactory little tale." Again, the clues offered by the books of "Une Circassienne" as cultural commodities are insufficient to secure attribution: the different critical registers used in the evaluations of the two types of books with which Forestier-Walker was associated demonstrate the reality effect that attached itself to harem literature but do not resolve the impossibility of attribution.

The response to the "fascinating" evidence offered in *Romance of a Harem* is not unlike that given to Melek Hanım's 1913 account of palace intrigues, *Abdul Hamid's Daughter*. Published a decade after *Romance of a Harem*, and edited by Ellison, Melek Hanım's book tells the story of Princess Aïshe, a daughter of Abdülhamid (who succeeded his brother Mourad when insanity caused him to be removed from the throne). Aïshe's life is ruined when her cousin Princess Leyla plots against her, stealing her beloved husband and attempting to poison her in revenge for her uncle's role in deposing Leyla's father Mourad. The plot is foiled, thanks to Aïshe's loyal servants. The book is framed with an introduction by Ellison, giving her impression of the unhappy princess whom she met when staying in Istanbul in the winter of 1913/14, by which time her father Abdülhamid too had been deposed by the events of the Young Turk revolution and counter-revolution. Melek Hanım was able to claim veracity for her account, based on her own knowledge of the princess and the eyewitness recollections of the princess's treasurer. The *Times Literary Supplement*, which had reviewed Zeyneb Hanım's book in March 1913, that same year gave attention to Melek Hanım's, listing it as jointly authored with Ellison and tying it directly to the life history and literary associations of the two sisters:

> Mrs Ellison, it will be remembered, edited "A Turkish Woman's European Impressions," giving therein the letters of Zeyneb Hanoum, sister of Melek Hanoum (the two being the heroines of Pierre Loti's "Désenchantées"). During their life in the harem they frequently visited the Sultan's daughter. Melek has written the tragedy of her Imperial hostess, from notes given her by the Princess's Treasurer; and Mrs Ellison adds her own impression of life at the Ottoman court, throwing over the story, "for obvious reasons, a veil of fiction."[35]

Here, the sisters' experiences of the imperial harem, combined with Ellison's reputation as an authority on Turkish female society (her almost daily dispatches to the *Daily Telegraph* as "An Englishwoman in a Turkish Harem" had just finished in February of that year), are conjoined with their fictional status in Loti's *roman-à-clef* to validate the veracity of their account. The testimony of the treasurer (the most senior female operative in the princess's household), when passed to a named Turkish Muslim woman, secures the reliability of this albeit somewhat glossed account as originating safely from an "Oriental" source – though we must not forget that the authority of Melek Hanım and Zeyneb Hanım was challenged in terms of both the authenticity of their ethnicity and the prominence of their role in the concoction of the Loti narrative. But, however nebulous their grasp on authenticating Oriental authorship, their books can still be more securely identified as Oriental or Ottoman sources than can *Romance of a Harem.*

Was an Oriental point of origin even necessary for the production of *Romance of a Harem*? A non-Oriental author could have read the several accounts in circulation and/or spoken to Western women travelers and concocted the same tale. The author need not even be female – external sources could be used as much by men as by women. The status of the books by "Une Circassienne" looked set to remain uncertain, and I was quite happy for it to continue that way. As books without a secure point of origin they served very effectively as a limit case to unsettle the surety of authorship ascribed to other texts within harem literature. Given that I wanted to illustrate how harem literature was a field of cultural production in which the commodification of authenticity took on a significance beyond its usual role in literary conventions of the author function, the liminal status of "Une Circassienne" suited me just fine. Having done all I could to trace her historically, I was content to have the validity of her real identity remain a mystery. But then, just as I was about to go into print, the wonders of the internet brought me a response from Irvin Schick informing me that "Une Circassienne" could in fact be identified as the French writer Madame Pilon-Fleury. Further digging revealed a first name, Marguerite, but no additional biographical information (though perhaps now more will turn up). Traces of the author also appear in a first-edition copy of the French original, *Islam: La Courtisan de la montagne; roman par une Circassienne*, presented with an author's inscription to the British writer Thomas Hardy in 1901. So, it would seem, there was an actual French woman author – and one who retained a veil over her identity for the reading public, allowing only the select few to be in the know. Having attempted to explain and justify the authorship of *Romance of the Harem*, Forestier-Walker's preface to the second edition also sought to lend credibility to its contents, announcing that: "It was the reading of this story and its successor 'La Courtisane de la Montagne' [referenced in a footnote as "English edition entitled, 'The Woman of the Hill'"], in the original, that His Majesty, the present Sultan, issued an irade, forbidding the employment of European governesses in Turkish Harems."[36]

In both books by "Une Circassienne," foreign governesses are given a bad press with a repetition of what were at the time common complaints: that foreign women of dubious repute duped Turks (read Muslims) into thinking them respectable; that they took little care of their charges; that they allowed girls to read unsuitable foreign literature; and that Turkish children should be raised by Muslims from their own society. The *irade*, or decree, issued in 1901 against the employment of foreign governesses, was reported in the English-language press in Istanbul with some concern, noting that women "of very immoral and improper manners have been admitted into Musselman houses under the title of governesses, nurses, etc," and that the resultant "manner of education and this way of living are even condemned by right thinking Christians."[37] Treading a difficult line between distancing itself from dissolute governesses (a not uncommon concern for parents in Europe) while protecting European interests but not offending the sultan, the *Oriental Advertiser* offered muddled support for the *irade*, with the caveat that the "fanaticism" which often accompanied the protection of "fortune, life and honor" should be guarded against. As the newspaper report makes clear, imperial concern about the infiltration of Western governesses (and other female staff) into Ottoman households was part of a longstanding political agenda for the Ottoman state: Forestier-Walker's claim that the writings of "Une Circassienne" played a central role in the development of imperial policy, while quite probably overstated, show his (and possibly her) awareness of contemporary Ottoman social discourse and how it might be harnessed to the books' advantage. By marking her out as important within Ottoman debate, Pilon-Fleury is also differentiated from the European women of bad repute who were criticized by the decree: as a European who allegedly had free access to Ottoman and Muslim households, her reputation must be distinguished from those Westerners felt to be a danger to the morality of the Ottoman empire.[38]

Yet, though the second edition of *Romance of a Harem* offered biographical information to substantiate the validity of the books by "Une Circassienne," the author herself remained hidden. In a period when women authors in Britain and France were routinely publishing under their own names, the taint of transgression that had once surrounded women writers could no longer have been a consideration. The retention of the pseudonym functions rather to construct and maintain an Oriental indexed author position that would help sell the books in a way that "Marguerite Pilon-Fleury" would not. The value of "Une Circassienne" as a recognizable brand,[39] even after the existence of the French author had been revealed, is illustrated by the publication in 1911 of *Adile Sultane: Roman* by "Une Circassienne" and Victor Barrucund. Not translated into English, and appearing without any explanatory preface, this final volume continued the theme of royal romance still presented under the guise of Circassian rather than French authorship. Although there was a clear market for harem accounts written by Western visitors (all of whom took pains to elaborate the degree of their access to Ottoman homes), the books by "Une Circassienne" do not present themselves as outsider accounts. Positioned within a field that prioritized female access, these two examples of harem literature oscillate between registers of fact and imagination:

> For many a long year I lived in a harem, and of that time I have the sweetest remembrances; comparisons that I have been able to make since the chances

> of fortune led me to share the life of European women, only strengthen the tender melancholy of those souvenirs.[40]

As the evocative opening lines of *Romance of a Harem* immediately make clear, the location of the narrator is central to the effective utilization of Orientalist tropes. With its emphasis on eyewitness experience and cultural immersion, the preface appeals to the conventions of ethnographic observation which, as Billie Melman observes, came to exert a profound influence on harem literature from the mid-nineteenth century.[41] As the reliable depiction of other cultures came to be validated through an ideology of objective observation, women's authority came under threat from their very proximity to the Oriental object of study that made their accounts a valuable commodity. As Melman has shown, the female connections and presence in the harem that gave Western women something to sell also downgraded their work as empathetic rather than scientific.

Western women sought in various ways to retain and recode the value of their special access, operating in uneasy alliance with an ethnographic authority that was relentlessly gendered. But for Ottoman women, themselves far too embedded in the harem's enervating atmosphere, the ability to access the superiority of an often imperial ethnographic gaze was inevitably compromised. The fanciful mix of historical narrative and personal drama in the volumes by "Une Circassienne" illustrates the combination of narrative form against which, as Mary Louise Pratt argues, ethnographic writing in the early twentieth century came to define itself.[42] With ethnographic authority depending (especially post-Malinowski) on the "scientific" rendition of the personal fieldwork experience, the first-person narrative was increasingly dismissed to the margins, operating as uncomfortable collateral for the objective social scientist's analysis of other worlds.[43] For harem accounts published in the early twentieth century, operating within a publishing category that relied absolutely on personal experience in the field, the calibrations of identity that secured experience as reliable were very finely drawn.

Conclusion: Blurring Boundaries of Genre and Identity

Harem literature has never been a definable genre: by its very nature it has always been relational to other forms of writing (themselves also evolving). Generically unstable and intrinsically porous, the one constant in harem literature has been its authenticating female point of origin. In this an "Oriental" authorship has had a particular premium. But though this would imply an allegiance to life writing, the picture concerning authenticity is further complicated when we remember that, for example, both Vaka Brown and Halide Edib, in addition to memoirs and autobiography, wrote fiction set in the Orient. The market for their fiction relied on its extra-textual relationship to the author function of their names and the other writings validated by it, which gave their fiction an "authentic" feel. In order to understand how and why harem literature's generic permeability and spectacularly contested authorship affected their work and their reception, I needed to widen my sample and include less securely "Oriental" and female sources – such as turned out to be the case with "Une Circassienne."

The case of Leïla Hanoum challenges also any lexicon of classification in terms of both author and genre. Her book, *A Tragedy in the Imperial Harem at Constantinople* (1883, first published in French in 1879), tells another version of the story of Abdülaziz's deposition. Published only a few years after the events occurred, it also presents palace intrigues through the eyes of insiders but is told in the third person. In this tale, the coup is set against an even more complicated plot of love and betrayal. As in *Romance of a Harem*, we encounter again Hassan the Circassian and his sister, Mihri, who had found favor with Abdülaziz. But the story of the coup this time is told in relation to the lovely young orphan Aïshe, whose love for Abdülaziz's aide-de-camp Salaheddin Bey is foiled by an evil plot concocted by the sultan's sister, Adile Sultan, whose husband had been Aïshe's father. Hidden identities, thwarted romances, dynastic ambitions, young women charged with important political secrets, and picturesque details of harem life are joined by a political discourse that details the machinations of the Great Powers in trying to control Ottoman events. The English edition begins with a translator's preface outlining the dastardly role of Russia and sketching in the tenets of Islam, based on the male translator's six years in Egypt serving the ex-Khedive Ismail in a military capacity. The book concludes with three appendices on slavery, polygamy, and harem life reprinted from named and unnamed Western sources. In its mix of romance, history, and detailed political debate, *A Tragedy in the Imperial Harem at Constantinople* is clearly addressed to a Western audience, aiming to explain Ottoman politics and society through inside information. Framed by ethnographic appendices and a scholarly preface itself based on the author's military immersion in the region, the book does everything it can to locate itself as trustworthy and realistic. While the overtly romanticized style of the harem narrative might seem to sit at odds with this, within the generic hybridity typical of harem literature, this potentially contradictory mix of literary registers serves instead to reinforce the "reality" of the account. Framed by supporting external verification, the wild rendition of the palace tale can be confirmed as reliably "Oriental."

But Leïla Hanoum – a proper-sounding Ottoman identification – is also identified by outside sources as Adriana Piazzi (née Delcambre), a woman of French descent (later married to an Italian) whose father moved as a doctor to the imperial court and converted to Islam. Does this make her an "Oriental" woman?

Examples such as these reveal the problems of classification and of reading that other books are relatively free from. Clearly, one of the elements that sold Halide Edib and Demetra Vaka Brown's books was their implicit and explicit claim to tell it like it was and to reveal the secrets of the hidden harem. That their purpose in this was to challenge Western stereotypes while earning a living did not lessen the market for their work. Contradictions like this were inherent in the publication of the always presumed to be revelatory harem literature, and can be seen in its packaging and promotion. Female authors' books frequently appeared with the word harem in the title and a disclaimer on page 1 that there was nothing obscene or improper within its pages. But, as the "publisher's note" at the start of Annie Reichardt's *Girl-Life in the Harem*, from 1908, demonstrates, these refutations were sometimes more of an incitement than an dampener:

> The Publishers respectfully beg to intimate that there is not a single line in this book that the most scrupulous person may not read. There is absolutely no objectionable matter whatever, though the account is replete with thrilling incidents.[44]

Publishers were not beyond performances of opportunistic outrage to activate stereotypes of Oriental sexual excess,[45] and if the name on the spine looked Oriental, the marketing opportunities were greater.

But the ability to spot a fake, fundamental to the citational practices of Orientalist discourse and publishing, had a particular importance in securing the always threatened authority of women's cultural practices in harem literature and travel writing. When two articles on "Life in the

Harem" by "Adalet" appeared in the British journal *The Nineteenth Century* in 1890, Lucy Garnett was quick to denounce them as frauds. Fulminating that the author demonstrated an "ignorance of so elementary a fact as [the rules of veiling], and other similar errors which might be cited," Garnett, herself compiling an ethnographically thorough study of Ottoman women, used her superior, acquired (not inherited) knowledge of Eastern life to reveal that "Adalet" was probably a European governess and not "a genuine 'Voice from the harem'."[46] The appearance of articles such as that by "Adalet" and the swift response of female authorities in the field highlights the importance of harem literature as an area of cultural activity available to Western women. In defending the integrity of the field, Western authors buoyed up its significance and protected the value of their expertise. Garnett policed the boundaries of harem literature again in her 1911 volume *Turkey of the Ottomans.* Here she decried the credibility given to *Les Désenchantées*, arguing that, by

> all who possess an adequate knowledge of Eastern life this work is . . . condemned as presenting an entirely false view of the aspirations and ideals of representative Osmanli womanhood. There are no doubt in Turkey, as in every nation a certain number of frivolous and foolishly sentimental women, but they are not regarded as typical of their countrywomen generally, nor must the type depicted by this brilliant French writer be looked upon in any degree as representative.[47]

Though the instances I have covered in this essay may seem more marginal than the attributable autobiographies I have dwelt on elsewhere,[48] their liminal status is important in delineating the contours of those accounts considered central to harem literature. For a field to have status it must have boundaries, and to analyze it one must have protocols. The problems of reading these strange sources reveal the ways in which contemporary critical practice invests in concepts of truth and authenticity even as it seeks to undercut them.

This is a necessary and unavoidable contradiction, and it is one of the reasons why it is important to deal with these books as cultural commodities; as items with a history of production and reception that, alongside writing conventions, all served to construct a racialized point of gendered origin for their narratives. But there were competing definitions of authenticity at play: if Ottomans recognized the transitional elective identities of converts, the West wanted pure bloodlines based on inheritances of fixed and detectable racial origins. The various purposes (political, social, religious, cultural) served by these different concepts of authenticity could not always stand the transculturation inherent in harem literature, where Ottoman authors faced Western readerships that could not recognize the terms of their identifications. The impossibility of securely attributing some of these sources highlights the necessary fiction of current attempts at ascribing authorial integrity to sources from a more secure point of origin.

Notes

1 R. Lewis, *Rethinking Orientalism: Women, Travel and the Ottoman Harem* (London: I. B. Tauris, 2004).

2 By author function I mean the identity that readers, without even necessarily realizing it is a literary convention, project onto the books' imagined point of origin.

3 Lady Mary Wortley Montagu, *Embassy to Constantinople: The Travels of Lady Mary Wortley Montagu* (1763), ed. C. Pick, introd. D. Murphy (London: Hutchinson, 1988).

4 For examples and discussion see J. Beaulieu and M. Roberts (eds.), *Orientalism's Interlocutors: Painting, Architecture, Photography* (Durham, NC: Duke University Press, 2002); J. F. Codell and D. S. Macleod (eds.), *Orientalism Transposed: The Impact of the Colonies on British Culture* (Aldershot: Ashgate, 1998); R. Lewis, *Gendering Orientalism: Race, Femininity and Representation* (London: Routledge, 1996); J. M. MacKenzie, *Orientalism: History, Theory and the Arts* (Manchester: Manchester University Press, 1995).

5 B. Melman, *Women's Orients: English Women and the Middle East, 1718–1918: Sexuality, Religion and Work* (Basingstoke: Macmillan, 1992).

6 For examples of elite Ottoman women's cultural agency prior to this period see L. Peirce, *The Imperial Harem: Women and Sovereignty in the Ottoman Empire* (Oxford: Oxford University Press, 1993).

7 The Ottoman education system was overhauled during the reforms of the Tanzimat period (1839–76) when the Ottoman state was keen to acquire for itself the scientific advances that seemed responsible for Western economic and political superiority. Though designed to meld Western science to Islamic values, the new civilian and military education establishments fostered a sea change in their (male) students' sense of themselves. Individuals came increasingly to value the secular ties of civic association over the religious abjuration to dynastic obedience. The political and personal ramification of these educational developments extended into the lives of students' families and

communities, having an effect far beyond those actually enrolled in the new schools. See B. Fornta, *Imperial Classroom: Islam, the State and Education in the Late Ottoman Empire* (Oxford: Oxford University Press, 2002).

Though most of the Tanzimat education system was concerned with boys, state schools for girls were opened in 1858 and expanded in the 1860s, with daughters of the progressive Ottoman elite receiving a Western-style education from tutors and governesses at home. See E. B. Frierson, "Unimagined Communities: Woman and Education in the Late-Ottoman Empire," *Critical Matrix*, 9/2 (1995), 55–90.

8 On the Ottoman women's press see E. B. Frierson, "Mirrors Out, Mirrors In: Domestication and Rejection of the Foreign in Late-Ottoman Women's Magazines," in D. F. Ruggles (ed.), *Women, Patronage, and Self-Representation in Islamic Societies* (New York: State University of New York Press, 2000); E. B. Frierson, "Cheap and Easy: The Creation of Consumer Culture in Late Ottoman Society," in Donald Quataert (ed.), *Consumption Studies and the History of the Ottoman Empire 1550–1922* (New York: State University of New York Press, 2000). On the women's press in Egypt see B. Baron, *The Women's Awakening in Egypt: Culture, Society and the Press* (New Haven: Yale University Press, 1994).

9 S. Deringil, *The Well-Protected Domains: Ideology and the Legitimation of Power in the Ottoman Empire, 1876–1909* (London: I. B. Tauris, 1999).

10 See Z. Çelik, *Displaying the Orient: Architecture of Islam at Nineteenth-Century World's Fairs* (Berkeley: University of California Press, 1992).

11 For more details see Lewis, *Rethinking Orientalism.*

12 In Ankara, Edib served in the army as translator, and nursing and relief co-ordinator, reaching the rank of major.

13 When her first husband took a second wife without her consent and she insisted on a divorce (still difficult for a woman to obtain at that time), Edib faced unwelcome notoriety.

14 H. Edib, *The Turkish Ordeal: Being the Further Memoirs of Halidé Edib* (London: John Murray, 1928), 190

15 *Times Literary Supplement*, November 29, 1928, 921.

16 On the politics of Edib's accounts as a riposte to *Nutuk* see H. Adak, "National Myths and Self-Na(rra)tions: Mustafa Kemal's *Nutuk* and Halide Edib's *Memoirs* and *The Turkish Ordeal*," *South Atlantic Quarterly*, 102/2–3 (Spring/Summer 2003), 511–29. See also her discussion of how the memoirs, not available in Turkish until the 1950s, were "translated" by Edib with many alterations that mitigated her criticisms of Kemal.

17 Melek Hanoum, "How I Escaped from the Harem and How I Became a Dressmaker," *The Strand Magazine* (February 1926), 129–38.

18 H. Edib, *Memoirs of Halidé Edib* (London: John Murray, 1926), 198–200.

19 Melek Hanoum "How I Escaped."

20 Lewis, *Rethinking Orientalism.*
21 *Times Literary Supplement,* March 13, 1913, 107.
22 Marc Hélys (pseud. Marie Léra), *L'Envers d'un roman: Le Secret des Désenchantées* (Paris: Perrin, 1923).
23 Melek Hanoum "How I Escaped," 133. On the sisters' relationship with Loti and with Hélys, see Y. Ternar, *The Book and the Veil: Escape from an Istanbul Harem* (Montreal: Véhicule Press, 1994).
24 See D. Quataert, "Part 4: The Age of Reforms 1812–1914," in H. Inalcik, with D. Quataert, *An Economic and Social History of the Ottoman Empire, 1300–1914* (Cambridge: Cambridge University Press, 1994).
25 Not independently wealthy, Vaka Brown faced the prospects of limited employment choices or whatever sort of marriage could be contracted for a girl without a proper dowry.
26 D. Vaka Brown, *Haremlik* (London: Constable, 1909), 12–13.
27 See Lewis, *Rethinking Orientalism.*
28 In a parallel plot to the imperial coup, Prince Halim hopes that his support for the unprecedented intervention by ministers of state into the Ottoman throne will result in a change of his fortunes, he having been ousted from his position as heir apparent when the Khedive departed from convention by making his son rather than his nephew the designated successor to the Egyptian throne.
29 Referred to here as the Sultana, though this title applied only to the daughters of the sultan, not his consort.
30 For a fuller discussion of debates about signature see Lewis, *Gendering Orientalism.*
31 R. Barthes, "Pierre Loti: *Aziyadé*" (1971), in Barthes, *New Critical Essays,* trans. R. Howard (Berkeley: University of California Press, 1990), 107.
32 Barthes, "Pierre Loti," 107.
33 Clarence Forestier-Walker, preface to "Une Circassienne" (pseud. Marguerite Pilon-Fleury), *Romance of a Harem,* trans. Forestier-Walker, 2nd edn. (London: Greening & Co., 1904).
34 All quotations from the fly sheet of "Une Circassienne" (pseud. Marguerite Pilon-Fleury), *The Woman of the Hill,* trans. Clarence Forestier-Walker, 1st edn. (London: Greening & Co., 1902).
35 *Times Literary Supplement,* October 16, 1913, 450.
36 Forestier-Walker, "Une Circassienne," *Romance of a Harem* (1904 edn.).
37 "Foreign Governesses and Musselman Families," *Oriental Advertiser,* July 17, 1901.
38 The tendency for visiting or resident Westerners to publicly distance themselves from disreputable Perotes/Westerners is seen in many accounts from this period. See Lewis, *Rethinking Orientalism.*

39 The Orientalized specificity of the regional location of "Une Circassienne" makes it far more effective than the generic "A Lady."

40 "Une Circassienne" (pseud. Marguerite Pilon-Fleury), *Romance of a Harem*, trans. Clarence Forestier-Walker, 1st edn. (London: Greening & Co., 1901), 1.

41 Melman, *Women's Orients.*

42 M. L. Pratt, "Fieldwork in Uncommon Places," in J. Clifford and G. E. Marcus (eds.), *Writing Culture: The Poetics and Politics of Ethnography* (Berkeley: University of California Press, 1986).

43 As Pratt points out, even with the postmodern turn to subjectivity in ethnography, the scandals of the late twentieth century centered on "fraudulent" accounts of fieldwork written without direct experience and sometimes appropriating "native" accounts as well as those of professional ethnographers. The *cause célèbre* of Florinda Donner's *Shabono: A True Adventure in the Remote South American Jungle* in the 1980s proved again that one could "construct a convincing, vivid, ethnographically accurate account of life in another culture *without personal experience in the field.*" Pratt, "Fieldwork in Uncommon Places," 29, original emphasis.

44 A. Reichardt, *Girl-Life in the Harem: A True Account of Girl-Life in Oriental Climes* (London: John-Ouseley, 1908).

45 See also I. Schick, *The Erotic Margin: Sexuality and Spatiality in Alteritist Discourse* (London: Verso, 1999).

46 L. Garnett, *The Women of Turkey and their Folk Lore*, 2 vols. (London: David Nutt, 1890–1), 471.

47 L. Garnett, *Turkey of the Ottomans* (London: Sir Isaac Pitman & Sons, 1911), 241. Garnett was not alone in arguing that the heroines of *Les Désenchantées* were untypical, but her vilification of Loti's characters (the "brilliance" of his writing serving for her to emphasize its artifice) highlights the extent to which the *désenchantées* became a touchstone in the representation of harem women. For Grace Ellison, who worked directly with the original *désenchantées*, bringing Ottoman women into print extended the field of harem literature and helped in her political project of harnessing British sympathy for Turkey at the same time as it enhanced her status as a reliable authority on Ottoman matters.

48 Lewis, *Rethinking Orientalism.*

5

The Sweet Waters of Asia: Representing Difference/ Differencing Representation in Nineteenth-Century Istanbul

Frederick N. Bohrer

The exotic is not a unique invention of the nineteenth century. Rather, throughout the histories of many world cultures, articulating who one is has necessitated also saying who one is not. There is a host of evidence – psychological, cultural, political, anthropological – that an individual's or group's self-definition can be fundamentally bound up with, and even partly asserted through, contrast with an external, alien figure of difference: a shifting, inchoate "other."[1]

This situation surely accounts for much of the appeal of exoticist imagery in European and American visual culture during the nineteenth century. It was essential for assimilating, for controlling and making sense of, the burden of discovery of the vast variety of world cultures which came to the attention of the West during the period. Considerable scholarship in art history and other disciplines has ably demonstrated how such imagery participates in, indeed enacts, the desires, anxieties, and confusions bound up in Western conceptions of a "non-Western" world: a curiously generic elsewhere both spatially and temporally distinct from the European metropole.[2] This approach has also highlighted the attendant power relations through which Western dominance has cast an inferior East as its counterpart. Central to this work, starting with Edward Said's seminal *Orientalism* of 1978, is an assumption that the arrangement between parties is fundamentally hierarchical and binary. That is, such analysis is conceived in determinate pairs – West–East, colonizer–colonized, "us"–"them," etc. – from which power is not evenly shared but rather exerted by the stronger, "Western" party over the weaker, "Eastern" one.

The inspiration of this first generation of post-colonial writing remains important to art history and visual studies. At the same time, it seems clear that the vast, nebulous, and contradictory images of the East that flourished throughout the nineteenth century say more about the period than binarism alone can capture. Indeed, after more than two decades of post-colonial and cultural studies, such binary arrangements have been questioned from many directions, by scholars such as Homi Bhabha, Nicholas Thomas, and Mary Louise Pratt (as well as Said himself in more recent work).[3]

Taking these later developments into account means not simply rejecting binarism as it has informed art history, but rather resituating it within the larger, polyvalent scope of visual culture. This is not in any sense to minimize the dramatic force of colonialism and imperialism on the lands beyond the West. Rather, as Thomas especially has argued, it is to make the impact of these modern dislocations more comprehensible today, more connected to the realities of our time.[4] At the same time, this resituating cannot be the simple addition of a supplement to an otherwise unquestioned approach. James Herbert has explored how some of the principles of post-colonial theory present a radical challenge to fundamental epistemologies of traditional art history.[5] In this brief essay I want to consider a related challenge posed by this new context. Examining some representational transformations during the nineteenth century of a tangible place in Ottoman Turkey confronts us with questions of motivation and instrumentality in political and cultural terms that supplement the established art-historical literature on Orientalism. At the same time, it makes clear that these concerns cannot be seen apart from the work of the same images to problematize representation itself. Considering the Western vision of the Orient, that is, must be to question tenets of realism and representation *per se* as much as the truth or falsehood of Oriental subject matter. In a study of French nineteenth-century painting, Darcy Grimaldo Grigsby posits that "Orientalist discourse represents its own incompleteness."[6] I present here material to establish a related structural principle, that Orientalist imagery is always incomplete *as representation.*

If there is any place where the meeting of East and West could be presented as a naturally binary situation, one literally inscribed in the landscape, it is Istanbul. Then as now an essential stop for the traveler to the East, the city uniquely spans both Europe and Asia, while also holding the two apart, divided by a watery boundary. To examine in more detail the city's geography, as represented in the nineteenth century, must also be to examine related assumptions of what characterized the different continents and their inhabitants. In fact, within the city's bounds are two spots whose traditional Western names directly juxtapose the two continents. The shores of the Golden Horn and the Bosphorus, the major bodies of water that divide the city, are interspersed with level, grassy fields, often gently shaded with trees and foliage while irrigated by rivulets running from the distant hills. Two of the best known of these park-like areas were known respectively as the Sweet Waters of Europe, a large expanse at the top of the Golden Horn on the western edge of the city, and the Sweet Waters of Asia, a smaller area on the eastern side of the Bosphorus toward the north of the city. The striking parallelism of these names suggests that what differentiates the places is what differentiates Europe from Asia. At the same time, their linguistic basis also suggests that the binary conception itself is not objective or universal but rather a Western conceit. For the Turkish names of these places, Kiathanesu and Küçüksu, bear no trace of a continental opposition, but simply identify them both as places with proximity to water ("su" = water).

Yet the binarism that could be construed through the opposition of continents plays a clear role in the exposition of the city by Western tourist guides. Thus an 1854 edition of Murray's guide, *A Handbook for Travellers in Turkey*, by far the most popular series of its time, states: "we find that the Asiatic shore has been the more favored and beloved residence of the Ottoman Sultans than the Western and European shore, along which the Greeks and Franks have preferred constructing their summer residences."[7] In fact, royal residences could be found at both the Sweet Waters. Indeed, the principal imperial palace, the huge and gleaming Palace of Dolmabahçe, completed a year earlier, in 1853, dominated the western, not the eastern, shore of the Bosphorus. More generally, the physical fabric of Istanbul was then very much in flux, the result of a sweeping project of modernization directed by a succession of Ottoman sultans, supporting fundamental changes in architecture, transportation, and city planning.[8]

There is a sense in the guide's description, then, of an inherited, even nostalgic, order of things. A tourist's expectations are to be flattered. They might be filled in or somewhat deflected, but not directly countered. One detects a similar assumption in the later notation of a 1914 guide by Baedeker (whose format is directly modeled on that of Murray) that between the two rivers that feed the Sweet Waters of Europe "in 1913 the big electrical plant was built."[9] Whatever else flowed into the Golden Horn from the European side, it was introduced to the reader as a fount of modernization. More generally, this binarism of East and West offers a version of what Susan Stewart has called "the containment of representation."[10] The guidebooks' accounts do not merely describe the visual field around them; they discipline it to adhere to, or naturalize, a systematic, ideological preconception.

In fact, whatever sorts of differences needed to be posited about the two places, they had quite a lot in common. One of the most lyrical of late nineteenth-century guides writes of the Sweet Waters of Europe: "There may be seen a beautiful kiosque of the Sultan, many elegant villas, groves of trees, and fine meadows... During the spring and summer this place is much frequented [although not so much so as formerly]."[11] This description is comparable in many ways to the same guide's treatment of its counterpart:

> Near *Kandili* is the delightful place of resort called the *Sweet Waters of Asia*, "shaded by sycomares, oaks and planetrees, and dominated by an imperial kiosque which is surrounded by large gardens fairly blushing with roses... A fountain of white marble, embroidered all over with arabesques, storied all over with inscriptions in golden letters, and capped by a great roof with strong projecting eaves and by small domes surmounted by crescents" points to the traveller this charming resort and place of gathering for the wealthy.[12]

Both places were clearly described as pleasant expanses of flowing, tree-shaded meadows adorned with a kiosk. Further, they are functionally comparable. Both are described as grounds for promenade, available especially to upper-class visitors. At the same time, as this guide clearly intimates, the Sweet Waters of Asia inspired a far greater enthusiasm, of much longer and more loving description. More than half of the entire description, notably, is devoted to the place's elaborate marble kiosk.

This relative valuation of the two locations in the guide is completely concordant with their relative treatment in nineteenth-century visual representation. Throughout the range of visual media of the time, the Sweet Waters of Asia was portrayed much more often than the Sweet Waters of Europe. This clear European preference for one over the other is symptomatic of the Orientalist fixation on its other. Yet, looking more closely at one example of this subject (unusual only in its degree of detail), we can see how this other is both constructed and domesticated.

Johann Michael Wittmer's painting, *An die süssen Wassern Asiens* (At the Sweet Waters of Asia) of 1837 (figure 5.1), was made as souvenir of a tour – from Italy to Asia Minor – of Crown Prince Maximilian of Bavaria. The itinerary was typical of the time. Wittmer clearly presents the site as the "place of gathering for the wealthy" described by the guide. Upper-class families and groups lounge or stroll about the lawns, accompanied by their servants, elaborately decorated coaches, and a host of unique objects, most prominently the many-colored rugs and *narghile* of the man in the foreground. It is a festive scene of domesticity, rendered with an eye toward ethnographic detail of costume and implements.

The scene is strikingly varied, juxtaposing men and women (without their exactly intermingling), but also bringing together a variety of both Greek and Turkish cultural groups, with fezzes evident among the turbans. But the variety is not as great as it first appears. Reinhold Schiffer observes of such scenes, "ethnic and social differences have been smoothed out in order to achieve an over-all Ottoman quality."[13] The tone of seemly upper-class leisure is only heightened by the beggars, dancing waifs, Ottoman servants, and Jewish merchants circulating, at respectful distances, throughout the scene. A further clue to the ideal social order of the scene is the group of Europeans present, middle-distant at right. They include the artist himself and his patron, Crown Prince Maximilian.[14] The inclusion of the Europeans distinguishes this image from more commonly known Orientalist imagery, testifying to the painting's function as souvenir to the Crown Prince himself. At the same time, this inclusion makes uniquely explicit the relation between the painting's European viewers and its Ottoman subject.

The group of Europeans is decentered within the image, in just the same manner as the carefully detailed kiosk at left, which it visually balances. Together, both assert the artist's presence, his claim to having witnessed the scene. And yet, particularly through these Europeans at ease in the crowd, we can see the importance of representing the entire grouping as of a suitable social class and deportment for the small party to be pleasantly lost in. A Latin inscription at the bottom of the painting records the

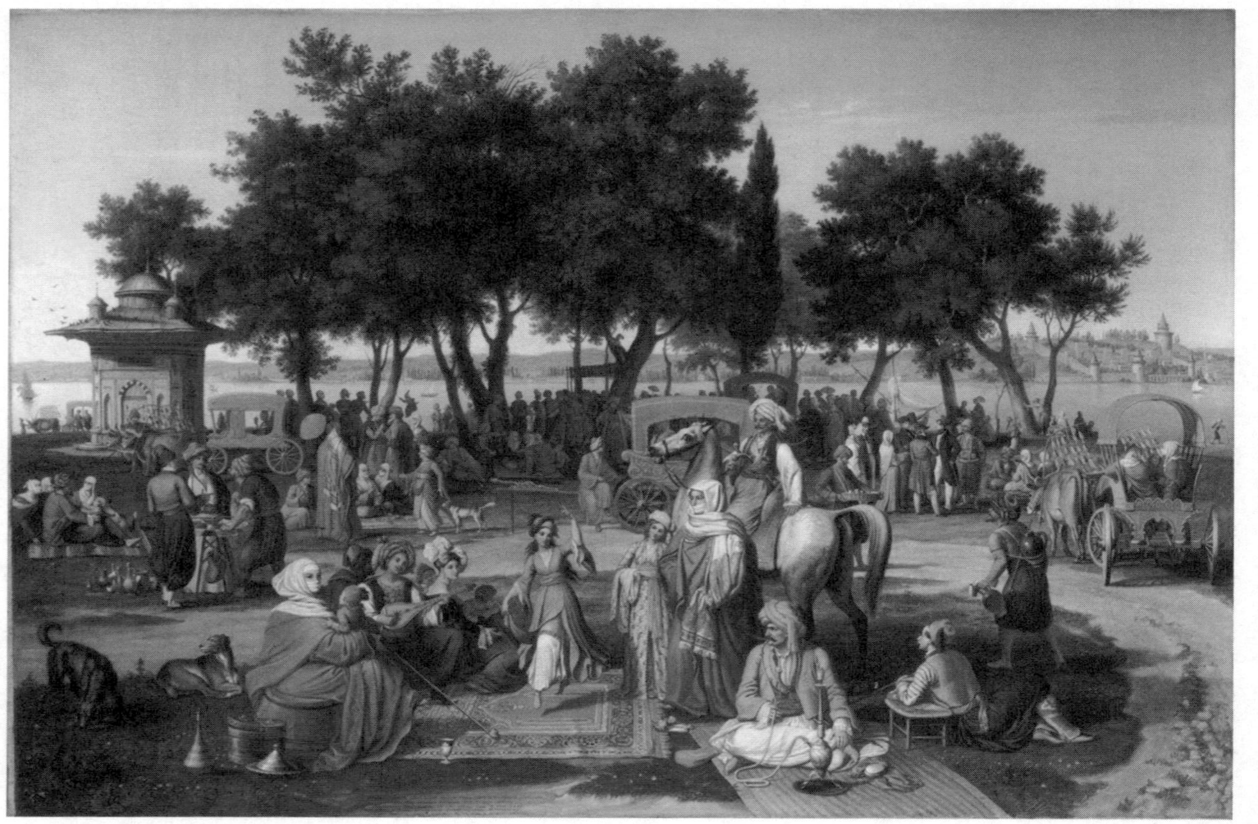

Figure 5.1 Johann Michael Wittmer, *An die süssen Wassern Asiens* (At the Sweet Waters of Asia), 1837. Bayerische Staatsgemäldesammlungen, Munich, Inv. 13690. Oil on canvas

party's experience as the pleasant promenade ("PERAMBULANS.RECREABATUR") of a particular date.

The Sweet Waters of Asia here emerges as both sight (of difference) and site (of power). Wittmer's image clearly details many physical and cultural details of a particular Turkish locale. Just as clearly, it places this conception in the context of a particular subject-position: one discreetly dominated by the hierarchy of power incarnated by his royal patron, as well as the related position of visual sovereignty of the image's Western viewer. Wittmer's image clearly enacts a vision of the Sweet Waters of Asia which was powerful in Europe throughout the nineteenth century. But, despite its own claims to the contrary, this does not mean that its representation captures or fixes the actuality of the place. We can best gauge what is unique and what is inevitable about Wittmer's conception by comparison with another image of the Sweet Waters of Asia by a slightly later traveler.

Théophile Gautier's visit to Istanbul in 1852 became the subject of an entire book. His *Constantinople* includes a description of the Sweet Waters of Asia, which makes clear it was for the author the most interesting site on the entire east coast of the Bosphorus. Gautier begins with the kiosk, which he describes as "A charming fountain of white marble, adorned with arabesques and covered with gilded inscriptions, topped with a steeply slanted roof with small domes surmounted by crescents."[15] This description, very similar to that of the guidebook, also essentially accords with Wittmer's image. Moreover, it plays the same sort of rhetorical role here, one first analyzed in Orientalist imagery by Linda Nochlin: the catalyst of a Barthesian "reality effect" strategically decentered in order to enhance the (more problematic) claims to veracity for the ethnic and cultural types placed by Gautier at the center of the scene.[16]

Although these two descriptions coincide, they do not, for that, objectively construe the Sweet Waters of Asia as a single, agreed-upon place. Gautier's interest, even more than Wittmer's, is centered on the people enacting the Friday ritual attached to the Sweet Waters of Asia. However, unlike Wittmer, he does not depict it as a place suitable for a European aristocrat, but rather a voyeuristic pageant from which the European (male especially) is specifically excluded. In Gautier's Sweet Waters of Asia, "upon their Smyrna carpets, lounge the idle beauties of the harem." He continues:

> Black eunuchs, switching their white trousers with a whip, walk among the groups, watching for any furtive glance, or covert sign of intelligence,

> watching above all if any Giaour is seeking to penetrate, from afar, the mystery of the yamachak or feredgé. Sometimes the women fasten shawls to the boughs of the trees, and rock their infants in improvised hammocks. Some eat rose confiture or drink iced water. Others smoke narghiles or cigarettes. All are chattering among themselves, some speaking against the Frankish women, who are so brazen as to show their faces uncovered and walk in the streets among men.[17]

Gautier presents the Sweet Waters of Asia as an open-air harem, its women to be protected from the penetration of the Western infidel. The women are juxtaposed to a variety of male subordinates, from black eunuchs to Bulgarian peasants to "Israelites . . . with that low and servile air which belongs to the Jews of the East, always on guard against the fear of insult." This visit to the Sweet Waters of Asia, then, presents it not as a place of decorum suitable for the recreation of a European aristocrat. Rather, it is closer to a licentious fantasy-space of racial and gender difference, less appropriate to palace than peepshow.

Part of the difference between these images might be related to differences between visual and verbal media. Gautier's description of the women's conversation, for instance, bears no obvious analog in Wittmer's painting. Still, both works might well be interpreted through the binarist model of the nineteenth-century exotic. Both present a vision dominated by, indeed created for, a European viewer. Further, both employ a characteristic strategy of artistic realism (especially through the ever-detailed kiosk) to persuade the viewer of the veracity of that vision, reveling in details of place and costume.

Yet even as these are both visions of Oriental difference, of an Eastern "other" constructed as a foil to Western norms, they are strikingly different *from each other* as well. Though anchored by the same elaborate description of what is clearly the same kiosk, they hardly seem like the same place at all. Gautier's place is one of implicit intrigue and enforcement of segregation, both by gender and between Ottoman and European. The scene presented by Wittmer, by contrast, is one of greater mixture and circulation, not least in situating the European viewer *within* the scene itself. Juxtaposing these images tells us at least as much about cultural and temperamental differences between Gautier and Wittmer (and their different implied audiences) as about any place in Istanbul.

The juxtaposition of Gautier and Wittmer highlights the mobility of the exoticist signifier, its remarkable openness to inflection in a variety of contexts and media.[18] The particular complexities imposed by this choice of images also point to the limitations of conceptions of European exoticism based solely on French, or English, examples. While the centrality of these countries to projects of colonialism and imperialism is undeniable, the multicultural variety of Europe, and of individual nations and regions during the nineteenth century, must also be taken into account. The more we see how the image of the Orient varies in European representations of the nineteenth century, the more we must acknowledge the variability of Europe itself. Indeed, basing conclusions solely on a few of the most common English or French examples risks privileging or naturalizing the particular imperialist claims of these countries during the nineteenth century. In all, these concerns highlight the tension involved in exoticist representation, undermining the possibility of one-to-one correspondence between the image's Eastern subject and its referent. On closer scrutiny, then, neither party in the binary model of exoticism can be treated as an integral unit. There is neither a simple "Us" nor "Them." Rather, both parties are fractured and variable, constructed in a dynamic relation to each other.

These conclusions would be less surprising were it not for the powerful claims to realism of the representations we have considered.[19] In fact, expanding the scope of imagery, and media, of the representation of the Sweet Waters of Asia, it becomes evident that the nineteenth-century drive to ever greater realism pressures to the point of exploding the capacious model of binarism, which becomes wholly inadequate as it is pressed farther.

Perhaps the nineteenth century's fundamental innovation to representations of the East lies in the imagery of the very medium invented during the period: photography. While the use of photography beyond Europe has been studied in some detail, the larger cultural import of this imagery, and its relation to other modes of exoticism, remains little examined.[20] Turning, then, to a nineteenth-century photograph of the same subject elaborates the stakes involved, precisely by focusing on the same locale, in its claim to greater, if not unmediated, realism.

Serving much the same Western audiences as paintings and literary accounts of the East, photographers fixed upon much the same choice of subjects. Again, photographic imagery abounds of the Sweet Waters of Asia. In a characteristic example, a photograph by Sébah (figure 5.2), we find an image of the place which is indisputably identifiable, but radically different. This photograph is centered on the place's main physical feature,

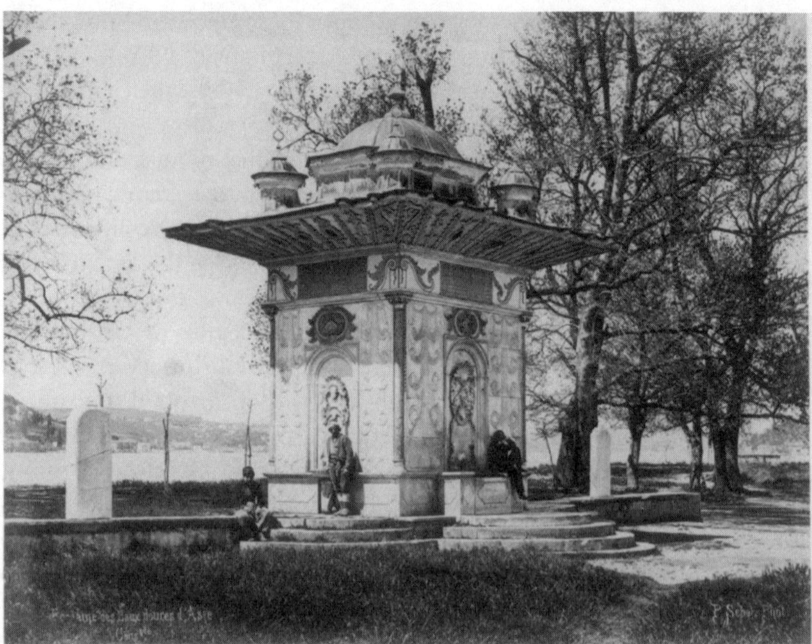

Figure 5.2 Pascal Sébah, "Fountains of the Sweet Waters of Asia," ca. 1870. Photograph. Library, Getty Research Institute, Los Angeles, the Pierre de Gigord Collection (96.R.14)

the kiosk (called a fountain in the photo's caption). However, even as it validates much of Wittmer's (or Gautier's) description, it also, effortlessly, corrects their descriptions of innumerable details, both of the kiosk itself and its setting.

But that is the least of it. This photograph fundamentally transforms the Sweet Waters of Asia. Artful as the image may be, and undeniably true for the Western viewer in a way inaccessible to the painter or writer, it is also a shock. Rather than a place of high pomp and display, the Sweet Waters of Asia is now an empty and rather drab spot of land. The kiosk itself is not used here to validate something else in the picture. Rather, it now serves as the very center of the image, rising a bit incongruously behind a few indolent locals who stare back at the photographer.

In the camera's eye, moreover, the Sweet Waters of Asia is not only differently peopled, but also differently gendered. The women described by Gautier and represented by Wittmer are nowhere in evidence. Instead, the quotidian, physical reality of the place occludes the once-a-week pageantry for which it was previously recommended. In fact, most of the time the large open space of the area was sparsely populated, a pastoral backdrop for the elaborate mansions and palaces nearby, on which local peasants grazed their animals, and those of lower social class could loiter. The camera's unparalleled realism, and the drive to "know" the East behind it, wrench the site from its previously established identity. It is here decentered from the guidebook description quoted above: a "charming resort and place of gathering for the wealthy."[21]

This image's intervention into the conventional Western conception of the Sweet Waters of Asia may be associated not only with the nature of the photographic medium but also with the cultural identity of the photographer. For this is the work of an Ottoman photographer: Pascal Sébah. Sébah was among the most successful Ottoman photographers of his time, establishing an immense photographic repertory of Turkish peoples and places for Ottoman clients as well as Western tourists.[22] Thus even while Sébah's choice of subject responds to the same touristic interests as the other images, its differences from them may be seen to figure the photographer's different relation to the site and the people pictured within, one distinct from that which would apply to a Western visitor at the site.

Between the images of Wittmer, Gautier, and Sébah, the Sweet Waters of Asia appears as anything but the fixed pole of a binary arrangement. Rather, it is a sort of floating signifier, which elaborates visually the sort of theoretical device that has come to replace binarism in post-colonial studies: hybridity. To emphasize the hybridity of these images is to emphasize their unfixedness, or resistance to a single account. Seen as a group (which could easily be extended), each image critiques the totality or sufficiency of the others. The Sweet Waters of Asia itself, specifically the kiosk that is its defining physical feature, serves as a sort of pivot point around which different kinds of representations are differently conceived. Appropriately, the kiosk itself is designed in the "Ottoman Baroque," itself stylistically hybrid.

While this group of images by both Western and Ottoman makers varies greatly in medium and emphasis, it is still one fundamentally designed to respond to external, touristic interests and preconceptions. As we have seen, this sort of interest is played to, in different ways, by the majority of images of the Sweet Waters. Yet photography also offered a unique way to counter the tenets of Western exoticism, using the camera's objectivist conception to testify to a contemporary Ottoman reality in a way that could redirect or amend the viewer's assumptions. The representation of the Sweet Waters also offers a paradigmatic case of such photographic reuse, further expanding the representational range available through photography.

In 1893 the Ottoman Sultan Abdülhamid II presented to America a series of photographic albums. These 51 albums of photographs, made by Ottoman photographers at the behest of the Ottoman ruler, cover Istanbul in detail, in a way "designed to present the Turkish domain of the Sultan in a progressive light."[23] Here, in a context designed to counter rather than flatter Western assumptions, there are more than three times the number of photos devoted to the Sweet Waters of Europe than the Sweet Waters of Asia. Zeynep Çelik has identified these albums as key monuments of a drive toward "speaking back" to Orientalist discourse in the Ottoman empire of the time.[24] Certainly their relative attention to the different locations of the Sweet Waters supports this conception, as it literally, and uniquely, goes against the otherwise dominant tendency in the representation of these two places.

Seen individually, in their own time, these images may address the nineteenth-century discourse of cultural binarism, either by depending upon it or speaking back to it. But seen together, from a contemporary standpoint, they are a range of hybrid conceptions, each shaping the experience of a place in a different way for different motivations. Bhabha states that "Hybridity intervenes in the exercise of authority not merely to indicate the impossibility of its identity but to represent the unpredictability of its presence."[25] In their hybridity, these images do indeed intervene in the authority of their makers. Such intervention is even implicitly acknowledged by the exaggerated assertion of authority imposed by their makers within the images, such as Wittmer's inscription or Sébah's labeling, or the elaborately stamped bindings of the Abdülhamid albums, which forms a framework for their presentation. The "unpredictability" represented by this group of images is precisely their resistance to binarism and, indeed, objectivity. What one image can stand for the reality of a place? This very question is figured in Bhabha's "impossibility," suggesting instead a sense of identity that is partial and never fully revealed. Instead, the image of the Sweet Waters of Asia (like the Sweet Waters of Europe) is inflected through the manifold variations of its image-makers.

This group of images turns the tables on another authority beside that of the makers, namely that of the very media through which they are conceived. In this sense, the differentiation of the Sweet Waters of Asia as subject pictures the representational capabilities of different media: painting, text, photography. This is just the beginning of the range of media available for constructing images in the nineteenth century (one might also consider images in broadsheets, panoramas, theatrical representation, book illustrations, etc.), but it intimates the complexities, confusions, and hybridities thereby fostered across the range of visual culture. The East, in this sense, serves as a mirror of representation *per se*, as practiced in the nineteenth century. Undermining the claim of each medium to a totalizing, self-sufficient realism, it points instead not only to the insufficiency of each mode individually, but also to the incommensurability between them. This too is underlined by Bhabha's term "impossibility." Both effects testify to the nature of Orientalist imagery posited at the start of this essay: that it is always incomplete as representation.

A final root of unpredictability is apparent here as well: the alterity of the past. For the contemporary viewer, the Sweet Waters are dislocated not just spatially, as for the nineteenth-century traveler, but also temporally. A 1991 Blue Guide, the Baedeker of our time, has this to say about the Sweet Waters of Europe:

> For centuries the meadows and banks of the Sweet Waters were the site of royal palaces, mansions, gardens, and pavilions ... But today the area is a squalid industrial slum of the worst sort, the Sweet Waters are a sewer, and only a few pathetic ruins remain of the pleasure domes that graced its shores in Ottoman times.[26]

Even as the judgmental tone continues an aspect of the nineteenth-century view of the East, and palpably indicates some real consequences of Western dominance, this passage also reminds us that many of the objects of the nineteenth-century representation no longer exist. Even as imagery continues to circulate, from paintings to postcards, there is an unbridgeable gap between past and present. The encroachment of modernity we have seen approvingly noted at the site by an earlier guide is now registered only as detritus, its origin in modernization unacknowledged. Similarly, my own visit to the site of the Sweet Waters of Asia in 1996 found a wasted work zone with fires flaring from oil drums, the now damaged kiosk hidden behind a formidable fence, awaiting restoration.[27]

From this position, explicitly acknowledging the present concerns and location of the viewing subject, we look back at the Istanbul of the nineteenth century. From here, at the beginning of the twenty-first century, it has never been farther away. Yet, as we look anew at the nineteenth century, within a perspective shaped in the framework of visual culture and post-colonial theory, we can hear within the voices of the nineteenth century itself an alternative view to the binary conception that has long dominated ideas of the relation between "the West and the rest." Rudyard Kipling's well-known (and paradigmatically binarist) assertion "East is East and West is West, and never the twain shall meet" can no longer be an unquestioned touchstone. In fact, on closer inspection Kipling's own poem, *The Ballad of East and West*, goes on to undermine its distinction between East and West even in the process of establishing it.[28]

Even more, just as this essay, in the process of enlarging the scope of European renderings, has considered a German painting of an Ottoman subject against more commonly known French and English Orientalist treatments, so too can the maxim of a central German writer serve to further complicate the views of imperial motivation centered in the great colonial powers. That is, one can find a completely different view from Kipling throughout the earlier, and today far less quoted, exoticist work of Goethe, his *West-Östlicher Divan* of 1819. Rather than the confrontational quality, and implicit hegemonic interest, of Kipling, Goethe's work assumes a worldliness and circulation whose ultimate effect is to dissolve the very borders between East and West. As he puts it: "Wer sich selbst und andre kennt /Wird auch hier erkennen /Orient und Okzident /Sind nicht mehr zu trennen" (Who is familiar with himself and another /Will understand [that]here as well /Orient and Occident /Can no more be divided).[29] For Goethe, then, the binary structure of Eastern versus Western cultural difference is no sooner acknowledged than discarded, replaced by a plurality of differences, potentially as subtle and varied as the shades of Western individualism.

Hybridity's challenge to binarism, then, offers not just a perspective *on* the nineteenth-century image of the other derived from contemporary post-colonial theory, but in fact is specifically rooted *within* the nineteenth century itself. Far from being an imposition or external critical tool, it is a fundamental aspect of the burgeoning, unstable image of the East which emerged during the nineteenth century, yet one which has only in recent decades come into sight. Productive as they may have been, the distinctions between West and East, or Self and Other, must be mapped on a wider, more polyvalent range of representations, a nineteenth century whose contours and complexities are still to be revealed.

Epilogue

I have lived in Washington, DC, for more than a decade, which I'm sure affects my views of exoticism and representation. Surely no other city in the world today stands more for the same concentration of power and aspiration to dominance which emerged earlier in London and Paris in the nineteenth century. And yet, even at the heart of the imperial structure, fissures and differences, moves to resistance, are almost always apparent when one takes time to look

Most of this essay was completed in summer 2002. Even as war in Iraq was then being made to seem more inevitable, demonstrations against military action were mounted with increasing urgency. One of the earliest, little covered by national news media, ended with a rally about a block from my apartment, at a traffic circle very close to the official residence of the Turkish ambassador. On the grounds of that circle, for months, a group of Kurds had lived in a makeshift structure, in an attempt to make visible for a new audience the plight of this homeless and divided people. On one wall, facing the ambassador's residence, and legible to innumerable motorists, was painted in uneven lettering "HEY TURKEY, FREE THE KURDS!"

Speakers at the anti-war rally denounced the American government's already obvious war plan, not least its assumption that Turkey would allow full American use of its military facilities. Speakers for the Kurdish cause discussed their own horrendous treatment by the Turkish government in a parallel, and related, critique of totalizing power, and an imperial capital's denial of the concerns of its people. Despite representations to the contrary of both government and media, voices both American and Turkish rose up against representing either country as unitary or monolithic.

I returned to my apartment, and questions of the imagery of Ottoman Turkey and the East in the nineteenth century. Yet I did not feel that I had completely left the site of the demonstration. Even as I sat at my computer, voices from the rally rang through my windows, open for the typically hot weather. Further, though political action and historical scholarship are quite distinct things, questioning representation and questioning power are related projects, as exoticism makes especially clear. The call to war in Iraq was accompanied by extraordinarily tendentious representations of Arabs and Islam, not completely different in kind from those of nineteenth-century Orientalist painting. In this context, forging a link between present realities and historical patterns in the Western view of the Middle East may itself be seen as an act of resistance. Moreover, the incompleteness of representation itself can serve as check to claims of knowledge and calls to national aggression. More generally, just as we cannot fail to acknowledge the irreducible alterity of the past, and of cultural difference, so too we must acknowledge seeing them through the equally complex concerns of the contemporary viewing subject.

Notes

1 M. Harbsmeier, "On Travel Accounts and Cosmological Strategies: Some Models in Comparative Xenology," *Ethnos*, 50 (1985), 273–312; T. Todorov, *Nous et les autres: La Réflexion française sur la diversité humaine* (Paris: Seuil, 1989).

2 Within art history, see the still matchless essay by L. Nochlin: "The Imaginary Orient," in *The Politics of Vision: Essays on Nineteenth-Century Art and Society* (New York: Harper & Row, 1989), 33–59.

3 Compare these two formulations by Said, separated by 15 years: "Orientalism was ultimately a political vision of reality whose structure promoted the difference between the familiar (Europe, the West, 'us') and the strange (the Orient, the East, 'them')" (*Orientalism* [New York: Random House, 1978], 43); "some notion of literature and indeed all culture as hybrid (in Homi Bhabha's complex sense of that word) and encumbered, or entangled and overlapping with what used to be regarded as extraneous elements – this strikes me as *the* essential idea for the revolutionary realities today" (*Culture and Imperialism* [New York: Knopf, 1993], 317).

4 N. Thomas, *Colonialism's Culture: Anthropology, Travel, and Government* (Princeton, NJ: Princeton University Press, 1994).

5 J. D. Herbert, "Passing Between Art History and Postcolonial Theory," in M. A. Cheetham, M. A. Holly, and K. Moxey (eds.), *The Subjects of Art History: Historical Objects in Contemporary Perspective* (Cambridge: Cambridge University Press, 1998), 213–29.

6 D. G. Grigsby, "Rumor, Contagion, and Colonization in Gros's *Plague-Stricken of Jaffa* (1804)," *Representations*, 51 (1995), 1–46: 2.

7 *A Handbook for Travellers in Turkey*, 3rd edn. (London: John Murray, 1854), 118.

8 Z. Çelik, *The Remaking of Istanbul: Portrait of an Ottoman City in the Nineteenth Century* (Berkeley: University of California Press, 1993).

9 K. Baedeker, *Konstantinopel, Balkanstaaten, Kleinasien, Cypern. Handbuch fur Reisende von Karl Baedeker*, 2nd edn. (Leipzig: Karl Baedeker, 1914), 220. All translations are my own unless otherwise noted.

10 S. Stewart, *Crimes of Writing: Problems in the Containment of Representation* (Durham, NC: Duke University Press, 1994).

11 G. des Godins de Souhesmes, *A Guide to Constantinople and its Environs*, trans. G. P. Cacavas (Istanbul: A. Zellich, 1893), 61.

12 Ibid. 213. Italics and quotations in original.

13 R. Schiffer, *Oriental Panorama: British Travellers in 19th Century Turkey* (Amsterdam: Rodopi, 1999), 211.

14 For details of the subject, see *Neue Pinakothek München* (Munich: Bayerische Staatsgemäldesammlungen, 1982), 370.

15 T. Gautier, *Constantinople* (1853; Paris: Christian Bourgeois, 1991), 400–1.

16 Nochlin, "The Imaginary Orient," 38.

17 Gautier, *Constantinople*, 401.

18 F. N. Bohrer, "Eastern Medi(t)ations: Exoticism and the Mobility of Difference," *History and Anthropology*, 9/2–3 (1996), 293–307.

19 Beyond the obvious conclusion that Western representations of the East are biased is an intimation that an objective representation of the locale is almost structurally impossible. Thus James Clifford's early and influential critique of Said's *Orientalism* notes that "Sometimes [Said's] analysis flirts with a critique of representation as such": "On *Orientalism*," in *The Predicament of Culture: Twentieth-Century Ethnography, Literature, and Art* (Cambridge, MA: Harvard University Press, 1988), 261.

20 For example, N. N. Perez, *Focus East: Early Photography in the Near East, 1839–1885* (New York: Harry N. Abrams, 1988); Y. Nir, *The Bible and the Image: The History of Photography in the Holy Land, 1839–1899* (Philadelphia: University of Pennsylvania Press, 1985); K. S. Howe (ed.), *Excursions Along the Nile: The Photographic Discovery of Ancient Egypt*, Santa Barbara Museum of Art, exhibition catalog (Santa Barbara, CA, 1993).

21 Godins de Souhesmes, *A Guide to Constantinople.*

22 On the photographer, see E. Özendes, *From Sébah and Joaillier to Foto Sabah: Orientalism in Photography* (Istanbul: Yapı Kredi Yayınları, 1999).

23 W. Allen, "The Abdul Hamid II Collection," *History of Photography*, 8/2 (1984), 119–45: 119.

24 Z. Çelik, "Speaking Back to Orientalist Discourse," in J. Beaulieu and M. Roberts (eds.), *Orientalism's Interlocutors: Painting, Architecture, Photography* (Durham, NC: Duke University Press, 2002), 19–41.

25 H. K. Bhabha, "Signs Taken for Wonders: Questions of Ambivalence and Authority Under a Tree Outside Delhi, May 1817," in *The Location of Culture*

(London and New York: Routledge, 1994), 102–22: 114 (1st published in *Critical Inquiry*, 12 (1985), 144–65).

26 J. Freely, *Blue Guide: Istanbul* (London: A. & C. Black, 1991), 290.

27 I revisited the site in July 2004. The kiosk and palace have now been meticulously restored, and will soon open as a public park. But this salutary development still serves to distance the contemporary experience of the site from that of the nineteenth-century viewer, occluding its history, and the challenges of cultural difference staged upon and around it.

28 R. Kipling, "The Ballad of East and West," in *Poems and Ballads* (1889; New York: Caldwell, 1899), 11. It continues: "But there is neither East nor West, Border, nor Breed, nor Birth, /When two strong men stand face to face. Tho' they come from the ends of the earth!"

29 J. W. von Goethe, *West-Östlicher Divan*, in *Goethes Werke* (1819), ed. R. Müller-Freienfeld (Berlin: Wegweiser, 1923), 149.

6

The Work of Translation: Turkish Modernism and the "Generation of 1914"

Alastair Wright

> In these narrative graftings, I have attempted to offer a productive tension, a perplexity that derives from a multiplication of journeys.
>
> (Homi K. Bhabha, "DissemiNation")

Start in Asia, on the eastern banks of the Bosphorus. Move west toward Europe – moving west, but always at a tangent. Board the ferry at Üsküdar, and wait as it pulses hesitantly out across the strait. Watch eddies of water play against the hull, turning this way and that beneath our feet as the warm waters from the Marmara Sea meet colder currents from the Black, caught in the uncertain zone between Europe and Asia. The boat connects the two great land masses, but also keeps them at bay, its rigid trajectory holding the banks apart, refusing to allow them to collapse together.

Disembark in Europe, in Dolmabahçe. Cross the square in front of the ferry port, continuing to walk westwards, our backs to the rising sun. Turn left, keeping close to the edge of the water. Walk through what used to be the Catholic quarter before that population was swept away in the aftermath of World War I. Pass the Deniz Museum and move on into a courtyard further down the street. Take care not to turn to the right – into the blank-faced offices of the Turkish secret service; the guards would not, in any case, let us make this mistake. Turn instead to the left, through the dark wooden doors of the Istanbul Museum of Painting and Sculpture.

Light streams into the entry hall, gathering in turgid pools on the dusty stone floors. Contemporary sculptures emerge from shaded corners, but it is not for them that we are here. We are interested in an earlier moment, a time when such international modernism was not so ubiquitous, when the nature of Turkish art was up for grabs, when battles were being fought over the Turkishness – or otherwise – of Ottoman painting. The guide-book tells us where to go: "One climbs next the monumental stairway," up to a series of rooms with "a view over the Bosphorus." And there, at the end of the corridor, is the work that catches our eye.[1]

* * *

We are facing Mehmet Ruhi Arel's *Stonebreakers 1924* (figure 6.1). Three men at work in a quarry. On the left, the rock face resembles a mysterious system of half-submerged hieroglyphs, incomprehensible in its division of strata and crazy of aspect. To the right, a barren rock suggests the ruin of a stone wall, a tower, a blockhouse. And the three workers, who themselves appear solid, so still and stable do they stand before us. Even the track of light from the westering sun shines smoothly, without the animated glitter that speaks of the imperceptible respiration of skin and muscle. The straight line of the flat picture plane joined to the stable rock, edge to edge, with a perfect and unmarked closeness.

An art historian stands in a museum in Istanbul in front of a Turkish painting. And immediately the art-historical machine sets itself in motion. Something here seems familiar, something calls forth memories of paintings and painters seen elsewhere. The first to come to mind is Cézanne. The repeated constructive brushstrokes, the solidity of the figures, even the rounded hat of the figure to the right: each of these traits seems to have migrated from Cézanne's Provence, from the quarry in Bibémus that he so often represented, to Turkey. And behind this lie other journeys. The tools lying in the foreground, the figures who strain to pull the rock apart, have perhaps arrived here from Jean-François Millet's *The Quarriers* (ca. 1846–7; Ohio, Toledo Museum of Art).[2] Ruhi's claustrophobic quarry answers to Millet's, though in the process of translation the French artist's drama – his figures' Sisyphean exertions amid a smokily indistinct atmosphere – has ceded to a calm that bespeaks orderly work, just as his brushwork has ceased to flicker. Something has congealed along the way. Millet viewed through the prism of Cézanne, facture and space closing down, compressed between the picture plane and the wall of rock.

Another memory echoes even more insistently, another European precedent: Gustave Courbet's *Stonebreakers*, with its own laboring figures and its own suffocatingly claustrophobic setting. Courbet himself had seen *his*

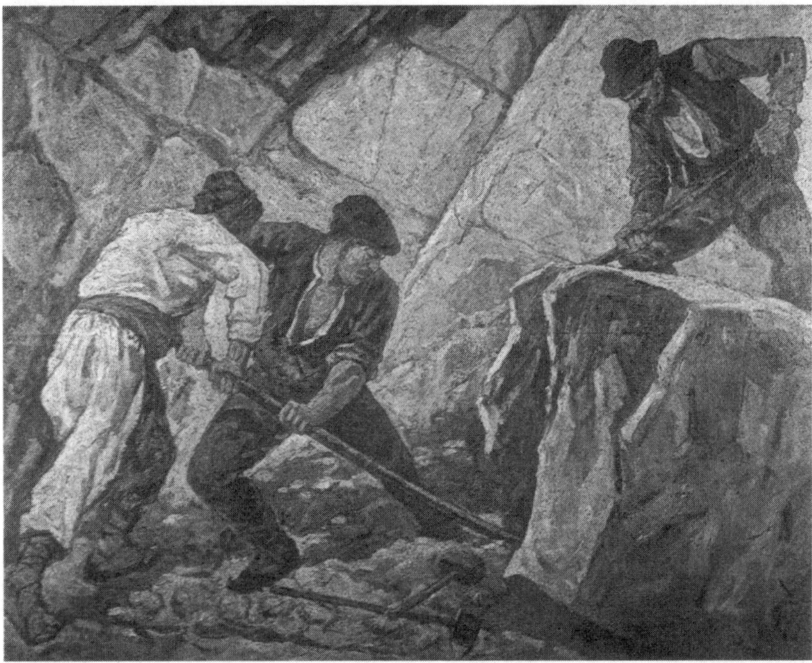

Figure 6.1 Mehmet Ruhi Arel, *Stonebreakers*, 1924. Istanbul Museum of Painting and Sculpture. Reproduced in Engin Özdeniz, *Türk Deniz Subayı Ressamları* [Turkish Naval Officer Painters] (Istanbul: Türk Deniz Kuvvetleri Komutanliği, 1994), 100

figures while on the move, on the road near his home in Ornans. They in turn had traveled to the painter's studio in Ornans to pose. From there their image would travel to Paris, to be shown in the Salon of 1849–50. And from there, after one or two detours, to Dresden, to be devoured in 1945 in the firestorm delivered by the RAF. But along the way, before that blazing conclusion in Germany, another journey awaited them. From a French canvas to a Turkish; from a road near Maisières to Paris and on into the canvas of Ruhi.

The echoes are partial; the familiar is defamiliarized. Cézanne, but not quite. Courbet, but not quite. The feeling is of listening to someone else's language, a language that speaks otherwise – that speaks from elsewhere – even as it echoes ones with which the European art historian is more familiar. Just as, when he looks across at the wall label, words jump out – "muze," "koleksiyonu" – that allow the text to start coalescing into fragmentary meaning. He begins, falteringly, to "read" Turkish, but not really to read it; simply to hear echoes, to hear the marking of an alien tongue by his own.

* * *

Something gets caught, something snags, an eddy in time. One word after another, one gesture after another, holding on to something of their identity yet acquiring new accents – and this in every sense. Courbet's image moves on in time, out to a quarry in Turkey; Cézanne's constructive brushstrokes move on to Istanbul. One journey is adding to the next. And we have another to consider.

They stand on the street corner, a tight group, posing for the camera (figure 6.2). A mixture of the confident and the studiedly casual. This is our corner, our patch, their varied poses assert. Behind them, the Parisian café, with its brief notations of prices, its fragmentary indices of the interior, of roasting coffee and bitter Pernod, of mixed stimulants in the morning. Ruhi is here. Like others of his generation, he had made the journey to Paris in 1909, and like them he would stay until the outbreak of war. Here we see him in his new environment, third from the right, restrained in pose, with his ever-present pipe and fez (the fez that would be outlawed by Atatürk in 1927; for now, though, it is safe to wear). Some of his companions seem more willing to dress the Parisian part: Hikmet Onat, posing jauntily off to the right with his *chapeau melon* and gold watch-chain, with his waistcoat wrinkled and belly thrust out; over at the left, a tall man, another *chapeau melon* and a cravat: this is Ibrahim Çalli, posing as the proper French gentle-painter; and another colleague, straw-hatted, standing elegantly side-on – he knows how to pose, this one – cigarette held casually within an open palm, a Turkish Oscar Wilde. And again, Ruhi himself: arm cocked under an imaginary palette; legs set squarely on the ground, feet shoulder-width apart; none of the foppishly relaxed contrapposto of the man to his side; echoes of the military perhaps, of a former officer, never fully at ease.

Turkish painters in Paris. They trained together, for the most part, in the studio of Fernand Cormon. On this street corner they hold on to a network of old friends in the great art capital, yet disperse into it; some maintain their Turkish habits, others are more willing to adopt Parisian modes of dress. And, of course, of painting. What, then, did it mean for Ruhi, born on the shores of the Bosphorus, to travel to Paris, to learn his craft at the epicenter of advanced European art? What was at stake as he

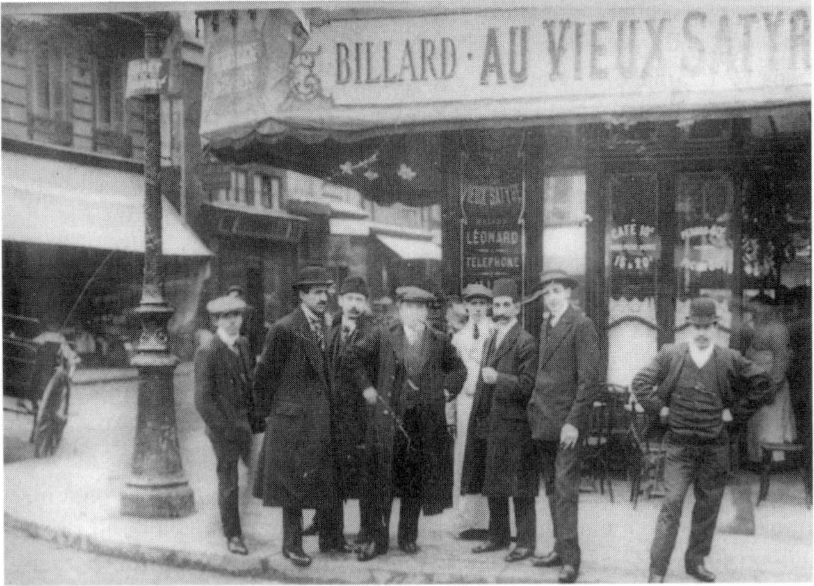

Figure 6.2 Photograph of Ruhi and colleagues in Paris, 1912. Reproduced in *Türk Resim Sanatinda: Şişli Atölyesi ve Viyana Sergisi* (Istanbul: İstanbul Resim ve Heykel Müzeleri Derneği, 1997), 39

painted the *Stonebreakers* in the first year of the republic? What are we to make of this translation from one culture to another?

* * *

> "His migration [was] like an event in a dream dreamt by another... [He] watch[ed] the gestures made and learn[ed] to imitate them... the repetition by which gesture is laid upon gesture, precisely but inexorably, the pile of gestures being stacked minute by minute, hour by hour... He learnt twenty words of the new language. But to his amazement at first, their meaning changed as he spoke them... The gesture continually overlaps and accumulates... [T]he Turk leads the life of the double, the automaton."[3]

Gesture upon gesture, one mark added to the next. What we see in Ruhi's work is an act of imitation – or better, of adaptation, of translation; of what John Berger, in a different context, has called production at one remove (Cézanne, but not quite). The experiences being described, we should note, are not the same. Berger's Turkish immigrant worker in

Germany occupies a radically different position to that taken up by Ruhi in Paris and – crucially – upon the artist's return to Istanbul. Berger's worker is judged by German eyes, his actions and words read by alien organs. Ruhi, in 1924, paints for his own people (this, as we shall see, will be one of the great claims made about his work). Nevertheless, something of the difference-in-repetition that Berger so piercingly identified is present also in the painter's work. Something shifts as a style crosses a border, as Turkish brush meets Cézannesque stroke; meanings change.

Ruhi is perhaps best understood as occupying what Homi Bhabha has described as a "space in-between."[4] Writing about the British imperial presence in India, Bhabha argues that when European discourse is repeated in non-European settings, i.e. when it becomes colonial discourse, it is no longer quite itself. It undergoes a process of displacement, distortion, dislocation. It splits. Difference exists not on the outside – not in the colony – but rather on the boundary, at the point where colonizer meets colonized; and this difference threatens not the colonized but the colonizer, for as colonial subjects mimic their masters an ironic reversal undermines the original's claim to be the model. Mimicry, the figure of a doubling, gazes back at the colonizer, reducing him to a partial presence, denying him his essential unity.

Bhabha's model speaks well to what we see in Ruhi, even though, as a subject of the Ottoman empire (and later, when he painted the *Stonebreakers*, as a citizen of the newly formed Turkish republic), the artist was neither colonizer nor colonized. The relationship between the Ottomans and France was very different from that between Britain and India. Those young men on the Paris street corner had been sent by the Ottoman court, part of an effort to protect the vitality of the empire, to acquire the military and economic resources held to be necessary for that project; if these resources were drawn at times from the West, the act of borrowing was carried out from a position of (admittedly waning) power. Yet if Bhabha's model does not quite fit – if something shifts as theory translates from one setting to another – a certain echo of the doubled nature of the colonial mimic nonetheless structures Ruhi's painting. The *Stonebreakers*, whatever the relations of power that underlay its production, occupies the in-between zone described by Bhabha. And as in the context described by Bhabha, this position, this hybrid identity, should not be seen as the repression of native traditions (though this, as we shall see, was how later Turkish nationalists were all too ready to view European influences). It is, rather, the sign of a breakdown, a rendering fluid of borders, the production of an inside/out:outside/in space that undermines – productively, I would suggest – the binary opposition of racial and cultural groups upon which processes of segregation and domination rest.

* * *

Walk back down the corridor in which the Ruhi hangs, step into one of the large adjoining galleries, and turn to face Osman Hamdi's *Guardian of the Tomb*. The painting represents what might seem at first a conventionally Orientalist theme, an apparently timeless subject rendered in precise detail. Cold light cascades into a darkened interior, picking out the blunt edges of marble tombs in crisp outline, silhouetting the motionless figure. We see here the unmistakable influence of Jean-Léon Gérôme, with whom Hamdi trained in Paris (he also studied with Boulanger) and to whom he owes the clearest of allegiances. Gérôme himself had visited Istanbul in 1875 and 1879, moving east along the trajectory that Osman Hamdi would later trace in the opposite direction: always a crossing of regards and of bodies, moving back and forth across the Bosphorus. On returning to Istanbul, Hamdi brought back Gérôme's quasi-photographic technique, his fetishization of marble and metal surfaces, and his attachment to the principles of academic training (Hamdi immediately set about founding a Fine Arts Academy modeled on the École des Beaux-Arts in Paris, staffing it for the most part with foreign instructors).

Gérôme, but not quite. Where Gérôme's paintings served to fix an image of the East as frozen in time, an exotic and picturesque other to Europe's modernity, Hamdi's images necessarily carried a different significance. As Zeynep Çelik has argued, Hamdi adopted a "critical stance as an insider within the outside," chipping away at the stereotypes and misrepresentations of conventional Orientalism.[5] Even the act of adopting Gérôme's style necessarily pries the East away from the fantasy of stable otherness, for here the East speaks with a modern voice (not that Gérôme's style was particularly modern; in Paris, this brand of documentary precision was far from cutting edge).[6] If Hamdi's desire to speak a European language is clear, we should not forget that he translates that language into his own voice. If he traveled to Paris to learn his craft, we should not forget that upon his return he helped draft legislation preventing wholesale European export of antiquities. Openness to the West and a certain protectiveness of Ottoman culture could easily exist hand in hand.

Such complexity continues to mark Ottoman painting even at its most apparently Europhilic. Back along the corridor, somewhere between

Guardian of the Tomb and the *Stonebreakers*, hangs *Beethoven in the Saray*, painted by Abdülmecid, son of the Sultan Abdülaziz and last caliph of the Ottoman empire before the Turkish republic swept the role away (he would end his life in exile in Europe). Here we see the elite of the Ottoman court, dressed, for the most part, in Western clothing (Abdülmecid himself reclines in military attire over to the right), their chamber concert overlooked by a European-style seascape on the wall and by a bust of Beethoven himself. We see a piano, a violin, and a cello. We are listening to European music, to Beethoven, displaced from one royal court to another, across the hinterland of Europe and out to the edge of the continent.

Here the turn toward the West seems complete. The European fashions, as Çelik has argued, distance the painting from conventional Orientalism.[7] Yet if the work signals its distance from one European tradition – the Orientalist imaging of the East as timeless – it does so precisely by revealing the alignment of Abdülmecid and his guests with another European tradition – that of modern European music and, crucially, painting. This is signaled in the very style mobilized by Abdülmecid, largely indistinguishable from any number of later nineteenth-century French naturalists. And with this painting one of the motors that drove this Occidentalization comes fully into view: the Ottoman court itself, which was, as Abdülmecid's painting makes clear, often deeply Europhilic in its outlook.

Ever since the eighteenth century the court had been eager to modernize – and for the most part this meant to Westernize. In 1828 Sultan Mahmud II, as part of a wide-ranging reform of government and military institutions, reclothed the army in European-style uniforms, a move extended to civilian administrators in 1829. Turbans and caftans were replaced by capes, trousers, boots, and fez. (Note the irony: Mahmud comes to the throne in 1808, the year that Byron, yet to travel outside England, orders a Turkish costume for a masquerade in England; an Eastern costume wings its way westward to satisfy a romantic dream, following the route along which Western designs will soon travel to the east to meet the demands of a modernizing empire.[8]) Those painters on a Paris street corner, then, were perhaps not adopting local French modes; some of those suits might have been packed before leaving Istanbul. But Ruhi's fez and Onat's bowler nevertheless speak different sartorial languages – the fez a declaration of otherness, a refusal to bow to local custom.

Alongside European clothing, Sultan Mahmud II would promote the production of Western-style portraiture as a means of promulgating his image, a tactic adopted even more enthusiastically by his successor, Sultan Abdül Mecid.[9] A taste for European painting and the concurrent tendency for some Ottoman artists to respond to Western visual influences became one of the more visible signs of the court's modernizing inclination.[10] Abdülaziz, the successor to Sultan Abdül Mecid and father of Abdülmecid (the creator of *Beethoven in the Saray*), founded an Ottoman school in Paris in 1860 to which young Ottomans – among them many artists – were sent to train.[11] And his son, Abdülmecid, produced the canvas that renders this preference for things Western utterly visible. Listening to Beethoven, the Ottoman court is represented by the heir to the throne in a pictorial style utterly identified with Europe. And the painting is large, dominating the gallery in which it now hangs, declaring these Western allegiances loud and clear, today as it did then. This was a court that wore its Europhilia on its sleeve.[12]

* * *

And yet, if the court was often deeply Europhilic, there were also periods of withdrawal (though it would perhaps be more accurate to say that the two tendencies existed side by side, a contradictory push-pull of Europhilia and nationalism in a permanent stand-off on the Bosphorus). Sultan Abdülhamid II (1876–1909), brought to power in part in reaction against the modernizing programs of his predecessors, was anti-reform and publicly none too keen on the influence of Europeans. Such positions were, however, never clear-cut. In his spare time he listened to Offenbach and read imported detective novels.[13] Such ambivalence was reflected in government policy. Despite his aversion to European involvement, Sultan Abdülhamid had by the 1890s overseen a rapid growth of foreign investment in the empire, in particular in the area of railways.[14] And in the sphere of art, despite his public disavowal of European influences, he maintained the practice of inviting both home-grown and foreign artists to paint portraits of former sultans and pursued the creation of a museum at the Yıldız Saray complex.[15] The "muze" begins its inexorable rise.

The Ottoman relationship to the West would always be marked by this push-pull dialectic. Sultans sending students to Paris to learn about military technology would subsequently become alarmed over these same young men's dangerous exposure to European models of democratic political organization.[16] Sultan Abdülaziz, even as he dispatched young Ottomans to Paris, would begin to sponsor a revival of Ottoman architecture. The immense tome *Usul-i Mi'Mari-yi 'Osmani*, published as part of a larger effort by his government to represent the empire at the 1873 Vienna World Exposition, served both as a historical account of Ottoman architecture and as a rallying cry for its revival.[17] Abdülaziz the modernizer and Abdülaziz the traditionalist, always in tension, the two tendencies swimming against and through each other at all times like the water switching back and forth underneath the boat. Note that the 1863 Sergi-i Umumi Binasi (National Exhibition Hall), which quickly became one of the motors of Ottoman revivalism in architecture, was designed by the French architects Bourgeois and Parvillé: again the exchanges of glances between East and West multiply, rendering questions of identity and tradition ever more dizzyingly unsettled.[18]

A complex moment, then. And other players were beginning to appear on stage. If the imperial court had a complex relationship to notions of modernization and Westernization, the same was equally true of the Young Ottoman movement.[19] The court's Western allegiances – Abdül Mecid's Tanzimat regime, in particular – were lambasted as a superficial imitation of Europe.[20] So, too, the cosmopolitan foreign economic interests who had an interest in keeping the sultan on the throne were decried.[21] Yet the same Young Ottomans who offered these critiques would turn to Europe for alternate political models. Their opposition to the court system, and their support for ideas of representative parliamentary democracy, would draw heavily on European philosophical and political traditions – it is not coincidental that many Young Ottomans spent their frequent periods of exile in Paris.[22] In the early years of the twentieth century, as the Young Ottoman generation ceded to that of the Young Turks, mistrust of European influences would increase.[23] The ideologists of the Committee of Union and Progress would begin to argue ever more forcefully that modernization must be joined to the principle of cultural nationalism.[24] Yet still the attachment to the West would thrive.

In painting, for example, Ottoman painters would continue to follow French precedents, as the influence of Gérôme gave way to that of Impressionism.[25] This was the "Generation of 1914" – Ruhi's generation – who traveled to Paris with the support of Abdülmecid just after the formation in 1908 of the constitutional government, Meşrutiyet.[26] The later galleries of the museum are choked with sun-filled views of the Bosphorus, boats rocking gently in the light-flecked water, bright pigment loosely applied according to the tenets of *plein air* painting. Though Impressionism changed as it was refracted in its various second homes – the United States, Australia, Japan, the Ottoman empire – these simple celebrations of local landscape align themselves fairly obediently with Impressionism. Yet even as these canvases dried, the orientation of the visual arts towards Europe began to be challenged by a more assertive nationalism.

* * *

Another old photograph (figure 6.3). The year is 1917, and war is on everyone's mind. Ruhi and his colleagues have been called back to Istanbul at the outbreak of hostilities and put to work in the Ottoman war effort. In the photograph we see them once more, most of the friends who had posed for that earlier photograph in the balmy days before the war. They stand now in the studio provided for them by the government in the Istanbul suburb of Şişli, a studio filled with props – cannons, rifles, uniformed models, and so forth – to be included in images of the glorious feats of the Ottoman army.[27] Abdülmecid stands in his suit, the figure of authority, surveying the work of one of his charges. Off to the right – perhaps he never was quite at home in this group – stands Ruhi, as though ready to fence, to spar with his colleagues.[28] His left hand, once again cocked under an imaginary palette, perhaps a brush in his right, held up toward the distant painting. In the center, in front of a large canvas, it is Çalli who goes through the motions, aping the act of painting for the camera.

For artists such as Ruhi, this affiliation between painters and military was a natural outgrowth of their training. That young man who stood stiffly to attention outside the Paris café had learnt to paint at the Naval Academy, graduating in 1900 and beginning his professional career as an assistant painting teacher in the Naval High School. At the same time, he enrolled in Hamdi's Fine Arts Academy, from which he graduated in 1909, resigning from the navy with the rank of lieutenant and journeying to Paris on a government scholarship.[29] Now he was back working for the military once more.

The studio in Şişli was essentially a propaganda machine, and the paintings that came out of this workshop both lionize and humanize the Turkish forces. Çalli's *Turkish Cannoneers* of 1917 – the canvas before which he sits in the photograph – is typical.[30] If the painters and models could step aside we would see a cavalryman astride a rearing horse, urging the artillerymen onwards, up toward the dramatic sky, toward the sunlit mountains in the distance. Ruhi, working in the same studio, produced

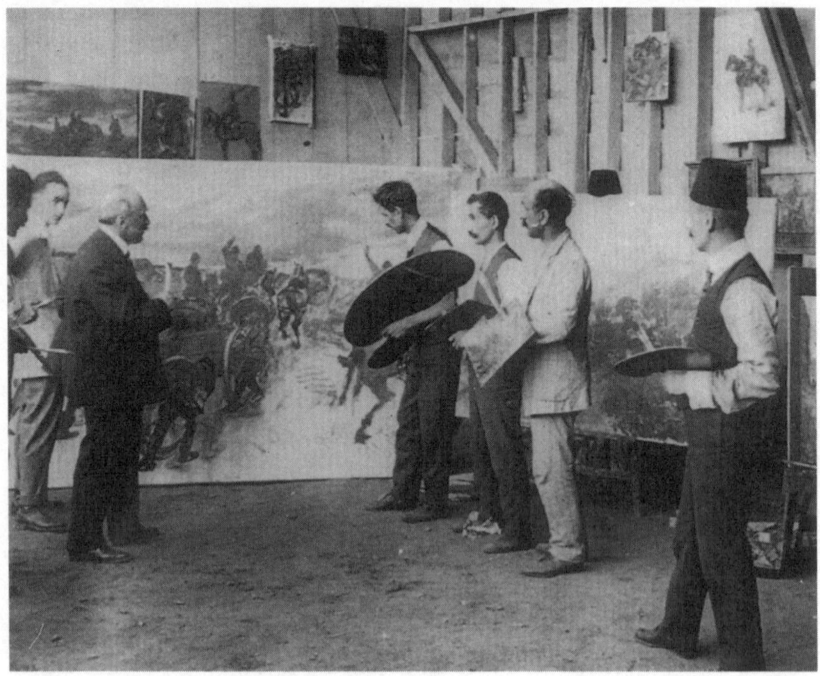

Figure 6.3 Photograph of Ruhi and colleagues in the studio at Şişli, 1917. Reproduced in *Türk Resim Sanatında: Şişli Atölyesi ve Viyana Sergisi* (Istanbul: İstanbul Resim ve Heykel Müzeleri Derneği, 1997), 41

equally heroic images: brave warriors, resplendent in traditional Turkish uniform, standing to attention; generals and colonels, uniforms starched, moustaches waxed; and Ottoman soldiers resting in the aftermath of the victory at Gallipoli.

The patriotic import of such subjects is clear enough – and understandable, given the year. What, though, of the politics of style? Of adopting a Western pictorial vocabulary? By 1917, earlier doubts about foreign influence had begun to crystallize. The Committee of Union and Progress had done its work. And in the years immediately following the war, with the British occupying Istanbul and with a puppet sultan responding obediently to their manipulation of the strings, the reaction against such meddling, and against European influence more generally, would come to a head. Atatürk's resistance movement began to stir in central Anatolia, coming fully to life when the British handed over areas of the Asia Minor coast to the Greeks. In 1922–3, after a final stand-off around Istanbul, the British withdrew, and the republic was proclaimed.

* * *

Now the backlash could begin in earnest. The distrust of European intentions manifested itself most concretely in the political and economic thrust of Atatürk's nationalization plan.[31] But it also impacted the realm of art and art criticism. Turkish painting, it was argued, had been colonized by the West, a view that would reverberate in the Turkish academy for the next half-century and more. Nerullah Berk, writing in the 1950s, would complain that Turkish art fell into decline because of its inability "to resist against European importations" – just as the court was obliged to accept "the disastrous regime of the Capitulations."[32] Zahir Güvemli, in 1987, would be equally dismissive: "[In] the nineteenth century... [Turkish painting] moved out of its own orbit... [I]ts future development fell into the hands of a group of painters completely isolated from the society to which they belonged... Instead of continuing the tradition of true Turkish painting [i.e. miniature painting]... they returned to their own country having learned to use paint and canvas in the manner of their European masters" (Güvemli, we might note, was none too keen on Hamdi).[33]

It was not strictly accurate to put the blame wholly on the nineteenth century. European influences had been felt much earlier than this (as had Turkish influences in Europe: the situation was one of continuous give and take).[34] But for later nationalist writers, the turn toward the Occident in the nineteenth and early twentieth centuries became their principal bugbear. Listen, for example, to Adnan Turani:

> while the fall of the Ottoman empire was daily expected... [i]n occupied Istanbul art exhibitions were opened (they were attended by conceited foreigners and arrogant officers, and French was the language of the catalogues), concerts were held, and balls were given at the great houses bordering on the Bosphorus. These were the Sodom and Gomorrah years... when so many people (in imitation of the Western fashion) moved out to suburban areas... to live in apartments, and the French language was idolized and cosmopolitanism the aim of all. Turkish painters... still let themselves be deceived by the outworn glamour of the Impressionist movement.[35]

The mixture of populism and nationalism in such pronouncements is typical of republican rhetoric. It takes aim in part at the deposed court, at men such as Abdülaziz, who in 1867 had traveled to Paris and London and had returned with armfuls of French paintings – Boulanger, Harpignies, Daubigny, Ziem, Gérôme – with which to fill the salons of the Dolmabahçe Palace.[36] Such collecting became a mark of disloyalty to the homeland, and in the early years of the republic painters began to respond to this shift in outlook. Ruhi was no exception. He already had links with leading members of the Committee of Union and Progress, the vehicle of the most radical of the Young Turks, and in his paintings he began to concentrate on subjects drawn from local life, often turning his hand to the depiction of figures in traditional dress engaged in time-honored labors.[37] On the level of style, too, his work began to lay claim to indigeneity. He turned increasingly to a naive style which, the nationalists would claim, was tied to popular art and thus to a domestic artistic tradition free of the taint of Western influence (free, in particular, of the influence of Impressionism).[38]

Consider, in this light, his *Çulha Weaver* of 1926. The *çulha* is a rough-woven kilim, a heavy fabric, simple, of the common people. And Ruhi's painting aligns itself with these qualities. Yet another translation has taken place, this time into the vernacular. The old man weaves the simple design just as Ruhi weaves his composition out of the simplified geometry of the hand-operated loom. The deliberately indicated contours of the man's hands, the reduction of modeling, the flattening out of light: each of these aspects speaks to – speaks in the language of – the popular. A refusal of sophistication, of the Europhilic drive toward the esthetic, toward Art. And he would continue in this vein. The explicitly nationalist subject-matter of *Atatürk with the Peasants* is transposed into a style that bespeaks down-to-earth simplicity. Here, the painting seems to say, is Atatürk, man of the people, meeting his people, in the style of the people.[39]

This is what Ruhi would come to be known for. Güvemli, after lamenting the Sodom and Gomorrah years, celebrated the artist for having "adopted western techniques without becoming slavishly western," for having "felt and made others feel what was really meant by nationalism and local color," for having moved toward a "popular style" characterized by "ingenuousness" and "clumsy spontaneity."[40] Such claims had earlier been made by Berk in a text written (significantly enough) in French:

> [though Ruhi] studied in the Occident, his works do not reveal the slightest foreign influence, but on the contrary are in the form of [*affectent*: also, significantly, to feign, to sham; Berk's French perhaps reveals more than was

> intended] an essentially national character. His technique itself, with careful, meticulous brushstrokes, as well as the harmony of his colors, recall Turkish embroideries and printed fabrics. As for his subjects, Ruhi took them moreover from the life itself of his country. Ruhi is a populist painter, in the most noble sense of the word. [41]

* * *

"In the form of" – but also "feigning" – a national character. This is the key to Ruhi's painting. Its reception in Turkey had everything to do with the effort to construct a national identity in paint, to imagine a visual language free of foreign accents (by 1987 Güvemli was willing to acknowledge the impact on Ruhi of "western techniques"; Berk, writing in the more fiercely nationalist 1950s, sought to exclude all such traces[42]). Yet while Ruhi's painting might have *passed* for the indigenous in 1926, the *Çulha Weaver* still bears the marks of the Western influences that his supporters would try so hard to dismiss. Even the claimed allegiance to popular traditions bears little scrutiny, for there is nothing in Ruhi's work that speaks to domestic Ottoman or Turkish traditions of folk art.[43] The simplification of outlines and the reduction of chromatic complexity speak, if anything, to the popular imagery of posters, but this popular culture – more properly mass culture – was itself a (relatively) modern phenomenon that, in the Ottoman empire as elsewhere, derived from imported technologies of mechanical reproduction and a formal vocabulary utterly removed from earlier folk art traditions. Here we might recall Courbet's own parallel move, 60 or so years earlier, toward a language of the popular, of the clumsily naive. Ruhi's painting, in its drive toward a fantasy of the popular, bears the echoes of these other voices, visual languages that disrupt the putative national unity of his style.

These are echoes to which the nationalists would remain willfully deaf. Writing in the extended afterglow of the Kemalist revolution, they would seek to construct a unified narrative of Turkish identity in the arts. Yet their efforts foundered on the fractured, polysemic surfaces of Ruhi's canvases. Here the *Stonebreakers*, painted one year after the foundation of the republic, is exemplary. It sits on a knife-edge between West and East. Inclining toward France, toward Cézanne and Courbet and Millet, it begins at the same time, in its translation of these sources, to unpack – to unpick – this affiliation. Those blocks of color, patiently laid down in the manner of Cézanne, crafted into a solid and timeless edifice of pigment, are levered apart by Ruhi's eager workforce, lifting one from the other, prising apart the schema of Cézanne's painting – of Western painting. And Courbet's workers are transformed into citizens of the young Turkish republic. No more poverty; here we see only energetic hard work. No more cracked sabots and tattered waistcoats; here we see loose-fitting garments, laced ankles, open-necked white shirts – the uniform of the Turkish worker. So, too, the features of the central figure speak aggressively, demonstratively, of local flesh and bone. And if Ruhi's French sources have been indigenized, this is true at the level of style as well as of content.

Earlier I suggested that in Ruhi's painting the painterly flicker of Millet had been extinguished by Cézanne's repeated strokes. But now I see something more – a congealing that goes beyond Cézanne and on toward a naively literal depiction that spoke – in 1924 – to the fantasy of a re-emergent Turkish popular culture. Yet the beauty of the painting lies in its resistance to this move, in the way that, even as it pushes toward an essentialized national identity, it speaks otherwise. A point of transition, a point of contact, it speaks a hybrid tongue, resisting the efforts of later scholars to make painting speak a single language. The very quality that nationalist discourse points to in its effort to claim for Ruhi an indigenous identity opens out immediately into its other: the popular refuses to sit still, refuses to collapse into domestic traditions. It is this that elicits the ongoing attempts on the part of critics and historians to suppress the alien accent, to persuade the domestic audience that this is a purely Turkish art. For in Turkey – as elsewhere – the polyglot spreads fear.[44]

* * *

We have one more moment of transition, one more point of contact, to consider. Another grainy photograph. This is Ruhi's *Triptych* of 1917. Not the painting itself, but the reproduction that appeared in the catalog of the Ausstellung türkischer Maler (Exhibition of Turkish Painters) held in Vienna in May of 1918. More propaganda. In the center panel, the fighting in Çannakale, the great battle for the Gallipoli peninsula. On the right, the starting-point: a young man takes leave of his family. On the left, the aftermath: the same man returns a veteran. A painting, then, that reads from right to left, against the expectations of the European viewer who reads by habit – with paintings as with text – from left to right. Perspectives begin to rotate, forcing us to read otherwise. The painting's orientation, its inversion of European convention, offers an apt metaphor for everything we have been discussing (and yet: if we read from right to left this falls in line not with the Turkish text but with the Arabic; yet more accents emerge to complicate our narrative).

The *Triptych* was just one of a number of paintings sent from the studio in Şişli to Vienna early in 1918. The Great War was still grinding on, though it was entering its last months, and the exhibition represented a cementing of the axis between two empires both drawing their last breath (though neither knew it yet): the Austro-Hungarian, to be dismantled in the dying days of the war, and the Ottoman, itself facing the end, the final break-up of a once glorious empire that had stretched across the Middle East and even, in the seventeenth century, as far as the gates of Vienna itself.

Vienna, 1918. Turkish painters, European styles; Turkish battles, a central European public. In this constant shuttling back and forth we sense the porousness of the boundaries between cultures. We see it in the exhibition and we see it in Ruhi's painting, sitting in a hall in Vienna, spanning the divide between continents. Even *Atatürk with the Peasants*, for all its Turkish populism, is marked by a European accent (Atatürk himself never shed his attachment to the West). The leader's leather boots, his trenchcoat, the military insignia – all of this, in the 1930s, could as easily be Germany as Anatolia. Almost. Once more, then, that tense stand-off – the in-between pinpointed by Bhabha. And the painting's style speaks a similarly hybrid language. Its deliberate simplicity, its lack of sophistication, would be held by Turkish scholars to signal a rejection of European modernism, yet once again the painting owes much to Western painting. Soviet realism – or national socialist realism – are perhaps the most obvious points of reference here. The painting represents a strange collation of the modern and the timeless, insisting that it speaks an up-to-date language – a language of the new Kemalist generation – even as it claims to speak an unchanging Turkish idiom. A temporal ambivalence that, as Bhabha notes, typifies the rhetoric of nation-building: up to date *and* venerable, "the disjunctive time of the nation's modernity."[45]

* * *

Courbet's image moves on, out to a quarry in Turkey; Cézanne's constructive brushstroke moves on through time also, out into a canvas in Istanbul. And Ruhi's work moves too, from Şişli to Vienna, to Dolmabahçe, and on, finally, at a remove, to us. The graininess of the photograph of Ruhi's triptych, its inability to make Ruhi's painting present in front of us, speaks to the difficulty of getting hold of Ruhi across the decades that separate us from him. "Gathering the memories . . . of other worlds lived retroactively;

gathering the past in a ritual of revival; gathering the present."[46] This was Ruhi's project. And it is mine too. Like Ruhi, I look back. From London to Istanbul. From Istanbul to Provence. From Provence to Paris. From Paris to Ornans. And each displacement, each journey, introduces a certain distance, a slippage, a becoming grainy, as the past slips further from us.

We have heard, in the preceding pages, a mixture of voices, part fiction, part history: snatches from the writing of Joseph Conrad; a little John Berger; some Homi Bhabha; echoes of Robert J. C. Young; and a range of Turkish art-historical voices.[47] Like Ruhi, I have been picking up useful pieces wherever I have found them. My essay, like his painting, is marked by echoes of the voices of others, by ideologies and languages that twist and turn as they are translated into my own text. Like his painting, my essay does not quite hold together; my view of him will always be partial, contingent, marked by echoes (echoes that both reproduce and distort). In the fragmentary quality of my own text we sense the fragmentary nature of our access to him; but we also glimpse the fragmentary nature of Ruhi's engagement with French painting and of subsequent attempts to construct an image of "Turkey" in his painting.

In the end it is the boat trip that first took us to the painting that speaks best to Ruhi's painting, suspended as it is between Europe and Asia, in the turbulence between the two great land masses. Looking at Ruhi's work, watching his migration across cultural boundaries, tells us something about the slipperiness of the divide between East and West, about the permeability of that border, of the edges of empire, of those edges so often held to be fixed, absolute, eternal – and this by observers on both sides. And looking at his work, sensing its distance from us, tells us something too about our own position on the borderlines of histories, nations, and traditions, about our own constitution from memories, from migrations through time and across space. An idea of "Europe" was constructed in Ruhi's day – by Ruhi and his colleagues – just as it continues to be today. But in our dialog with his dialog, in our looking at him looking at Europe, we grasp – and this, perhaps, is Ruhi's most important lesson – the always contingent status of all such constructions.

Notes

1 *Le Musée des Beaux-Arts d'Istanbul* (n.p., n.d.); my translation.

2 Repr. in G. Pollock, *Millet* (London: Oresko, 1977), 33; thanks to Roger Benjamin for this suggestion.

3 J. Berger, *A Seventh Man* (Harmondsworth: Penguin, 1975), 96, 118, and *passim*; cited in H. K. Bhabha, "DissemiNation," in *The Location of Culture* (New York and London: Routledge, 1994), 165–6.

4 H. K. Bhabha, "Of Mimicry and Man: The Ambivalence of Colonial Discourse," *October*, 28 (1984), 125–33; H. K. Bhabha, "Signs Taken for Wonders: Questions of Ambivalence and Authority Under a Tree Outside Delhi, May 1817," *Critical Inquiry*, 12 (1985), 144–65.

5 Z. Çelik, "Colonialism, Orientalism, and the Canon," *Art Bulletin*, 78/2 (1996), 201–5: 204. See also Z. Çelik, "Speaking Back to Orientalist Discourse," in J. Beaulieu and M. Roberts (eds.), *Orientalism's Interlocutors: Painting, Architecture, Photography* (Durham, NC: Duke University Press, 2002), 19–41: 21–5, where Çelik furthers her argument that Hamdi offers a critique of Orientalism from within, adopting its visual language but replacing Gérôme's world of blind faith and sexual depradation with depictions of scholars engaged in intelligent debate and women who read rather than strip.

6 Note also that, like Gérôme, Hamdi shows nothing of Istanbul's transformation into a modern industrial capital, a transformation much bemoaned by European visitors; see S. Germaner and Z. İnankur, *Orientalism and Turkey* (Istanbul: The Turkish Cultural Service Foundation, 1989), 85.

7 Çelik, "Speaking Back to Orientalist Discourse," 22. For a fascinating instance of the adoption of European dress by the Ottoman elite, see Mary Roberts's account of the experience of Mary Walker, an amateur painter resident in the Ottoman empire, whose desire to represent her sitter in traditional Ottoman dress was stymied by the woman's decision to stay up half the night (according to Walker's account) copying a "Frank" dress from a Paris fashion magazine in which to pose. M. Roberts, "Contested Terrains: Women Orientalists and the Colonial Harem," in Beaulieu and Roberts (eds.), *Orientalism's Interlocutors*, 179–203: 191–4.

8 M. Levey, *The World of Ottoman Art* (London: Thames & Hudson, 1975), 112.

9 G. Renda, "Portraits: The Last Century," in *The Sultan's Portrait: Picturing the House of Osman* (Istanbul: Topkapı Palace Museum, 2000), 442–542: 442–56; "Westernism," Renda writes, "was now in all phases of social and cultural life" (p. 449).

10 Germaner and İnankur, *Orientalism and Turkey*, 82–5; E. Özdeniz, *Türk Deniz Subayi Ressamlari* [Turkish Naval Officer Painters] (Istanbul: Türk Deniz Kuvvetleri Komutanligi, 1994), 13. On the later nineteenth-century taste for European painting among the Ottoman ruling class, see M. R. Brown, "The Harem Dehistoricized: Ingres' *Turkish Bath*," *Arts Magazine*, 61 (1987), 56–68. On the efforts of the Ottoman court to stimulate European-style painting at home, see Z. İnankur, "Official Painters of the Ottoman Palace,"

in *Art Turc/Turkish Art*, proceedings of the 10th International Congress of Turkish Art (Geneva, 1999), 381–8; and S. Germaner, "Le Mécénat dans l'art turc: Du Sérail à la République," in *Art Turc/Turkish Art*, proceedings of the 10th International Congress of Turkish Art (Geneva, 1999), 345–7. Interest in the European arts was not restricted to painting: Western architecture was also much emulated; see Levey, *The World of Ottoman Art*, 129–38.

11 G. Renda, T. Erol, A. Turani, et al., *A History of Turkish Painting* (Seattle: University of Washington Press and London: Palasar SA, 1988), 111. Though the school only lasted until 1874, young Ottomans would continue to be sent to Paris; see R. H. Davison, *Essays in Ottoman and Turkish History, 1774–1923: The Impact of the West* (Austin: University of Texas Press, 1990), 166–79.

12 Semra Germaner writes that *Beethoven in the Saray* "shows the members of the imperial court impregnated with European culture, fervent admirers of romantic music and literature" (Germaner, "Le Mécénat dans l'art turc," 347; my trans.). At times the interest would be returned. Abdülmecid presented one of his paintings at an exhibition in Paris with – in an interesting twist – the help of Pierre Loti, the famous Orientalist novelist, author of racy tales of Frenchmen abroad and their romantic entanglements in the colonies (Renda, Erol, Turani, et al., *A History of Turkish Painting*, 121).

13 Levey, *The World of Ottoman Art*, 140.

14 E. J. Zürcher, *Turkey: A Modern History* (New York: I. B. Tauris, 1993), 77–84.

15 Renda, "Portraits," 461–2.

16 M. S. Hanioğlu, *The Young Turks in Opposition* (Oxford: Oxford University Press, 1995), 7–10 and 16–18.

17 A. Ersoy, "*Usul-i Mi'Mari-yi 'Osmani*: A Source of Revival in Ottoman Architecture," in *Art Turc/Turkish Art*, proceedings of the 10th International Congress of Turkish Art (Geneva, 1999), 291–5.

18 A. Batur, "The Subject of Style in Ottoman Architecture at the End of the 19th Century," in *Art Turc/Turkish Art*, proceedings of the 10th International Congress of Turkish Art (Geneva, 1999), 143–52: 145.

19 On the genesis of Young Ottoman thought, see Ş. Mardin, *The Genesis of Young Ottoman Thought: A Study in the Modernization of Turkish Political Ideals* (Princeton, NJ: Princeton University Press, 1962).

20 Zürcher, *Turkey: A Modern History*, 71–3.

21 Ş. Mardin, *Continuity and Change in the Ideas of the Young Turks* (Ankara: Robert College School of Business Administration and Economics Occasional Papers, 1969), 6–9.

22 Ibid. 4; Zürcher, *Turkey: A Modern History*, 74–5.

23 Davison, *Essays in Ottoman and Turkish History*, 243–64.

24 Renda, Erol, Turani, et al., *A History of Turkish Painting*, 159; Mardin, *Continuity and Change*, 4–5; and Zürcher, *Turkey: A Modern History*, 90–138.

25 Renda, Erol, Turani, et al., *A History of Turkish Painting*, 143.

26 Ibid. 149–52.

27 Renda, Erol, Turani, et al., *A History of Turkish Painting*, 155.

28 He was, we are told, "an artist who always lived alone, far from the world." N. Berk, *La Peinture turque* (Ankara: Direction Générale de la Presse et du Tourisme, 1950), 20; my trans.

29 Özdeniz, *Türk Deniz Subayi Ressamlari*, 196–7. Military and artistic training had been entwined in the Ottoman empire since the eighteenth century, when Sultan Selim III (1789–1807) added Western-style painting to the curriculum of the Artillery College in 1794 (the ability to record topography accurately in three dimensions had obvious military applications). When the Military College was founded in 1834, it included painting lessons, as did the military high schools that opened towards the middle of the nineteenth century. Hamdi's Fine Arts Academy opened up an alternate route for artists, though, as Ruhi's trajectory makes clear, individuals frequently moved between the two systems. On art education in the military schools, see S. Öner, "The Place of the Ottoman Palace in the Development of Turkish Painting and the Military Painters," in *Art Turc/Turkish Art*, proceedings of the 10th International Congress of Turkish Art (Geneva, 1999), 517–23; Özdeniz, *Türk Deniz Subayi Ressamlari*, 15–17; and Renda, Erol, Turani, et al., *A History of Turkish Painting*, 90, 92.

30 Reproduced in *Türk Resim Sanatinda*, 51.

31 Mardin, *Continuity and Change*, 11–12.

32 N. Berk, *Modern Painting and Sculpture in Turkey*, trans. B. Bather (Istanbul: Turkish Press, Broadcasting and Tourist Department, 1955), 6.

33 Z. Güvemli, *The Art of Painting and Turkish Painting* (Istanbul: Akbank'ın bir kültür hizmeti, 1987), 58, 76, 79. This, it might be noted, is also how the French saw the situation, though they were rather happier about the implications. Louis Réau's four-volume *Histoire de l'expansion de l'art français* (Paris: Van Oest, 1924–33), which first saw the light of day a year after the founding of the Turkish Republic, included a chapter on "The Expansion of French Art into Turkey." The chapter was divided into two sections: first, "The Influence of Turkey on French Art," by which Réau meant simply the appearance of Turkish themes in French art, which is to say Turkish subject-matter brought under the control of French pictorial conventions; second, "The Influence of French Art on Turkish Art," i.e. the artistic influence of the French school on the Turkish (*Histoire*, iii. 368 ff.). Underlying Réau's assumption that stylistic influence was a one-way street, moving from West to East, is the belief that European culture – and, by implication, European society – always occupies the position of master, to be followed, imitated, by its weaker neighbors. For further discussion, see A. Wright, *Matisse and the Subject of Modernism* (Princeton, NJ: Princeton University Press, 2004), ch. 6.

34 See L. Jardine and J. Brotton, *Global Interests: Renaissance Art between East and West* (London: Reaktion, 2000); Berk, *La Peinture turque*, 14; and Renda, Erol, Turani, et al., *A History of Turkish Painting*, 90. As early as 1479 Gentile Bellini had been brought to Istanbul to paint the portrait of Mehmet the Conqueror, returning to Venice with a taste for things Ottoman that spawned an early outbreak of "turqueries." On European artists in the Ottoman empire during the fifteenth and sixteenth centuries, see J. Raby, "Opening Gambits: From Europe to Istanbul," in *The Sultan's Portrait: Picturing the House of Osman* (Istanbul: Topkapı Palace Museum, 2000), 64–95 and 136–63, and Güvemli, *The Art of Painting*, 72.

35 A. Turani, *Bati Anlayisina Dönük Türk Resim Sanati* (Ankara: Türkiye Iş Bankaşi Kültür Yayınları, 1977), p. xix. For further comments on the outdatedness of Impressionism, see Güvemli, *The Art of Painting*, 76.

36 Berk, *La Peinture turque*, 14–15. Abdülaziz's engagement with European art was sustained and long-standing; he commissioned European (and Turkish) painters as palace artists over many years and ordered paintings for the palace collection from individual artists such as Gérôme and from dealers such as Goupil. Gérôme himself acted as a consultant for the collection, which was put together by one of his Ottoman students, Şeker Ahmed Pasha. See Germaner and İnankur, *Orientalism and Turkey*, 119–20, and Renda, "Portraits," 460.

37 Renda, Erol, Turani, et al., *A History of Turkish Painting*, 158.

38 Ibid.

39 Reproduced in Özdeniz, *Türk Deniz Subayi Ressamlari*, 109. On the relationship between Turkish nationalism and images of farming, see Z. Y. Yaman, "The Theme of Peasants and Farmers in Turkish Painting," in *Art Turc/Turkish Art*, proceedings of the 10th International Congress of Turkish Art (Geneva, 1999), 751–6.

40 Güvemli, *The Art of Painting*, 79–80.

41 Berk, *La Peinture turque*, 20; my trans.

42 Berk's writings were at times more ambivalent. In 1955, though still writing scathingly of the deleterious impact of European painting on Turkish art, he sought to align the two cultures – "With each succeeding year, Turkey makes a new step towards her complete incorporation in the cycle of the great Western nations" – and to distance Turkish art from "Arabo-Persian civilization." Yet these opening statements, pushing Turkey away from its eastern and southern neighbors and toward Europe, are immediately contradicted by claims for modern Turkish painting's ancestry in "the Seljuk and Ottoman tradition," which is to say in a decidedly non-European visual culture. Berk then switches course once more, however, arguing that European influences led to the revival in Turkish painting (Berk, *Modern Painting and Sculpture in Turkey*, 1–6). Such contradictions are symptomatic of the tensions that

marked Turkish nationalist rhetoric, with its uneasy combination of modernizing and traditionalist discourses.

43 On Ottoman and Turkish folk art, see M. Aksel, *Anadolu Halk Resimleri* (Istanbul: Baha Matbaasi, 1960).

44 French art criticism of the period is marked by similar efforts to produce a singular national tradition. There, too, nationalist critics railed against foreign influences, whether they be German or Arabic or Ottoman. And there, too, paintings often resisted such efforts to make art speak with a single language. See Wright, *Matisse and the Subject of Modernism*, ch. 6.

45 Bhabha, "DissemiNation," 142.

46 Ibid. 139.

47 The visit to the museum never took place as described. It is an invention, inspired in part by the opening pages of Robert J. C. Young, *Colonial Desire: Hybridity in Theory, Culture and Race* (London: Routledge, 1995), and constructed from, among other elements, a conversation with Gerar Edizel about his (perhaps faulty) recollections of the time he spent in Istanbul as an art student; a map of the city; and a museum guidebook, *Le Musée des Beaux-Arts d'Istanbul* (n.d.). The encounter with Ruhi's *The Stonebreakers* is, as with the rest of the visit to the museum, imagined; the opening description of the painting is an adaptation of the opening page of Joseph Conrad's *The Secret Sharer.*

7

Stolen or Shared: Ancient Egypt at the Petrie Museum

Sally MacDonald

> The treasure dug up is not gold but history
> (William Matthew Flinders Petrie[1])

> A museum is a dangerous place
> (William Matthew Flinders Petrie[2])

At the start of the twenty-first century the role of museums is being questioned in new ways. The expansion of international travel and the growth of the internet have tended to make museum audiences more diverse and more mobile, yet in the UK at least museums remain, for the most part, the exclusive preserve of the educated middle class. Current debates concern the extent to which such institutions should attempt to attract new audiences, redress historic biases, or attempt to effect social change. In many parts of the world groups who have had their pasts appropriated by museums are demanding control over the way their heritage is now presented, and sometimes the repatriation of objects taken from them under colonial or other unequal circumstances. Against this backdrop, the Petrie Museum is attempting to review its past and current practices to find more inclusive ways of presenting a complex and contested subject.

The Petrie Museum

The Petrie Museum is rooted in Egypt and the Sudan; almost all the 80,000 objects in its collection were dug up or bought – between 1880 and 1980 – in these countries. Yet these excavations and acquisitions, the formation and classification of these and other such collections, were essentially Western activities. Digs were led by European archaeologists, with foreign funding, and undertaken in a colonial and neo-colonial context.

William Flinders Petrie (1853–1942), after whom the museum is now named, was an exceptionally energetic and rigorous archaeologist. He excavated in Egypt each year from the early 1880s (coinciding with the British occupation from 1882) for almost 45 years. The Egyptian Antiquities Service, established by the khedival government, had first refusal, for the Cairo Museum, on finds from his digs. However, nearly all senior posts in the museum and the Antiquities Service were, in the nineteenth century, held by Europeans and operated in European interests.[3] Petrie was able to export each year vast quantities of ancient objects, the majority of which were offered in turn to the institutions and individuals who had funded his excavations, by way of recompense, ending up in around 120 public and private collections worldwide.

The objects not distributed entered Petrie's private collection, which he brought with him to University College London (UCL) in 1893 when he became the country's first Professor of Egyptology. Over the decades that followed he collected on behalf of the university, selling his own collection to UCL in 1913. The university's collection grew rapidly as a result of the excavations of Petrie, his students and successors, becoming one of the most significant ancient Egyptian collections outside Egypt.

It now numbers around 80,000 objects, and is one of the largest and best documented collections of Egyptian archaeology in the world, illustrating life in the Nile valley from Palaeolithic times to the twentieth century AD. The museum is full of objects of great public interest, including vast quantities of artifacts used in daily life in the ancient world (costume, jewelry, writing materials, tools); funerary material (the world's largest collection of Roman period mummy portraits); and important archaeological groups, such as the decorative art from Akhenaten's city at Amarna.

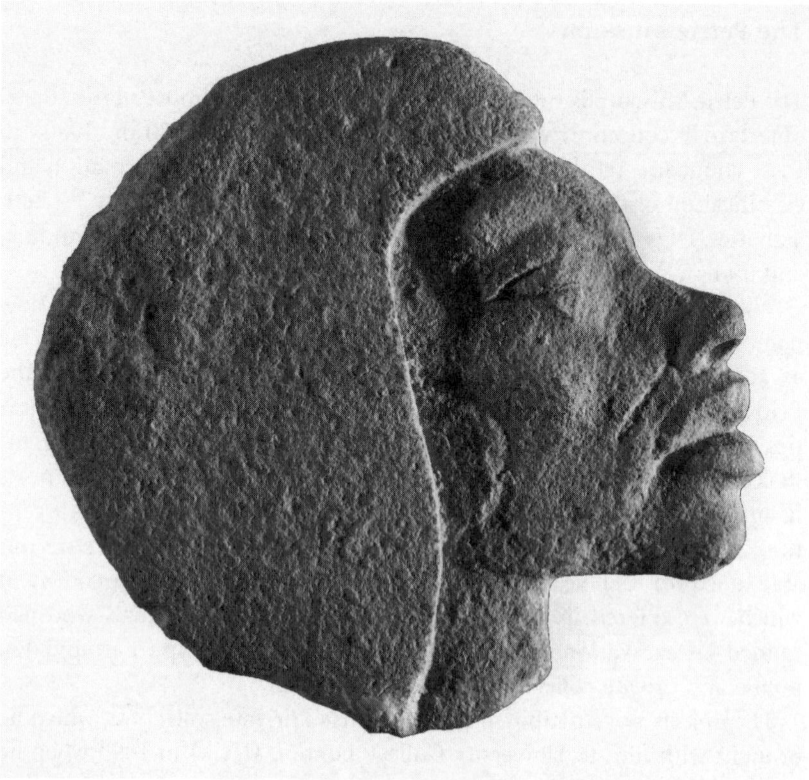

Figure 7.1 Ancient Egyptians: limestone carving of a man, from Amarna, Akhenaten's city, around 1350 BCE. Copyright Petrie Museum of Egyptian Archaeology, UCL, museum number UC 009

Despite the collection's popular appeal, the museum Petrie developed at UCL was a university museum, a teaching and research collection primarily to help train archaeology students, and although the quality and range of the collections inevitably attracted specialist academic researchers from all over the world, until recently it had no mandate to serve anyone outside academia. In the 1970s museum staff began to take steps to broaden its audience and to welcome interested amateur Egyptologists. External visitor numbers rose from around 200 per annum in 1970 to around 3,000 by 1997. As the museum became more heavily used by an "outside" audience, the inadequacies of its cramped accommodation, on the first floor of a university library building, grew more apparent and the need to find a safer, more spacious, and more accessible home grew more acute. The search began for a suitable site.

In 1998 management of the museum was reorganized with the specific intention of making the museum better known among the general public. At about the same time, the collections were designated by the government as being of national importance. Designation enabled the museum to access additional funding, on condition that it began to serve a broader, national audience.

Five years on, the museum attracts around 9,000 visitors a year. This includes its traditional academic audiences, but has broadened considerably to include school groups (ancient Egypt is a popular option on the primary history curriculum in England), adult and further education groups, young adults, families, and tourists, most of them with a special interest in ancient Egypt. Just over half of the museum's general audience comes from Greater London, but the international appeal of the collections means that specialists and tourists come from across the Western world. Less than 5 percent of visitors, however, describe themselves as having a cultural background in Egypt or another part of Africa.

The museum's new mandate to serve a national audience encouraged us, the museum staff, to reassess its strategic plan, and to review its audiences. Over the past two decades museums of all kinds – but particularly ethnographic and social history museums – have become more open to dialog with communities of users and stakeholders.[4] Some museums with collections acquired from abroad in colonial times are engaging in positive relationships with overseas source communities, seeking to alter the colonial dynamics of representation. Such collaborations are resulting in the reidentification of objects that were previously poorly documented, and in new displays and interpretations seeking to redress historic biases.[5] However, archaeological museums have been criticized for lagging behind, for failing, often, to see the relevance to their institutions and displays of such issues as cultural diversity.[6] As Moser points out, "displays of ancient human ancestors have yet to involve the contemporary cultural groups who are most affected by their representations, particularly people of African descent."[7] She argues that archaeological museums have a responsibility not only to present the latest available information but also to address the assumptions and outdated ideas that stifle visitors' interpretations of the subject.

Reassessing the strategic direction of the Petrie Museum and reviewing its audience base involved us in considerable discussion of which contemporary cultural communities were most affected by representations of Egypt, and of which interest groups were currently disenfranchised. The museum's current Strategic Plan – while acknowledging its duty to continue to serve an academic audience of teachers, students, and researchers – now includes within its target audiences school groups, and three audience groupings hitherto largely excluded: those with an "alternative" interest in Egypt, Egyptian and Sudanese people, and people of African descent. The commitment to begin dialog with these communities – with a clear stake in the presentation of Egypt's ancient past – appeared to us to be an ethical and academic imperative, entirely consistent with the mission of a university museum.

We have done so in the belief that the possession of a collection acquired in such unequal circumstances demands an ethical response, in which proactive sharing, the repatriation of information and understanding, represents a tentative first step. We also hope that the perspectives of these new audiences will influence the interpretation of the collections and enrich our understanding of the past and its relationship to modern audiences. This is particularly pertinent as we now have a site for a purpose-built museum – on the university campus but with a public front door – and the opportunity to reinterpret the displays to present new perspectives and ask new questions concerning the identity and legacy of those who inhabited ancient Egypt, and about our own perceptions of this inheritance.

Exploring Contested Territory

While acknowledging the need to extend public access, one might ask why a re-evaluation of ancient Egypt is necessary. Public fascination with ancient Egypt, in the UK, is considerable; so considerable that it is often taken for granted. Those analyzing recent British Museum visitor surveys comment that "as might be expected" the Egyptian antiquities attracted most favorable remarks; twice as many as any other display or feature in the museum.[8] In the report on the most recent survey by the British Museum Visitor Services Department (April 2000), the researchers conclude that "visiting the Egyptian exhibitions is the main reason why one third of all visitors come to the museum, particularly so for Europeans and parties with children." Research commissioned by the Petrie Museum in 2000 and conducted in five focus group sessions confirmed the widespread popularity of the subject and identified a number of "mythic themes" associated with ancient Egypt in the minds of general audiences: death, power, wealth, treasure, extinction, creativity, and religion.[9] Researchers concluded from the discussions that, at least for white audiences,

> Ancient Egypt is a concept. It is not only a country. It is not purely history. It is not just a tissue of myths and artefacts. It is an amalgam of all of these; a magic terrain where myths may be real. The concept is created by school, media, archaeology, myths and museums, and is completely self-contained and satisfying.[10]

Participants in the groups referred readily to images and memories from Hollywood films, Bible stories, and computer games as well as to more evidence-based presentations such as television documentaries or museum displays. Vengeful mummies and Indiana Jones are symbols as potent as the pyramids. Researchers noted an almost universal enthusiasm for the subject and at the same time a reluctance to have preconceptions challenged.

Clearly, few subjects have such power to attract people to museums, to stimulate an interest in archaeology and heritage, and one could argue that the stereotypes surrounding the subject are so strong that it is futile to attempt to challenge them. It can, however, also be argued that that this is largely a Western fantasy, owing not a little to Hollywood, and one that intellectually perpetuates the physical appropriation that took place with excavation and export.

In a recent UK survey researchers found that three out of four people believed that "the contribution of black people and Asians to our society is not thoroughly represented in heritage provision."[11] A number of institutional and professional initiatives are attempting to address this situation: funding bodies such as the Heritage Lottery Fund encourage applicants to address cultural diversity issues, while the Museums Association's *Diversify!* project aims to increase the number of black and minority ethnic museum professionals. The archaeology of Egypt presents interesting questions in this respect, in that it features heavily in UK museum displays and in the school history curriculum, yet is not presented as an African culture. Nor is it presented in the context of modern Egypt, or of the Arab world.

There is a long history of black scholarship on the subject of ancient Egypt and its relationship to the rest of Africa.[12] Some of the more extreme aspects of what is often called Afrocentrism have been criticized as being themselves racist,[13] and some academics argue that it is both misleading and dangerous to seek to establish, as many black scholars have done, what color the ancient Egyptians were.[14] To do so is, they argue, to apply modern concepts of race that did not exist in ancient Egypt. This reluctance to address the subject is reflected in the lack of solid bioanthropological studies, rooted in an Egyptian archaeological context.[15] Most Egyptologists would, however, acknowledge that, for almost two centuries, the study of ancient Egypt in the Western world has been distorted by Eurocentric and racist bias.[16]

Modern Egyptians can be regarded as another group excluded by traditional Egyptology. The growth of Egyptian Egyptology since the late nineteenth century has been fully documented only recently, and its significance for Egypt's modern national identity is only now being acknowledged in the West.[17] The achievements of indigenous Egyptologists are the more notable as they have taken place not only in a context of appropriation by Western scholars and archaeologists, but also against the background of pan-Arab politics, which has tended to favor a study of Islamic rather than earlier periods.[18] Hassan summarizes the modern Egyptian relationship with the country's ancient past as follows:

> the Pharaonic past is a political card. It can arouse passionate responses among certain intellectuals, but it has not effectively become an integral or a predominant element of the materiality of Egyptian life. Perhaps the only vibrant continuity with Egypt's Pharaonic past is the Nile River. But it no longer floods and is imprisoned within its bounded channel. Lined with high-rise Western hotels it belongs to the European and Arab tourists who can afford them.[19]

Scham argues that, while modern Egyptians and peoples of African descent have been similarly disenfranchised by Western appropriation of Egypt's ancient past, their approaches to Egyptology now differ radically from each other.[20] Modern Egyptians, she suggests, would describe themselves as Egyptians, rather than Africans, and are mainly concerned to lay claim to the presentation of their country's history to the rest of the world, increasingly focusing on a distinct Egyptian identity rooted in the distant past. Peoples of African descent, on the contrary, have tended to adopt a universalist outlook, reclaiming Egypt as part of the history of all black Africans. As Scham points out, while the claims of these two disenfranchised groups are sometimes in conflict, they both have much to offer the discipline.

That non-European perspectives may present a challenge to Western presentations is suggested by a study of visitors to the British Museum in 1998, which indicated that most visitors made no connection between ancient and modern Egypt.[21] This has been borne out in the research commissioned by the Petrie Museum in 2000. This research included in-depth interviews and focus groups with a range of people, and indicated that participants' cultural background can have a strong bearing on their views about ancient Egypt.[22] Participants in the research were asked to define their ethnic background, using the broad UK census categories then in use (e.g. white British, black British, black Caribbean, black Other). In fact nearly all focus group participants identified themselves as either white British or black British, though Egyptians interviewed tended to prefer to define themselves as Egyptian, rejecting the standard census classifications. The quotations that follow therefore refer to "white" or "black" or "Egyptian" respondents, though it is recognized that such broad terms bring their own problems and may obscure complex questions of identity.

The researchers found, for instance, that white people seemed untroubled by the mix of fantasy and fact in their vision of ancient Egypt, whereas black respondents were more conscious of distortions:[23]

> "I suppose I want to think that Cleopatra looked a bit like Elizabeth Taylor" (white adult)
>
> "People think it's European history, Richard Burton and Elizabeth Taylor" (black adult)

For black respondents ancient Egypt had a greater role, symbolizing "the theft of cultural capital" by white Europeans.[24] The research concluded that the question of color was an interesting and provocative one for all the adult respondents. White adults found questions about the skin color of the ancient Egyptians "profoundly disturbing and largely unexpected." There was evidence of a desire to maintain ancient Egypt as a part of Europe, although some respondents were clearly considering the question for the first time:[25]

> "Hollywood makes out they were white Europeans. Why didn't it dawn on me? I assumed they were all white and the dark ones were Nubian slaves" (white adult, Nile cruiser)

Black respondents felt passionate rather than threatened by the question. They were clear that ancient Egypt had been appropriated as part of white history:[26]

> "The black Africans were supposed to be ignorant, but we could build the pyramids" (black adult)

The researchers found that most of the focus group participants, particularly white respondents, made no connection between ancient and modern Egypt, which was "below nowhere on most people's agenda." "Modern Egypt is simply the country you have to get to so that you can physically experience the myth of ancient Egypt. Many people aren't quite sure where it is, but . . . this doesn't matter because spiritually they feel ancient Egypt belongs to them too."[27] The research noted that a passion for ancient Egypt regularly coexisted with strong anti-Arab feeling. Even those respondents who had visited Egypt seemed to have come away with negative views which suggested racial bias:

> "The monuments are too breathtaking for words. It knocks you away and now they can't mend your toaster" (white adult, Nile cruiser)

One of the Egyptians interviewed described the struggle to be accepted as a trainee on a dig in his own country:

> "Still, after all these years, you can see it in foreign expeditions digging in Egypt, it's all foreign, they are happy to take foreign students to train them, they never take Egyptian students to train them . . . I had to force myself onto anybody to take me for training; nobody was interested. They just don't take Egyptians." (Egyptian Egyptologist)

We concluded from this primary research that the Western consumption of ancient Egypt – as expressed in films, on television, in books, on package holidays, in museums – has engendered a set of familiar stereotypes and assumptions that limit our collective understanding of the past and may effectively exclude an indigenous speaking voice. That should be reason enough for a university museum to seek to challenge them.

But there are more specific reasons too. In the UK, following the murder of the black student Stephen Lawrence, the McPherson report made far-reaching recommendations on tackling racism, including changing the National Curriculum. It has been said that "Ancient Egypt is frequently chosen and taught as if this civilisation were actually white."[28] Certainly there are few currently available primary-level support materials that address questions of diversity or differences of interpretation in the study of ancient Egypt (though a resource pack produced by Dr Lance Lewis for Kirklees and Salford education authorities is under development), and this now has to be an issue for museums. Widespread concern about the under-achievement of black children has led to a boom in the provision of supplementary schools, many of them teaching African history as a means of raising self-esteem among young black people. Museums with ancient Egyptian material could play a critical role here.

At the same time the aftermath of the attacks on September 11, 2001 and the so-called "war on terror" have fueled anti-Arab and anti-Islamic feeling in some parts of the UK, leading to racist media coverage and physical attacks on Muslims. There appears to be little currently on offer in mainstream education or the popular media to challenge these anti-Arab sentiments, and small-scale positive initiatives can appear as cynical public relations exercises. Yet a museum might begin to make a difference by acknowledging that issues of race, ownership, and pride are live ones and that ancient Egypt is therefore contested territory.

Experiments

At the Petrie Museum we have begun to experiment with these ideas as part of trying to create a more inclusive and accessible museum, both in a physical sense and online. While in its current cramped premises the museum can only display 10 percent of its collection, we have concentrated on improving online provision. In April 2002 the museum launched its illustrated online catalog of its entire collection of 80,000 objects (www.petrie.ucl.ac.uk) as a first step toward sharing information about the collections with world audiences. Although each entry includes a photograph, we are well aware that some of the information in the catalog requires substantial revision, which we are undertaking in partnership with colleagues in Egypt.

The Petrie Museum's collection covers a huge chronological range, from the earliest farmers in the Nile Valley (around 5000 BCE) through Dynastic Egypt to Roman, Coptic, and Islamic Egypt. While the pre-Dynastic and Dynastic Egypt collections have benefited from long-term specialist input and are well documented as a result, the later collections have been comparatively neglected. Until the creation of the museum's online catalog (2000–2002), most of the Roman and Islamic material in the collection remained uncataloged, unresearched, and therefore largely unused. The collection of fragmentary Arabic and Coptic papyri is only now being conserved, and until they are conserved they cannot be read or interpreted.

The museum has been fortunate to attract external funding to employ specialists to edit the catalog entries for the thousands of Coptic and Islamic objects it holds. In 2003 it hosted an Islamic curator on secondment from the Islamic Museum in Cairo, and it is hoped to appoint a Coptic specialist in the same way. Our Egyptian colleagues bring with them a knowledge about and familiarity with Egyptian material culture that do not exist in this country, and are also helping us with our terminology and our understanding of the contemporary meanings of the objects in the collection. It is hoped that these secondments will lead to further staff exchanges.

These kinds of collaborations have begun to occur in anthropological museums engaging with source communities,[29] but are as yet exceptional in an archaeological context. A community archaeology project at Quseir on Egypt's Red Sea coast is most unusual in involving and training local people in a genuine attempt to develop truly collaborative practice.[30] As we reflect on our experience of the secondment of a specialist from Egypt to the Petrie Museum there are aspects of it that trouble us. Egypt currently has a shortage of experienced specialist curators in certain areas; in setting up such paid secondments and borrowing their expertise are we perpetuating the historically unequal relationship? Are we giving enough back? As Ames has commented, the experience of such collaborations raises sometimes uncomfortable questions about the internal politics and practices of the museum,[31] and we feel we have much to learn about hospitality and reciprocity.

At a very basic level we have decided to translate as much as we can of our online material into Arabic. The term "visual repatriation" has been used to describe the use of photography to return images of ancestors, historical knowledge, and material culture by museums to source communities.[32] We have sometimes talked about "virtual repatriation" when describing the aims of such online projects, although the use of the internet, with its impersonal and usually one-way communication flow, is in many ways inferior to the kinds of collaborative ventures being undertaken with photographs. We have recently created a 3,000-page online teaching and learning resource for higher education, *Digital Egypt for Universities* (www.digitalegypt.ucl.ac.uk). This site draws on the museum's collections but also includes speculative 3D recreations of the archaeological sites where they were excavated, and suggests ways of using this material to teach across a range of disciplines. We have begun to translate the site, in partnership with a translation company in Jordan and with substantial input from a colleague who is an Arabic-speaking Egyptologist, but have discovered that to complete the task will be a massive undertaking requiring substantial additional funding which we have yet to identify.

A further experiment concerned the interpretation of the museum collection in an exhibition context. In 2000 the Petrie Museum, in partnership with two other museum services in Croydon and Glasgow, put together a traveling exhibition, *Ancient Egypt: Digging for Dreams.*[33] The aims of the exhibition were to test new approaches in presenting Egyptian archaeology to a wider audience, and to encourage public debate on current approaches to presentation of Egyptian material in British museums. In addition both host venues – Croydon Clocktower and the Burrell Collection, Glasgow – wished to use the exhibition to attract new audiences and perceived the subject-matter as enabling them to do so.

The exhibition included around 120 ancient objects, and many more modern artifacts and props. The first section dealt with Western stereotypes and common assumptions about ancient Egypt, many of which have their roots in popular fiction: hidden treasure, the "glamor" of archaeology, the curse of the mummy. Visitors could use torches to examine ancient objects, some of which were fakes, laid out in a fictional tomb setting. Later sections discussed Flinders Petrie and his achievements, but contextualized them in relation to nineteenth- and twentieth-century archaeology as a colonial project. The exhibition went on to question the uses to which archaeology can be put: mummy portraits such as those excavated by Petrie, and displayed in the exhibition, were used by the Nazis as illustrations of the development of different racial types, and to demonstrate what they regarded as characteristically Semitic features.

The main part of the exhibition raises a number of questions about the ancient Egyptians, the most contentious of which centered around race and color. The displays featured several sculptural and painted figures and artifacts illustrating the different ways in which Egyptians depicted themselves and neighboring peoples over time, and discussed what these representations might and might not tell us about how the Egyptians looked. A further section displayed human remains, in a manner we hoped was respectful. These could be viewed under a shroud, and visitors were invited to comment on whether they thought dead people should be exhibited in public. The final section of the show, *Consuming Egypt*, commented on how ancient Egypt is marketed and commodified in Western society. Throughout the exhibition, interpretation included many voices, including "alternative" viewpoints, and ancient artifacts were deliberately juxtaposed with modern ones, to provoke questions about how we use the past.

Each venue organized extensive outreach programs to reach target audiences. For example, Croydon employed an outreach officer to encourage young people, particularly those from African and African Caribbean cultures, to visit the exhibition. The outreach worker contacted relevant groups – including homework clubs, youth clubs, scouts groups, and refugee associations – visited group leaders, and then the groups themselves, talking generally with them about black history and culture.[34] She then organized visits to the exhibition, with informal workshops where young people could discuss their responses. Media coverage of the exhibition in the black newspaper *New Nation* gave the project credibility with the young people. For Croydon this outreach work provided an important network to build on in future projects; for the Petrie Museum it was an opportunity to bring the collection to an audience that would not otherwise have visited the museum.

The exhibition attracted over 94,000 visitors to its two venues. Self-completion visitor surveys at Croydon suggested that 49 percent of visitors were spending 1–2 hours in the exhibition – a very long time for what was quite a small show, with 6 percent returning for a further visit. Face-to-face surveys indicated that visitors were surprised and intrigued by some of the issues raised by the exhibition, including the questions about race, the politics of archaeology, and the display of human remains. These responses are encouraging as we plan for more controversial displays on a new site.

Meanwhile we are working on other projects to get the collections into new contexts with new interpretations. Increasingly museums in the UK that seek to diversify their audiences have recognized the limitations imposed by their physical location and the need to employ staff who can operate as intermediaries. External funding has enabled us to employ two outreach staff, one African Caribbean, one Egyptian, to strengthen contact with our target audiences. This approach is currently working well, although our dependence on external funding calls into question the project's sustainability. The museum's African and African Caribbean Outreach Officer is building links with supplementary schools and youth groups, including young offenders, and is beginning to develop programs to bring these audiences into the museum, and to take ancient objects to them. Early discussions indicate there is considerable interest in this work among black communities. We are still exploring the best means of doing this and discussing ways of setting the objects in a meaningful context.

Our Egyptian Outreach Officer, who is also an Egyptologist, is working with a range of Egyptian and Sudanese groups to introduce them to the museum. He hopes to produce a series of television programs, based on aspects of the museum's collections, for broadcast in the Arab world. His conviction that many Egyptians and Sudanese people are interested in the ancient past – which directly contradicts traditional Western assumptions – was borne out at two study days held in 2002, organized by the Petrie and the Manchester museums. These discussion days brought together people from Egypt and Sudan and museum professionals from several UK museums to discuss the way in which Egypt and the Sudan are represented in museums, and how those representations might change. The discussions were lively, moving, and most productive, and it was agreed to continue them both at a broad and a more detailed level.

Initial discussions suggested that there is a real and relevant link between ancient and modern cultures in Egypt and Sudan. Conveying the vast chronologies involved is a problem, but we should start from where people are today, with the living cultures. Participants also felt strongly that it was important to present not simply the ancient past but also the colonial and post-colonial past, and to explore the reasons why things were collected and kept in museums. It was also felt to be vital to place ancient and modern Egypt and Sudan in a geographical and cultural context, dealing with wider networks through trade and war. Participants complained that museums and other parts of the education system in the UK tend to homogenize and package cultures under headings, rather than addressing issues of racial, cultural, and religious diversity, in both the past and the present. Finally those present felt there was a role for contemporary art and culture – music, literature, art – and for personal narratives and stories.

As a first step toward exploring the collections through Egyptian eyes, the museum invited Ahdaf Soueif, a novelist shortlisted for the Booker Prize in 1999, who is Egyptian but resident in London, to undertake a short residency, as part of the Year of the Artist scheme. She chose to sit and write in a corner of the museum near a display traditionally referred to within the museum as "the pot burial" (figure 7.2). The museum label reads:

> Pot burial 14857. Hememiah, north spur burial 59. Pot burial found in a settlement of the predynastic period with other intrusive burials. No associated grave goods. Body had been wrapped in a cloth or garment of linen. Brunton and Caton Thompson, Badarian Civilisation pl 69 3–5. ? Protodynastic.

Next to it is a small box labeled:

> Skin and cloth from skeleton in pot. Damaged by water 1985.

In the museum context even human remains become objectified, dehumanized. But need they be? Ahdaf's reinterpretation, her label, is reproduced here with her kind permission:

> The light splinters off the walls of the glass cabinets. You walk the corridor between them looking in at objects and the reflections of objects: fragments of stone murals, hieroglyphs, beads and jewellery, jars of alabaster and of pottery.
>
> The last cabinet holds a giant egg: topped as though with a sharp decisive knife leaving a curled rim into which the domed top had settled to seal in the girl. A web of parched-earth cracks spiders the surface. The girl sits with her back and head erect, her pelvis slightly tilted, cross-legged, her hands in her lap. Not twin boys to break out and wreak havoc but a solitary girl to sit straight and still until the distant knocking came and the voices and the scrape scrape scrape of trowels then fingers then a brush flicking the loose earth from the solid walls. The rocking and the tilting and the knocks and the scrapes – less tentative now, more resolute. The sudden glare of light and then the faces dark and dusty and lined and turbaned, the faces so familiar against the familiar sky –
>
> "May offerings be given her on the New Year's fast and every feast and every day, to the royal daughter, the royal ornament, Ni-sedjer-kai".
>
> Her bones have been pieced together, the missing sections replaced. Out of the sand, in her controlled climate cabinet, she can sit forever. No cramps

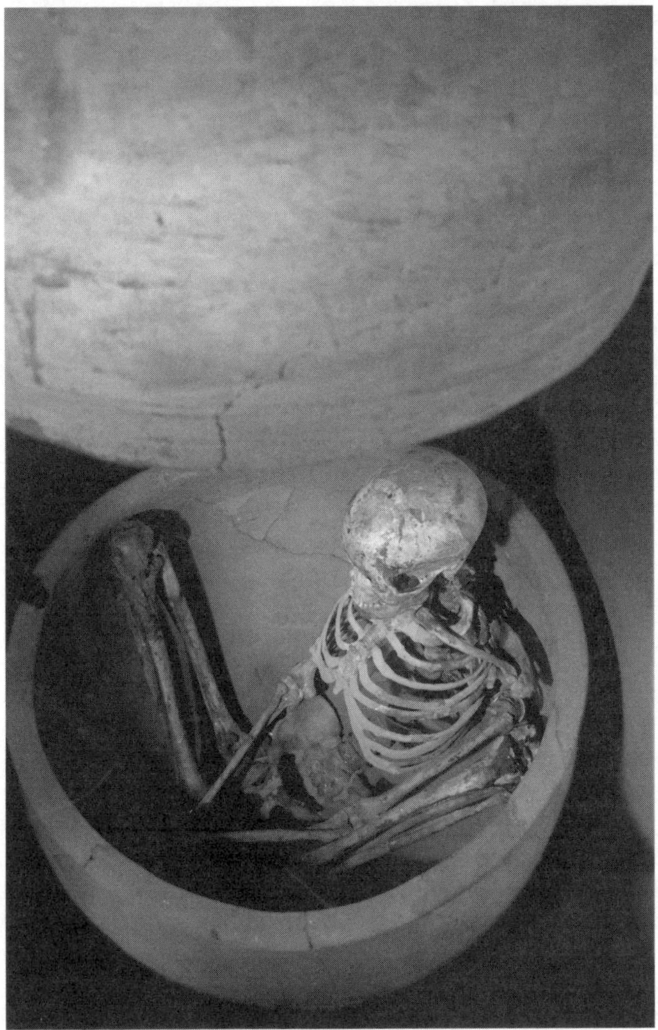

Figure 7.2 Ancient Egyptians: the "pot burial." Copyright Petrie Museum of Egyptian Archaeology, UCL, museum number UC 14857

can affect her bent legs, no hunger or thirst assail her, no boredom or despair. Only the curious, hushed stare of the rare visitor or the questing gaze of the woman who now sits facing her, her hand lying still amongst the brushes and pens on the table she has drawn to her side.

Who are you?

This interpretation, which both personalizes the exhibit and makes the visitor a conscious and active participant in a narrative, perfectly illustrates how new perspectives can literally breathe new life into the museum. How a stolen heritage can be shared.

The Petrie Museum is only just beginning to explore its own history and reflect on what its future role might be. The opportunity to relocate the museum in 2008 to a purpose-built site where the collections can be entirely reframed is immensely exciting. It is quite possible that in five years' time what will result is a smart new London museum that has gone through an exercise in consultation but is still essentially run by and for the European middle classes. The question is whether we have the time and the will to rethink traditional curatorial and managerial practices, to open up to other voices, or, as one indigenous commentator has put it, to let the right people furnish the house.[35]

Notes

1 W. M. F. Petrie, "A Digger's Life," *English Illustrated Magazine*, March, 1886, 440.
2 W. M. F. Petrie, *Seventy Years in Archaeology* (London: Sampson Low, 1931), 175.
3 D. Reid, *Whose Pharaohs? Archaeology, Museums and the Egyptian National Identity from Napoleon to World War I* (Berkeley: University of California Press, 2002), 93–5.
4 M. Simpson, *Making Representations: Museums in the Post-Colonial Era* (London: Routledge, 1996).
5 L. Peers and A. K. Brown (eds.), *Museums and Source Communities* (London: Routledge, 2003).
6 N. Merriman (ed.), *Making Early Histories in Museums* (Leicester: Leicester University Press, 1999), 3.
7 S. Moser, "Representing Archaeological Knowledge in Museums: Exhibiting Human Origins and Strategies for Change," *Public Archaeology*, 3 (2003), 3–20: 10.
8 M. L. Caygill and M. N. Leese, *A Survey of Visitors to the British Museum 1992–3*, British Museum Occasional Paper 101 (London, 1993).
9 S. MacDonald and C. Shaw, "Uncovering Ancient Egypt," in N. Merriman (ed.), *Public Archaeology* (London: Routledge, 2004), 109–31: 120.
10 S. Fisher, "Exploring People's Relationships with Egypt: Qualitative Research for the Petrie Museum" (Susie Fisher Group, unpublished document, Petrie Museum of Egyptian Archaeology, 2000), chart 16.

11 MORI, *Attitudes Towards the Heritage: Research Study Carried Out for English Heritage* (London: English Heritage, 2000).

12 A. G. Hilliard, "Bringing Maat, Destroying Isfet: The African and African Diasporan Presence in the Study of Ancient KMT," in I. Van Sertima (ed.), *Egypt: Child of Africa* (New Brunswick, NJ: Transaction Publishers, 1994), 127–47.

13 For example by S. Howe, *Afrocentrism: Imagined Pasts and Imagined Homes* (London: Verso, 1998).

14 For example C. L. Brace et al., "Clines and Clusters versus 'Race': The Case of a Death on the Nile," in M. K. Lefkowitz and G. M. Rogers (eds.), *Black Athena Revisited* (Chapel Hill: University of North Carolina Press, 1996), 129–64: 162.

15 A notable exception is S. O. Y. Keita: see "Studies of Crania from Northern Africa," *American Journal of Physical Anthropology*, 83 (1990), 35–48, and "Further Studies of Crania from Ancient Northern Africa: An Analysis of Crania from First Dynasty Egyptian Tombs, Using Multiple Discriminant Functions," *American Journal of Physical Anthropology*, 85 (1992), 245–54.

16 M. Bernal, *Black Athena: The Afroasiatic Roots of Classical Civilisation*, vol. i: *The Fabrication of Ancient Greece, 1785–1985* (London: Free Association Press, 1987), and vol. ii: *The Documentary and Archaeological Evidence* (New Brunswick, NJ: Rutgers University Press, 1991); R. J. C. Young, *Colonial Desire: Hybridity in Theory, Culture and Race* (London: Routledge, 1995), 118–41; D. O'Connor and A. Reid, *Ancient Egypt in Africa* (London: UCL Press, 2003), 4.

17 D. Reid, "Indigenous Egyptology: The Decolonisation of a Profession," *Journal of the American Oriental Society*, 105 (1985), 233–46; Reid, *Whose Pharaohs?*; F. Haikal, "Egypt's Past Regenerated by its own People," in S. MacDonald and M. Rice (eds.), *Consuming Ancient Egypt* (London: UCL Press, 2003).

18 B. G. Trigger, "Alternative Archaeologies: Nationalist, Colonialist, Imperialist," *Man*, 19 (1984), 355–70: 359.

19 F. A. Hassan, "Memorabilia: Archaeological Materiality and National Identity in Egypt," in L. Meskell (ed.), *Archaeology under Fire: Nationalism, Politics and Heritage in the Eastern Mediterranean and the Middle East* (London: Routledge, 1998), 200–16: 212.

20 S. Scham, "Ancient Egypt and the Archaeology of the Disenfranchised," in D. Jeffreys (ed.), *Views of Ancient Egypt since Napoleon Bonaparte: Imperialism, Colonialism and Modern Appropriations* (London: UCL Press, 2003)

21 S. Motawi, "Egypt in the British Museum," MA dissertation, Institute of Archaeology, University College London, 1998.

22 MacDonald and Shaw, "Uncovering Ancient Egypt."

23 Fisher, "Exploring People's Relationships with Egypt," chart 33.
24 Ibid., chart 13.
25 Ibid., chart 35.
26 Ibid., chart 37.
27 Ibid., chart 26.
28 H. Claire, *Reclaiming Our Pasts: Equality and Diversity in the Primary History Curriculum* (Stoke-on-Trent: Trentham Books, 1996), 12.
29 For example J. E. Stanton, "Snapshots on the Dreaming: Photographs of the Past and Present," in Peers and Brown (eds.), *Museums and Source Communities*; R. B. Phillips, "Community Collaboration in Exhibitions: Toward a Dialogic Paradigm," introduction to Peers and Brown (eds.), *Museums and Source Communities.*
30 S. Moser et al., "Transforming Archaeology through Practice: Strategies for Collaborative Archaeology and the Community Archaeology Project at Quseir, Egypt," in Peers and Brown (eds.), *Museums and Source Communities.*
31 M. Ames, "How to Decorate a House," in Peers and Brown (eds.), *Museums and Source Communities.*
32 Peers and Brown (eds.), *Museums and Source Communities*, 208–26.
33 S. MacDonald, "An Experiment in Access," *Museologia*, 2 (2002), 101–8.
34 L. Harris, "Ancient Egypt: Digging for Dreams: Museum Development Worker's Report" (unpublished document, Croydon Museum and Heritage Service, 2000).
35 Ames, "How to Decorate a House," 177.

Andalusia in the Time of the Moors: Regret and Colonial Presence in Paris, 1900

Roger Benjamin

It is unlikely that anyone living today remembers the great Universal Exposition held in Paris just over a century ago. One can't exactly "cast one's mind back" to an event one didn't personally experience, but a writer can undertake a kind of imaginative reconstruction, a sort of learned longing for a time and place that gains in allure through its relative remoteness. The persistence of objects can aid the task of reconstruction. Some of the best exposition architecture is still there – the Grand and Petit Palais, the Pont Alexandre III, even the Eiffel Tower of 1889 which presided over the Champ de Mars exposition site again in 1900. All four are exalted *lieux de mémoire*, rich in associations. Many of the 1900 paintings were reassembled in the year 2000 in a centenary display at the Royal Academy in London.[1] So it is possible to see the pictures visitors of 1900 saw, to imagine the architectural spaces their bodies occupied. Reimagining the Paris Exposition of 1900 is an act of nostalgia for the Belle Époque, before the terrible wars of the twentieth century, if not *regret* in the sense in which it will appear in this essay: that of mourning something lost through a failure of human action.

I sketch such a process of historical consumption because it was rampant in the 1900 Exposition itself. Although the familiar image of the 1900 Exposition conjures the marvels of futuristic technology, retrospective notions – millennial and centennial – were everywhere. The dozens of national pavilions used ideas of representative historical style in their architecture: the official Spanish pavilion on the Rue des Nations which lined the left bank of the Seine was Castilian Renaissance; the British pavilion was Elizabethan. Following the success of the popular Histoire de L'Habitation from 1889, the timbered village of Vieux Paris had been constructed nearby, replete with strolling actors in medieval costume. Yet few precincts so actively constituted a time lost as one all but forgotten to scholarship today: *Andalusia in the Time of the Moors* (*Andalousie au temps des Maures*). Produced by an entrepreneur as an elaborate entertainment, *Andalusia* was a spectacle through which the bodies of the consuming public might encounter an otherwise unknowable, but admirable, zone of culture and history.

The temporal procedure of *Andalusia* was a lamination of time, or better, of *times* brought from several wildly diverse points and superimposed on to the zero-point of the present at the year 1900. Such a laminar form of temporality was removed from the apparent unities of temporal representation in, for example, classical drama, history painting, or even their modern-day derivatives. Imagine today's British television or cinematic costume dramas after Jane Austen as a series of attempts at ever-increasing veracity, in which the sin to be extirpated is *anachronism* (in this sense, historically false detail), be it of costume, speech, or décor. The concept of historical falsity is itself questionable, as the historian Dipesh Chakrabarty has pointed out. He argues that anachronism is constitutive in the nomination and gathering of any data as historical. That is, to seek historical "evidence" is necessarily to subject material to an organizing principle outside the time that gave rise to it.[2] But, as will be seen, the fairground Andalusia flouted even the protocols used to produce a sense of unity in historical time. Instead, heterodox creative anachronism was its *modus operandi.*

Heterogeneity in the representation of times was presumably less a matter of intellectual decision than the result of the organizing showman's practical expediency, of answering the question, how could he, using the exhibitionary techniques of the day, give the greatest experiential immediacy to an era over 400 years distant in time? The answer lay, firstly, in a form of theater in which living bodies of diverse colonial origins and ethnicities substituted for historical types and personages; secondly, in facsimile reproductions of parts of famous buildings (never their wholes) that worked to induce an imaginative transposition in place as well as time. The third kind of visual embodiment was through museum displays:

Orientalist easel paintings and Islamic artifacts arrayed by the Society of French Orientalists, there to stand visually as an evocation of old Al-Andaluz.

The precinct *Andalusia in the Time of the Moors* was described as an "immense village" covering 5,000 square meters along the Quai Debilly, on the right bank of the Seine. It presented "all that is picturesque from ancient and modern Spain."[3] It was a commercial venture, like the dozens of other elaborate fairground attractions which vied with the official pavilions for the patronage of the paying public (16 million people visited the Exposition between March and November 1900). The man behind the project was J. H. Roseyro, an entrepreneur of presumably Spanish background and apparently a resident of Bayonne, on the French Atlantic coast close to the Spanish border and near Basque country. He was an editor associated with the populist weekly *L'Illustration* and the more august *Journal des débats.*[4] Initially Roseyro had received the support of the Spanish Minister of Fine Arts, the Count of Sequena, whose son took an active role in *Andalusia.*[5] This official backing from Spain is important: it implies the government was happy to expand beyond its sober national pavilion, with its didactic displays, to an attraction that could capitalize on the enormous touristic potential of the national heritage.

Roseyro spent (and possibly lost) a fortune on *Andalusia*: in 1902 he was exonerated by the Minister of the Colonies (who had administered the ensemble of colonial attractions in the Trocadero Gardens) from a debt of 40,000 francs. It had nevertheless been a paying entertainment: early plans called for an overall entry fee of 3 francs, with separate tickets available for the sections dedicated to the Gypsies, Moorish Women, the Aissaouas, and the Museum.[6] Roseyro had initially applied to have artisans on the site, plying trades he considered typical of the two cultures he was representing. He divided them by their products: "Moorish articles: 1. Flintlock rifles. 2. Carpets. 3. Leather (babouches). 4. Copper-work," and "Spanish articles: 1. Fans, castagnettes, tambourines. 2. Damasquinerie. 3. Pottery."[7] These "exotic" employees, of a type common to many other sections of the Exposition, are at once themselves, and ciphers for distant historical others. The curiosity of *Andalusia* is that it encompasses several systems of temporality and modes of representation: from the doubled actualization suggested by such Spanish artisans and their colonial (probably Algerian) counterparts, to the indexical realism of plaster-cast moldings.

On the physical fringes of the Trocadero colonial precinct that included all the French colonies as well as those of several other powers, *Andalusia* was distinct from it in mapping a deep time, at first sight far removed from the cares of the modern French empire. On the contrary, I would argue that *Andalusia* represents the bad conscience of the French colonial presence abroad: recognition that imperial expansion entails the destruction or mutation of cultures potentially richer than those that replace them. That is, the Spain of the Moors could be considered richer than that of the Christians in science, in poetry, in theology, in architecture, and in the centuries-long *convivencia* with the Jews (whose own theology, medical science, and literature are exemplified by the figure of Maimonides). Reconstructing Andalusia had the exculpatory advantage of recording a Spanish, not a French, elimination of this magnificent Islamic and Jewish culture. But there must have been French visitors who, reflecting on the history of southern Spain, would have drawn parallels with their own controversial invasion and settling of Islamic North Africa during the nineteenth century with the colony of Algeria and the protectorate of Tunisia.

Roseyro's Andalusia revolved in time around 1492, the terminus of the Reconquista, when the last Moorish Kingdom of Granada fell to the Catholic forces of Ferdinand of Aragon and Isabella of Castille. Andalusia had always been a meeting-point of cultures and ethnicities: Iberian Catholics descended from Romans and Visigoths, a Gypsy population, Sephardi Jews, and the so-called "Moors." These were originally descendants of Muslim soldiers from the Arabian peninsula and their North African Berber converts who, sweeping up across the Straits of Gibraltar, conquered the Iberian peninsula in the half-century following AD 711. Initially ruled from Damascus and then by Moroccan Berber dynasties, Al-Andaluz enjoyed Islamic rule for nearly eight centuries. From the twelfth century the Moors gradually witnessed the erosion of their power under the Nasrid dynasty, which, hampered by internal strife, lost territory to the Catholic monarchs until all that remained to Muslims was the southern kingdom of Granada. The last king of Granada, Abu'Abdullah, known in the West as Boabdil, capitulated to Ferdinand and Isabella after a long siege in the winter of 1492. With his court Boabdil went into exile in Morocco, while the Moors remaining in Al-Andaluz were forced to convert to Christianity and made subject to the Inquisition, much like the Jews with whom they had long coexisted during the *convivencia*, and who suffered a still more rigorous expulsion.[8]

In evoking this history, Roseyro drew upon a rich surviving tradition of festivities and thanksgiving in southern Spain: the annual celebrations of the "liberation" of specific towns and cities from the Moors, entitled the Fiestas de Moros y Cristianos. Natasha Staller has made a special study of these festivals, which she calls "performances of social and political subjugation."[9] She argues persuasively that the young Pablo Picasso was much affected by the annual parades of Moors and Christians in the Andalusian city of Malaga, where he grew up. Moorish heritage was an active issue in Malaga, due to the "racial" intermixing that was part of the city's history. That Picasso claimed on occasion to have Moorish blood indicates the positive cachet that some Andalusians still accorded the Muslim phase of their history.

It is easy to understand the appeal that this story of the clash of faiths and "races," set in a décor of medieval chivalry and exquisite architecture, had for the modern French. Spain was their great southern neighbor, which had been briefly controlled by France during the Napoleonic wars. The French defeat there by the Duke of Wellington's army and Spanish guerrillas was repaid following 1830 in colonial politics, with France assuming control of lands along the Barbary coast that had once been under limited Spanish sovereignty.[10] With the settling of Algeria and the annexation of Tunisia, France became a far more dominant colonial power in North Africa than Spain had ever been. One could argue that the Hispanophilia that was so marked in French art and letters during the nineteenth century was the fetishizing cultural expression of the political appropriation of a once great power in full decline.

Alhambraism and Architectural Décor

Within that Hispanophilia, the issue of the Moorish past was one of intense speculation, the more so as France was now a force within the Muslim world. Romantic authors had embroidered what is a centuries-old theme of Arabic letters: regret for the loss of Al-Andaluz, particularly as it was embodied in the great fortified palace of the Alhambra in Granada. As Gabriel Martinez and Sophie Makariou have shown, Spanish clerics and historians led the way in the scholarly re-examination of this monument, once considered a vestige of barbarity. From the later eighteenth century, authors such as Echeverria and de Argote began to reassess the Alhambra as an architectural treasure.[11]

They were followed by French authors such as the Vicomte de Châteaubriand, whose romantic novella *The Last of the Abencérages* takes as its décor this former palace of sultans, recounting the secret return to post-expulsion Granada of the scion of a great Moorish family exiled to North Africa. (Members of the Abencérages and their faction had been the victims of a notorious fifteenth-century massacre by their rivals in the halls of the Alhambra.) Living in disguise among the arcades of the Alhambra, the young man falls in love with the daughter of a Catholic duke. In a parable of miscegenation and religious belief, each implores the other to convert so that they might marry, but neither can deny their faith in order to do so. The young Abencérage returns to the bitterness of exile, the noblewoman spends her days in regret for his lost love. Châteaubriand's popular text, written in 1801 but published only in 1826,[12] coincided with Victor Hugo's poetic evocations of Granada in his *Orientales.* English writers, their attention drawn to Spain by the Duke of Wellington's alliance with the Spanish against Napoleon, weighed in with J. C. Murphy's *The Arabian Antiquities of Spain.* Washington Irving's *Tales of the Alhambra*, composed during the American writer's placement in Spain as a diplomat, was an entertaining oral history and travelogue that appeared in French in 1832 (and is still sold today at the Alhambra). The artists John Frederick Lewis and then Owen Jones published illustrated studies, plans, and elevations of the Alhambra, supplementing the work of the Frenchman Girault de Prangey. All such sources were well known to Théophile Gautier when he devoted 50 pages to Granada in his 1843 *Voyage en Espagne.*[13]

This brief review of literature is enough to show why the Andalusian precinct at the 1900 Exposition could be expected to capitalize on the interest in a region that was already, as Roseyro acknowledged, a mainstay of European winter tourism.[14] The writer Armand Silvestre explained: "With this magnificent reconstitution, one can relive the Arab civilization of the fifteenth century, which shone with such brightness in the south of Spain. For this the promoters of the enterprise have had only to draw upon the marvelous treasures of Moorish architecture that the monuments of Cordoba, Seville and Granada have preserved for us."[15] Indeed, the two major architectural works were the Lion Court, based upon the Patio de los Leones from the Alhambra (figure 8.1), and the tower of the Giralda from the Cathedral of Seville, reconstituted in 1900 to overlook the arena or Hippodrome (figure 8.2). The original buildings had been studied in Spain by the project's architect, M. Henri Malo, who traveled with Roseyro to Andalusia to select monuments and commission plaster moldings of the kind applicable to lightweight timber frames.[16]

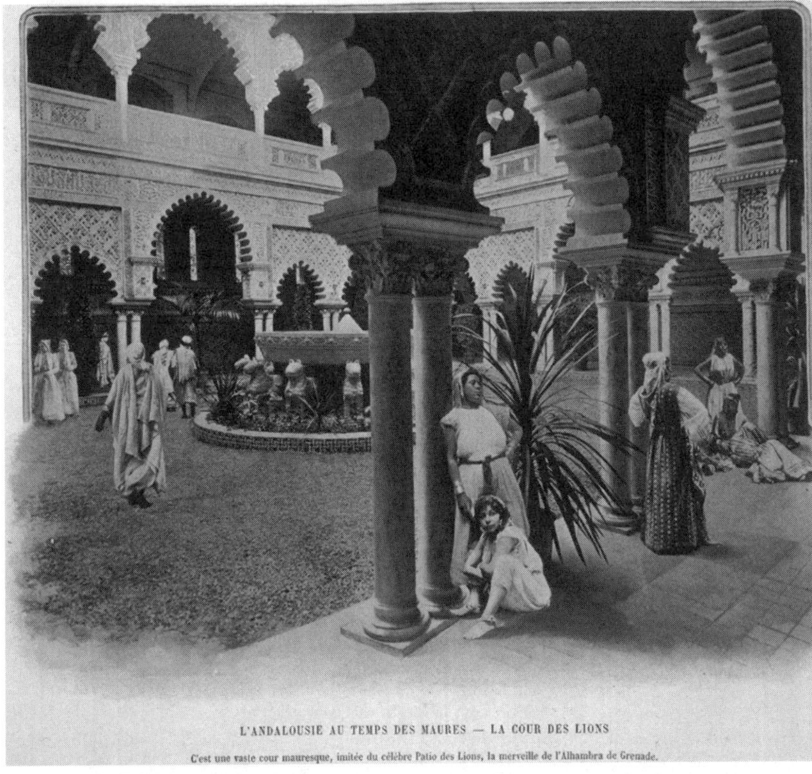

Figure 8.1 Lion Court, *Andalousie au temps des Maures*, Exposition universelle, Paris, 1900. From *Le Panorama, 1900*

The massive Giralda tower served as a visual advertisement and, as Roseyro wrote, "as entrance to both the general Exposition on the Quai, and to Andalusia. I hardly need to praise to you, M. le Ministre, the richness of this monument, one of the most important that Hispano-Moorish art has left to us." The tower well encapsulates the theme of cultural hybridity and accretion that animates *Andalusia in the Time of the Moors*, being "Moorish in its base, Renaissance in its bell-tower."[17] The first 230 feet of the real Giralda is the minaret of a great mosque built at Seville for the Almohad sultan in the twelfth century. In 1248 Seville fell to the Christians, who after 1400 began replacing the mosque with the world's largest gothic church; but they left the minaret, topping it in the

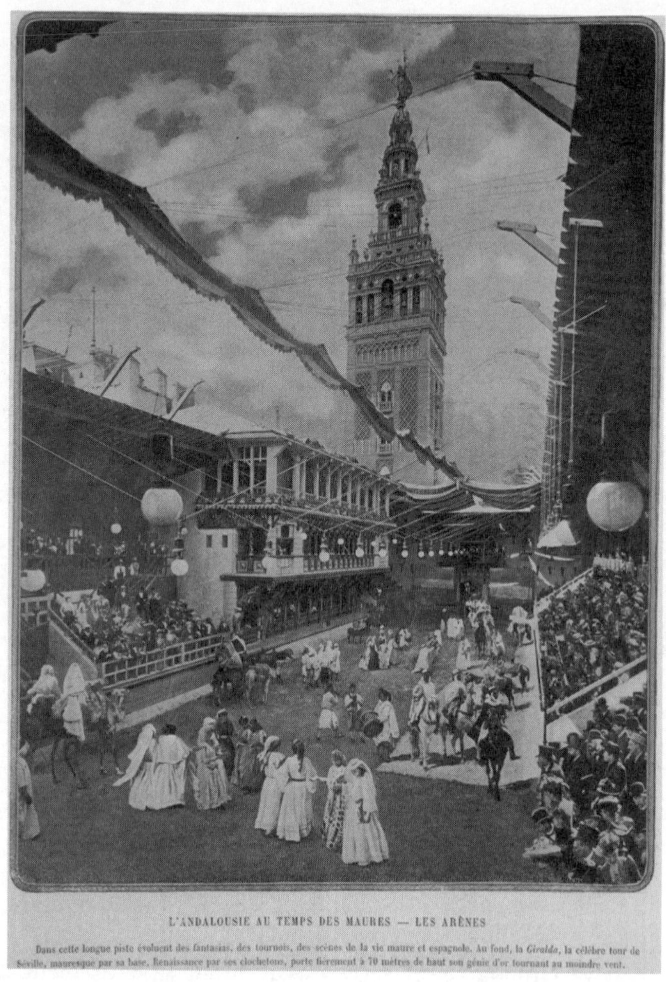

Figure 8.2 Tower of the Giralda with Hippodrome in foreground, *Andalousie au temps des Maures*, Exposition universelle, Paris, 1900. From *Le Panorama, 1900*

1560s with a new bell-tower culminating in the giant weather-vane figure of Faith (the "Giradillo").[18]

The second major architectural set-piece was the Lion Court from the Alhambra: "faithfully reconstructed using plaster moulds . . . [it] is the most delicate example of Moorish art," wrote Roseyro. Although built at full scale and physically impressive, faithful the Lion Court was not. The photograph republished from the deluxe album *Le Panorama* records a building whose arcades, with their scalloped arches and second-story balcony, are clearly also modeled on the Alcazar at Seville. Economy seems to have encouraged this liberty with architectural history: the Alcazar offered forms easier to copy in stucco than the ornate quadripartite columns, bees-nest coffering, and strapwork capitals of the original. The famous fountain that gives the Lion Court its name, with its shallow stone basin supported by 12 medieval lions, looks accurate enough.

Such a mélange of architectural monuments was endemic in the colonial pavilions of the Trocadero in 1900. The temporary nature and epideictic function of lath and plaster buildings invited an element of fairground fantasy, besides giving a nod to the indigenous architectural heritage of far-flung colonies. The government pavilion of French Algeria (nearby on the main axis of the colonial precinct) is a well-known example of this practice. Its architect, Albert Ballu, who had made detailed renderings of the historical monuments of Algiers as early as 20 years before,[19] combined salient features of a minaret from Tlemcen and the cupolas of the Djama el-Djedid in Algiers in arriving at his own building in "neo-Moorish" style. Yet this kind of pastiche, which received official sanction as a government style in Algeria in the decade after the Exposition, appears studious when placed beside the excesses of "Alhambraism" in Western cities in the inter-war years. The taste for Alhambraism led the designers of theaters, cinemas, coffee-shops, bathing-pavilions – almost any modern building associated with the pursuit of pleasure – to adopt the horseshoe arches, bees-nest ceilings, and scalloped pendentives loosely associated with the Granadan monument.

These two monuments aside, a variety of smaller façades and built spaces were used to vary the experience in *Andalusia.* They include a lane lined with timbered houses from Toledo, "with the jarring façades of its Romanesque and Renaissance houses and its shops occupied with an infinity of curious crafts: here the mantillas, the jewels encrusted with gold, the tambourines and guitars are made; in the background the illusion is completed by [a mural painting of] a 'sierra', harsh and jagged." The corner of a Moorish village or *gourbi arabe* recreated the vernacular mud-brick architecture from the Algerian Sahara: "all in white with its mosque and its whitewashed buildings and, in contrast, the rich products of the industry of its inhabitants: carpets, leathers, fabrics, and weapons of unparalleled opulence."[20] The sedentary performances of these artisans, producing and selling their goods, were at odds with the spectacular animations arranged for the two grander architectural spaces of *Andalusia.*

Moros y Cristianos: Peopling the Precinct

The year 1900 saw a continuation in North Africa of the primary political struggle in the Mediterranean basin for the previous millennium and more: that between Muslim and Christian powers. I would argue that the conception of the fairground *Andalusia* was both inflected by that fact and reliant on very old traditions of giving symbolic representation to such struggle.

The organizers of *Andalusia* tried to people built environments with a rich variety of costumed participants. In figure 8.1, a montage of present-day Maghrebins – males in full burnous and females in an implausible mixture of outdoor and indoor clothing (without the veil) – are inserted into the colonnades of the Lion Court. Nary a European can be seen. So photography sought visually to reinstall the exiled Moors of historical memory by using players (or *figurantes*, to use the music-hall term) from the present-day French colonies.

Roseyro's descriptions and the *Panorama* photographs indicate how he adapted the protocols of the traditional Moros y Cristianos parades in his *Andalusia*. Photographs published by Staller show that, in Malaga, players in Moorish historical costume (in turbans and burnous, often on horseback) were in the minority: the triumphalist ethos meant that Christians, often supporting the procession of religious icons to the local church or cathedral, predominated. In the French context, Roseyro redressed this balance, apparently giving equal weight to Muslim as well as Christian processions. Such a position again mirrors the acceptance, in certain circles in southern Spain of the day, that the Moorish or African heritage was vital to the Andalusian character and one of its indelible components.[21]

Thus from the 1900 Giralda tower there issued forth Catholic processions with costumes and accouterments copied from the famous *pasos* held during Holy Week in Seville and Cadiz.[22] The same was true of the Muslim cortèges coming from the façade of a mosque (based on the Tetuan mosque dedicated to the Aissouas, the still active sect which had been famously depicted in Delacroix's *Convulsionnaires de Tanger*). Another widely reproduced Exposition photograph shows a dozen men in burnous, carrying the banners of a religious confraternity, parading down a main thoroughfare next to the official Palace of Algeria.

In the Andalusian precinct itself the destination of such processions was the arena or Hippodrome. This is the space which constituted the most intense spectacle, and gave the most direct and physical representation to the historical conflicts I have glossed (figure 8.2). With its track of 60 meters and its seating for 1,000 viewers, the arena was "primarily intended for fantasias, for tournaments between Moors and Christian knights, for gazelle-hunts with sloughis or Arab greyhounds, for the attack of a caravan by Touaregs, for the ceremonies of a Gypsy marriage."[23]

This charivari of re-enactments and actions from historical and contemporary eras in both Spain and the Maghreb gives a sense of the degree to which Roseyro and company were reliant on the French North African colonies to provide "local color." This fact leads to interesting perturbations in the construction of time offered to the public by *Andalusia*. The attack of camel-mounted Touareg raiders on a caravan was an extreme example of the kind of anachronism known as *prochronism*, the error in chronology by which an event is referred "to an earlier date than the true one."[24] In 1900 and from the French perspective, the Touareg were a real threat to Saharan trade routes and to French attempts to extend their military rule into the far south of Algeria, where they were agitating for territory from the Moroccan sultan. Including the Touareg tribesmen had almost nothing to do with medieval Andalusia, but everything to do with the current French experience of resistant Islam in a colonial situation.

The "tournaments between Moors and Christian knights," symbolic fighting between individual men in the Hippodrome, was a theme as ancient, in French literature, as the medieval *Chanson de Roland*, which tells of the French knight of the Emperor Charlemagne who held back the all-conquering Saracen armies at Roncevaux in the Pyrenees in 778. It was also as recent, in French painting, as the adversarial struggle of faiths in the gigantic battle-paintings of Horace Vernet documenting the French campaigns against Abd el Kader in Algeria, or Eugène Delacroix's series (inspired by Lord Byron) of the *Pasha and the Giaour*. The "fantasias" mentioned by Roseyro (feats of arms executed at the gallop by massed North African horsemen) were a mainstay of Orientalist painting, but were also current in a theatrical context: as more than one color poster of the day shows, the permanent Hippodrome de Paris often featured entertainments of this kind.[25]

Andalusia's jousts were not only witnessed by modern tourists and visitors on the benches of the arena. As Roseyro states in his prospectus, "usually the Caliph Boabdil, last Moorish king of Granada, will preside at the fantasias that the Moors of Tlemcen with their horses, reputedly the best in Africa, enact with so great and so moving a *maestria*."[26] The advent of this modern incarnation of Boabdil on the benches of the 1900 arena is full of resonance. It is a curious performative figure, using a contemporary actor actualizing a historical figure as a witness, like a Roman emperor presiding over and judging the games in the Coliseum or the Circus Maximus. While nothing is revealed by Roseyro about Boabdil's identity, one may assume this was at least a dark-skinned actor, dressed with some sumptuousness, who would have occupied a box seat and possibly been called upon to adjudicate in certain of the competitions.

The Parisian Boabdil's task of witnessing, or *sur-veillance*, has historical and visual precedents. Gautier, for example, remarked in his *Voyage en Espagne* a rocky crag above Granada, the so-called Silla del Moro (Moor's Seat), "from which King Boabdil used to watch the Arab horsemen joust in the [valley of the] Vega against the Christian knights" during the city's siege of 1492.[27] Boabdil certainly had currency in neo-Romantic French painting, being the subject of the greatest single canvas by Alfred Dehodencq, *L'Adieu du roi Boabdil à Grenade*, today on show in the Musée d'Orsay. Dehodencq had made his reputation in the 1850s painting Spanish scenes which the young Manet admired, before moving further south, to Tangier, which became the location of his copious Orientalist work. Dehodencq's enormous canvas shows the famous tearful backward glance of the last Moorish king on quitting his homeland and his great palace of the Alhambra.

The opening page of Châteaubriand's *Adventures of the Last Abencérage* explains the scene:

> When Boabdil, last king of Granada, was obliged to abandon the kingdom of his fathers, he stopped at the summit of Mount Padul. From this high place one discerned the sea where the unfortunate monarch would embark for Africa: one also made out Granada, the Vega and the Xenil, beside which rose the tents of Ferdinand and Isabella. Upon seeing that beautiful country... Boabdil began to shed tears. The Sultana Aïxa, his mother, who was accompanying him into exile with the great folk who formerly had comprised his court, said to him: "Weep now like a woman for a kingdom you have been unable to defend like a man!" They descended the mountainside, and Granada disappeared from their sight for ever.[28]

To Aïxa's famous words, recounted in most travel books on Andalusia,[29] one should add the motif celebrated by Salman Rushdie in his novel *The Moor's Last Sigh*, which has as a historical leitmotif the tale of King

Boabdil's exile. Turning back for that last glimpse of his kingdom, Boabdil uttered a great sigh, so that the rock on which his horse stood is still known as "El ultimo sospiro del Moro." Boabdil was nicknamed the Unlucky (el Zogoiby) because, as Rushdie recounts, it had been foretold at his birth that he would preside over the downfall of Moorish power.[30]

In Dehodencq's picture, Boabdil's burnous-swathed body becomes an allegory of the contemporary submission of Islamic forces in the Maghreb before the Christian armies of the French. In 1868 (when Dehodencq made this painting) the French were still fighting to guarantee the security of southern Algeria, and the great Kabyle insurrection of 1871 was looming. But sympathy for the aristocratic Algerian elite had emerged in the 1865 visit of the emperor, Napoleon III, who unsuccessfully sought a power-sharing arrangement with that elite, and supported indigenous rights against the depredations of French colonists (mosques, for example, were being desacralized or destroyed at such a rate that 400 had been lost by 1900).[31] I believe a parallel cultural sympathy informs Dehodencq's Boabdil and cognate paintings of the old Andalusian Moors by Henri Regnault and Georges Clairin (inspired by their 1869–70 stays in Granada and Tangier in Morocco).

The choice of Boabdil to preside over *Andalusia in the Time of the Moors* is revealing in that he is a figure of the decline of Islam in Europe. It is not one of the conquerors who first established or extended Moorish power in the Iberian peninsula that Roseyro chose. This is in contrast to a later painted invocation of this history by the indigenous Algerian artist, Mohammed Racim (figure 8.3). Racim was a specialist in the pictorial representation of Moorish Andalusia as well as the reconstitution of the Barbary regency of Algeria (that is, in the period of Ottoman control, ca. 1520–1830). Effectively the founder of the Algerian school of miniature painting from the 1920s on, Racim combined a knowledge of Western perspectival representation (he was Francophone, with strong links with art circles in Algiers and Paris) with great learning in liturgical inscriptions, the Persian miniature, and the arabesque decorative traditions of the Maghreb and Andalusia. In 1919 the young Racim even traveled to Andalusia on a *bourse hispano-mauresque* provided by the Algerian government.[32]

Racim's Andalusian historical scenes give credence to the continuing nostalgia among Maghrebins for the loss of Al-Andaluz to the Spanish, of looking to Al-Andaluz as a golden age of Moorish art, science, and letters

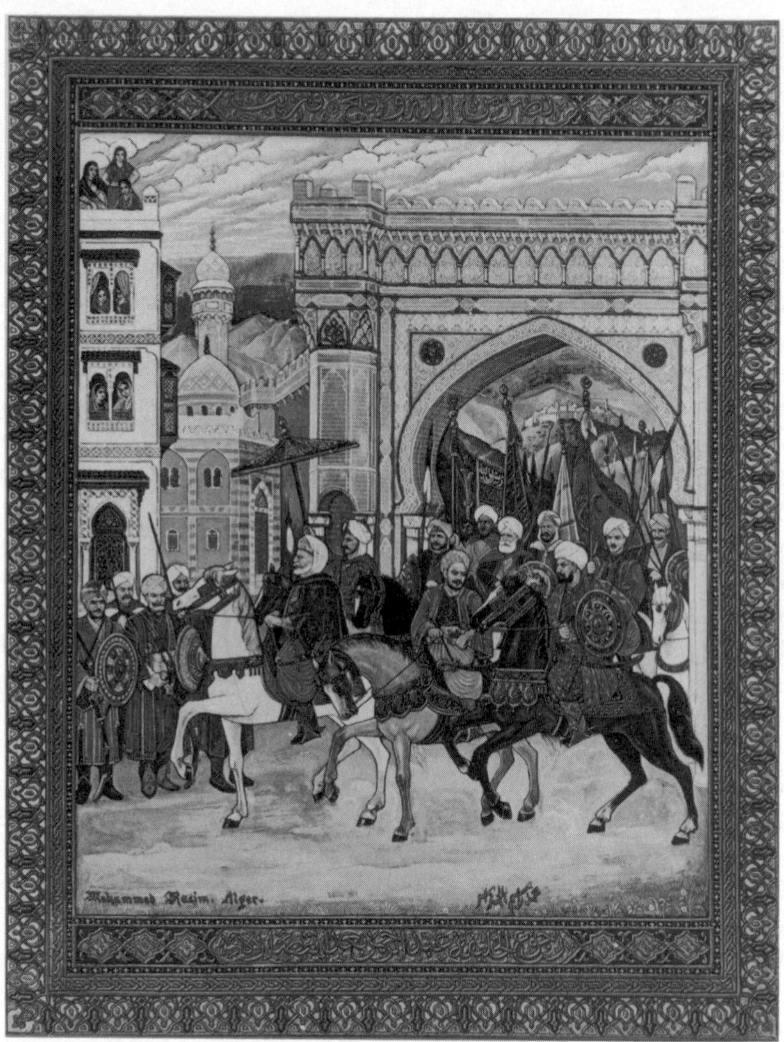

Figure 8.3 Mohammed Racim, *Retour du Caliphe*. Gouache and gold leaf on parchment. Whereabouts unknown

as well as military achievement. Perhaps surprisingly, some French commentators responded to *Andalusia* in just such terms. The *Livre d'or* of the Exposition deliberately deprecated Spanish cultural superiority: "The domination of the Moors is incontestably the most brilliant epoch in the history of Spain. These alleged barbarians in effect brought with them – together with perfect manners and a high degree of civilization – the arts and sciences which the Germanic invasions have erased from memory."[33]

In Racim's *Return of the Caliph* we see the victorious return of the Omayyad caliph of Cordoba, Abderrahman en-Nacir, from one of his campaigns against the Christian Visigoths who had assumed power in Spain after the decline of the Roman empire. In this work of sober Muslim triumphalism, Racim shows the pennons and standards of the religious confraternities, at once martial and devout. A great triumphal arch is visible behind the procession of uniformly stern-faced, bearded warriors, stereotypes of valor and determination. The critic Georges Marçais, while casting doubt on the scene's archaeological accuracy, noted its "psychological truth," writing: "very little, in his costume, distinguishes the Commander of the Faithful from the officers of his escort . . . but the nobility of his bearing, the gravity of his visage framed by a white beard and the white veil covering his turban, suffice for us to recognize a Muslim sovereign, convinced of being an instrument of Allah, 'from whom alone comes victory.' "[34]

Racim's earliest exhibited Andalusian scenes dated to just before 1920, the start of a decade in which an organized nationalist sentiment was on the rise among indigenous Algerians, who were largely disenfranchised by the French. Racim's brother, the more devout Omar (a practicing calligrapher), was associated with these movements. The symbolic value of Al-Andaluz and its heritage is evident when, for example, the Algerian nationalist politician Ferhat Abbas took the nom de plume of "Abencérage" to sign his 1930 manifesto *Le Jeune Algérien.*

Dehodencq's Boabdil could not be more unlike the caliph by Racim. Boabdil was a figure of transition, from whom power slips away. The contrast helps explain why Roseyro chose the last caliph as the presiding "genius" of the Hippodrome: he did after all did have to reconcile his Andalusian reconstruction with an important patron, the government of Catholic Spain, which might have been opposed to a more militant Islamic figure.

Despite being feminized by his mother's words, weep *like a woman*, Dehodencq's Boabdil is handsome, a traveler's burnous obscuring his rich garments, his figure etched against the stormy passes of the Sierra Nevada.[35] His apprehensive servant is a dark-skinned Numidian – an opposition common to Dehodencq's pictures of Jewish brides and a visual crossing held in common with his fellow Hispanophile Manet. Boabdil's twisting body enables the yearning glance at what is lost, beyond the picture frame. He is turning back to see the irrecoverable. It is an ancient literary figure: he is like Lot's wife turning back, against the warning of the angel, to see Sodom and Gomorrah in the moment of their destruction. In the Bible this forbidden backward glance results in a chastisement of sight worthy of the Medusa: Lot's wife is turned to a pillar of salt, and left forever standing in the desert. In the Greek myth of Orpheus and Eurydice, the hero, having braved the underworld to lead his imprisoned lover out from it, is warned never once to look back at Eurydice. Weakened by her repeated entreaties, Orpheus does so, and Eurydice is lost for ever in Hades.

But these are antique tales of supernatural intervention, whereas Boabdil was a historical figure literally witnessing the death of an era of history. For John Docker, Natasha Staller, and others, the exile of the Moors and the Reconquista defines the birth of the modern period as much as does the concurrent discovery of America. Boabdil is, in this painting, the embodiment of historical time, a *punctum* (in Roland Barthes's sense) both of a transfixing emotion of loss held in a single frozen moment, and a dagger-tip upon which human history swung. Behind the king lies the incomparable jewel he has lost, and ahead the anomie of exile and oblivion. Within the bounds of pictorial convention, his body is riven with emotion.

Performing Historical Dance

Dance, after the chivalric re-enactments, was the second great bodily signifier in *Andalusia in the Time of the Moors*. The problem with presenting historical dance is that its older forms are seldom recorded: they leave no permanent traces comparable to, say, the record of Moorish architecture or even historical costume. For a painter like Racim, ancient dance was a world of conjecture, evident when he sought to animate the Lion Court, in a miniature of around 1920, with a dancer of shaky pedigree. As Georges Marçais points out, her costume seems to be a combination of the Peris from the Persian miniature tradition, and the Apsaras of Hindu temple sculpture – neither of which seems relevant in an Andalusian context.[36]

Dance has been identified by Zeynep Çelik and Leila Kinney as a key marker of cultural identity as well as sexuality at the expositions. They studied the cross-overs between Egyptian and North African dancers and Paris music-hall performers, clarifying the doubtful authenticity of most exposition dance.[37] What Roseyro did in 1900 was employ troupes of dancers as signatures of various ethnicities, both of lost Moorish Andalusia and of modern Catholic Spain. The best documented of these was the troupe of Gypsy dancers who appeared in a photographic montage of the Spanish quarter at *Andalusia.* They were in fact Gypsy flamenco dancers from present-day Granada.[38] French perceptions of the cultural uniqueness and allure of Spanish Gypsies had been enshrined in nineteenth-century culture, starting with Prosper Mérimée's book *Carmen* of 1832 (reinterpreted as a light opera by Georges Bizet in 1875). For Somerset Maugham visiting Andalusia, the fascination of Gypsy song, dance, and music was that they remained very "Moorish," that they transmitted, as it were, the traces of the lost culture.

Flamenco performers and another dance troupe brought up from Spain, the "Sévillanaises" with their boléro, were fixtures at the theater of Andalusian dance and song, holding 600 spectators, which was located beyond the Spanish Village (figure 8.4). The theater's portico was composed of towers inspired by Maghrebin minarets, but inside the proscenium (and the idea of the theater itself) switched back to Catholic Spain, being formed by a giant baroque cartouche.

Treating the other side of the dance equation, Roseyro seems to have reasoned that, as the Moors of Andalusia had been largely Berber émigrés from the Maghreb, one could fairly study their lost dances via those of his day's most representative Berbers. Their performances were staged not just in the theater, but in zones that matched dance to the architectural décor. These included the quarters of the Hamadcha, the Jewesses of Tangiers, and the Ouled-Naïls. The Berber Ouled-Naïl women functioned symbolically and anachronistically as exiles from Andalusia, relics of a culture lost to Europe. But they were also figures of contemporary currency, exponents of an allure familiar to colonial tourists, to settlers, and to soldiers in the Algerian oasis resorts of 1900, where Ouled-Naïls still earned dowries by working as prostitutes. The image of these jewel-encrusted dancers was widely diffused in photographs, postcards, and academic Orientalist painting. The specialist on this last front was Etienne Dinet, a painter who utilized this imagery, as we will see, in the graphic work advertising *Andalusia in the Time of the Moors.*

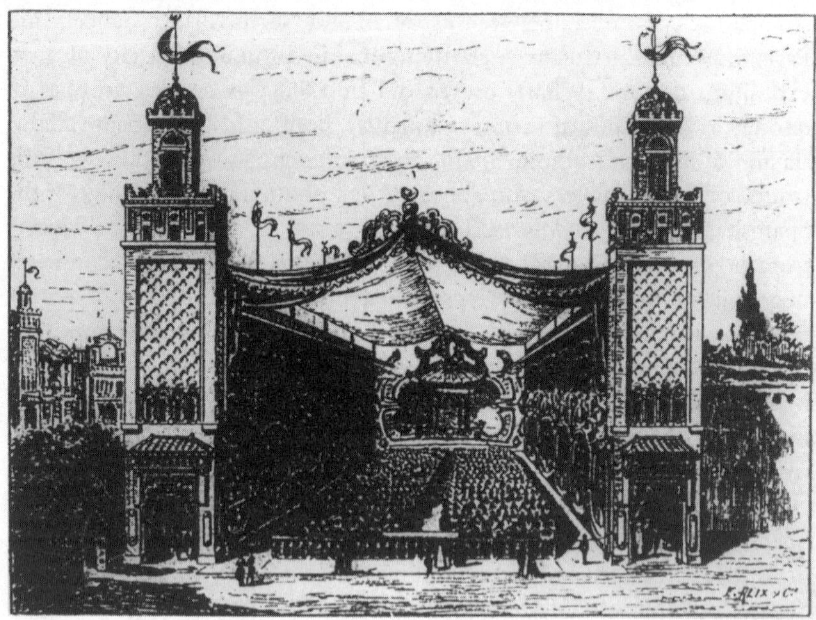

Figure 8.4 *Theater of Andalusian Dance and Song.* Woodcut. From *Le Livre d'or de l'Exposition universelle, Paris, 1900*

Orientalists on Show

Another layer of connection between *Andalusia* and the world of official colonial culture existed in the contributions of the Society of French Orientalist Painters. Founded in 1895 in the aftermath of an exhibition of historical and contemporary Orientalist art, the society established an annual art salon held at the Galeries Durand-Ruel, and worked to promote communication and solidarity among the dozens of professional French artists who traveled regularly to paint in the French colonies (not only in North and West Africa, but in Ethiopia and beyond, in Indochina and Oceania). With support from the Ministry of the Colonies arranged by their president Léonce Bénédite, the Orientalists stage-managed a growing number of exhibitions beyond their own salon. In 1897 they sent 100 works to an art festival at the Institut de Carthage in Tunis. For the 1900 Universal Exposition they mounted a series of interventions, which included a roomful of painting and sculpture for the official Algerian pavilion, the execution of colonial dioramas and panoramas for several other sites, and the gallery of pictures for *Andalusia.*

The logic of this art gallery was twofold: from the Parisian perspective Spain was regarded as the beginning of the exotic, the first country where landscape and sunlight, temperament and customs, were so different that they constituted a delectable alterity. So Spanish scenes (especially Andalusian ones) had been admitted to the Orientalists' salon since its inception; as one critic expressed it, "Spain is the liege-land of Orientalism."[39] Second, images of contemporary indigenous life from the Maghreb – Morocco as well as Algeria and Tunisia – could in the spectator's mind do duty for the lost Moorish life of old Andalusia.

Against the background of dance, bodies in conflict, and grand architecture, the Orientalist painters' presence was one of quietude and the immobile image. Their "museum" was a section of a building where "the Society of Orientalist Painters . . . has organized an exhibition of the finest works by its members. Next to these canvases so full of sun and of light we find a very complete retrospective exhibition of Muslim art."[40] Although I have not been able to locate a catalog of their display (if indeed one was printed), no doubt the Orientalists offered characteristic scenes of Maghrebin life in which no European presence was felt, to be read as a kind of time-warp back to the life of Al-Andaluz. The exhibition worked as a scattering of multifarious views that collectively constituted a panorama of lands once settled by the Moors. Photographs of typical Society installations of the day show paintings of the Maghreb, Spanish scenes – previous Orientalists' salons had regularly included works painted in Spain – Oriental carpets, clay sculpture on pedestals, and even arrays of Moorish weapons. Probably items such as the latter were incorporated into the little retrospective of Muslim art, most unlikely to be "complete," as the guidebook had it. But the Orientalist painters had mounted exhibitions of Islamic art before, with the help of curators from the Musée du Louvre or Bibliothèque Nationale, and leaning heavily for loans on Parisian private collections (some of them formed by leading Orientalists such as Jean-Léon Gérôme).[41]

Finally, the museum contained one last metonym for Andalusia: an exhibition dedicated to the "tauromachie" or bullfight. One can only speculate, as Staller does, on the appeal all this may have had to the young *malagueño* Pablo Picasso, had he strayed over to *Andalusia in the Time of the Moors* ("which Picasso would certainly have heard about, even if he did not see it") during his visit to the Paris Exposition.[42] At the

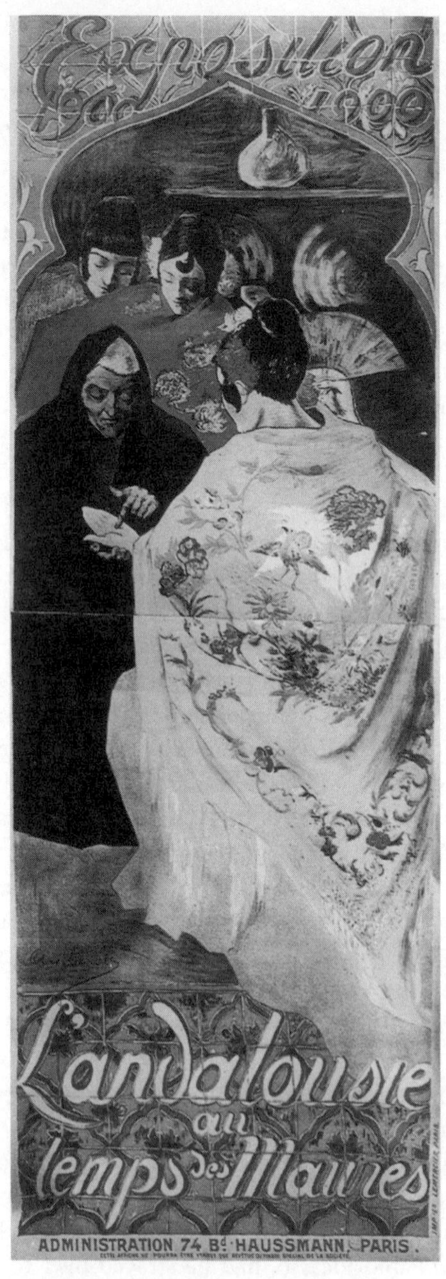

Figure 8.5 Alexandre Lunois, *Andalousie au temps des Maures.* Color lithograph poster. Slaoui Collection, Casablanca

Grand Palais, his melodramatic *Derniers moments* (which he soon painted over) was an official Spanish painting entry. But his own bread-and-butter paintings in 1900 were scenes of the bullfight and the café-concert.

As Staller shows, at the time in Spain there were various theories on the origins of the bullfight, recognized as a pinnacle of popular culture. Some held it to be an inheritance from the Moors, so that Christians could symbolically transpose the death of the bull into a ritual killing, every Sunday afternoon, of the invader from the south. Other scholars argued it was a relic of the Roman occupations of both the Iberian and North African provinces, and hence a common heritage of both Moorish and Christian Spain.[43] Roseyro's arena itself seems not to have featured bullfights (perhaps as a concession to safety). Indeed there were many more camels than bulls to be seen in his *Andalusia* (and to that extent, it was more African than Spanish).

A rare surviving color record of *Andalusia in the Time of the Moors* is a poster by the co-founder of the French Society of Orientalist Painters, Etienne Dinet. Featuring an over-life-size figure of a female dancer, this enormous chromo-lithograph is framed by panels of hand-painted Maghrebin tiles.[44] *Andalusia* as Dinet imagines it is straight from his studies of the Ouled-Naïl people of Bou-Saâda in Algeria, where he painted from 1890 on and lived from 1903. A tattooed young Berber woman in flowing robes, wearing the heavy silver jewelry that embodied her wealth, dances in a narrow horseshoe archway. Behind her, smiling Arab men smoke and wait in the crepuscular air – perhaps her admirers or clients. Taken together with its text, "Exposition Universelle, Paris 1900," this poster has an epideictic and display function (to use Philippe Hamon's terms): Dinet's dancer is like a *spruiker*, exhorting passers-by on the streets of Paris to step through the archway and pass into a different world.[45]

Dinet's poster, it turns out, had a pendant by Alexandre Lunois (recently published in a Moroccan collection of Orientalist posters). Lunois was the perfect complement to Dinet: a popular print-maker and pastellist, he specialized in Gypsy and Spanish scenes, but had a sideline in North African subjects and was, like Dinet, a member of the Society of Orientalist Painters. Lunois's poster emphasizes the Spanish as opposed to Dinet's Moorish: against a similar panel of arabesque tiles and a fictive horseshoe arch, an aged, black-clad woman reads the palm of a young, raven-haired beauty in a chignon, wearing an enormous yellow mantilla (figure 8.5). The opposition of young and old women in the context of fortune-telling evokes the character of La Celestina, the legendary Spanish procuress and fortune-teller also treated by Picasso in his Blue Period works.[46] The theme of chiromancy can be taken to indicate a persisting anti-rational otherness in Andalusian (and particularly Gypsy) life, one at loggerheads with the French intellectual preference for logic. Dinet's sumptuous Berber dancer appeals more directly to the eye, and adds an undercurrent of sex appeal for the Exposition public, despite her copious costume and jewelry.

In sum, both Orientalists posit *Andalusia* as a meeting with the contemporary exotic. But, at the same time, each image invokes the immemorial aspect of the costumes, traditions, and sites that cross back through time to the period of the Moorish presence in Spain. As for the elusive, brown-skinned actor who incarnated Boabdil in the Hippodrome of 1900, he inhabited more the realm of allegory, as a mythicized witness. Thus he embodied the overall metaphors of loss and imaginative restitution that animate this fairground homage to a distant past.

Notes

This text was first presented in "Time, Vision and the Body," a conference session convened by Deborah Cherry and Mieke Bal, at the Congrès internationale de l'histoire de l'art held in London in September 2000. It was repeated at the Humanities Research Institute, Canberra, in 2001. Translations are the author's unless otherwise noted.

1 See Robert Rosenblum, Maryanne Stevens, and Ann Dumas, *1900: Art at the Crossroads* (London: Royal Academy of Arts, 2000).

2 See Dipesh Chakrabarty, *Provincializing Europe: Postcolonial Thought and Historical Difference* (Princeton, NJ: Princeton University Press, 2000), especially 237–49.

3 Anon., "Les Attractions: Trocadéro," *Revue universelle*, 10 (1900), 298; a M. Roseyro is named as the commissioner of the precinct.

4 Adrian Rifkin suggested to me that Roseyro may be a Sephardi name (which might help explain the drive to recreate a time that saw the flowering of Jewish as well as Islamic high culture on the Iberian peninsula). His work as an editor is mentioned in the statutes of the company formed to undertake the *Andalusia* enterprise. The statutes were ratified in Bayonne, October 18, 1898 (Archives Nationales, Paris, F12–4355).

5 Most of the information on Roseyro's role and conception of *Andalusia* is drawn from a letter: J. H. Roseyro to M. the Commissaire-Général, Paris, October 15, 1897, Arch. Nat. F12–4355 ("Andalousie au temps des Maures:

Dossiers concernant les concessions diverses"). All quotations from Roseyro are from this source.

6 See "Etat des frais," September 5, 1898, Arch. Nat. F12–4355.

7 See letter from Roseyro to the Commissaire-Général, April 1, 1898, ibid.

8 A rich account of these events and their ramifications for world history is contained in John Docker, *1492: The Poetics of Diaspora* (London: Continuum, 2001).

9 Natasha Staller, *A Sum of Destructions: Picasso's Cultures and the Creation of Cubism* (New Haven and London: Yale University Press, 2002), 269–303: quote on p. 303. Staller gives the only analysis of *Andalusia in the Time of the Moors* I have found in secondary literature (pp. 302–3).

10 Staller, *A Sum of Destructions*, 291–6, 302.

11 Sophie Makariou and Gabriel Martinez-Gros, "L'Alhambra de Granada: Història d'un monument amb història," *L'Avenç* (Barcelona), 264 (December 2001), 12–19. I thank Gabriel Martinez of the Ecole des Hautes Etudes en Sciences Sociales for providing the original French version of this publication in Catalan.

12 "Les Aventures du dernier Abencérage" (1826), in *Œuvres complètes de Châteaubriand*, vol. iii, ed. M. Sainte-Beuve (Paris: Garnier Frères, 1861).

13 Théophile Gautier, *Voyage en Espagne* (1843), ed. Jean-François Revel (Paris: René Julliard, 1964); Washington Irving, *Tales of the Alhambra* (Granada: Miguel Sanchez, 1832); John Frederick Lewis, *Sketches and Drawings of the Alhambra* (London, 1835); Owen Jones and Jules Gourey, *Plans, Elevations and Sections of the Alhambra* (London, 1836–45); these are discussed in Michael Danby, *The Islamic Perspective* (London: World of Islam Festival Trust, 1983), 27 and 43 ff. Gautier's influential text drew on Washington Irving, but transformed the account of Andalusian places with a new esthetic sensibility. The poet and critic was an early champion of Spanish painting, which "arrived" in Paris with the exhibition of King Louis-Philippe's Galerie Espagnole; subsequently Napoleon III's marriage to the Spanish Eugenia de Montijo (from Granada) cemented French Hispanophilia, of which Edouard Manet's painting was a refined symptom. See Gary Tinterow and Geneviève Lacambre, *Manet/Velázquez: The French Taste for Spanish Painting* (New York: Metropolitan Museum of Art, 2003).

14 "From time to time the cathedral will give forth cortèges such as process around the streets of Seville and Cadiz during Holy Week. We know that this unique spectacle attracts thousands of tourists to Andalusia every year." Roseyro, letter to Commissaire-Général.

15 Armand Silvestre, *Guide Armand Silvestre de Paris et de ses environs et de l'Exposition de 1900* (Paris: A. Silvestre, 1900), 140. As well as publishing this guidebook, Silvestre ran a popular theater at the Exposition.

16 Presumably an architect who specialized in colonial expositions, I assume he was the author of Henri Malo, "L'Exposition coloniale nationale de Marseille," *La Nouvelle Revue*, NS 43 (1906), 43–59.

17 *Le Panorama: 1900, Exposition universelle* (Paris: Ludovic Baschet, 1900), 207.

18 Details from L. Russell Muirhead (ed.), *The Blue Guides: Southern Spain, with Gibraltar, Ceuta and Tangier*, 2nd edn. (London: Ernest Benn, 1958), 188–91.

19 See his superb 1884 rendering of the Mosque of Sidi Abd-er-Rahman, reproduced in Stéphane Guégan et al., *De Delacroix à Renoir: L'Algérie et les peintres* (Paris: Institut du Monde Arabe and Hazan, 2003), 206–7.

20 Both passages are from *Paris Exposition 1900* (Paris: Librairie Hachette, 1900) 341, trans. in Philippe Jullian, *The Triumph of Art Nouveau: Paris Exhibition, 1900* (Oxford: Oxford University Press, 1974), 164.

21 See Staller, *A Sum of Destructions*, 271–3.

22 "Costumes and accessories will be copied from those used for these solemnities." Roseyro, letter to Commissaire-Général.

23 *Guide Armand Silvestre*, 141.

24 *The Shorter Oxford English Dictionary* (1973 edn.).

25 See an example in Abdelaziz Ghozzi, *L'Affiche orientaliste: Un siècle de publicité à travers la collection de la Fondation A. Slaoui* (Casablanca: Malika Editions, 1997), 98.

26 Roseyro (1897); he continues: "The 'livre d'or' of the conquest of Andalusia by Ferdinand and Isabella the Catholic contains sufficient high deeds . . . for it to be easy to organize, in this vast arena, combats and tourneys between defenders of the Cross and sons of the Prophet."

27 Gautier, *Voyage en Espagne*, 277. He continues: "The memory of the Moors is still alive in Granada. One would say it was only yesterday that they left the city, and if one judges by what they left behind, it really is a shame."

28 From Châteaubriand, "Les Aventures du dernier Abencérage" (1826), 101.

29 For example W. Somerset Maugham, "Boabdil the Unlucky," in his *Andalusia: Sketches and Impressions* (New York: Alfred A. Knopf, 1920), 198–202.

30 See Salman Rushdie, *The Moor's Last Sigh* (London: Jonathan Cape, 1995). In Rushdie's retelling of the tale, the last Moorish king secretly loves a Jewess, who steals his crown and herself joins the diaspora to flee, via Egypt, to Puna in India where she is the precursor of Moraes Zogoiby (the Unlucky), protagonist of Rushdie's novel of twentieth-century Bombay. A modern rendition of Boabdil painted on horseback is at the center of a family intrigue which leads Zogoiby to back a castle in Andalusia for the climax of the tale.

31 See M. Elisabeth Crouse, *Algiers*, illustrated by Adelaide B. Hyde (London: Gay & Bird, 1907). On the episode of Napoleon's "Royaume arabe" and the visual arts, see Peter Benson Miller, "La Vision officielle de l'Algérie sous la règne de Napoléon III," in Guégan, *De Delacroix à Renoir*, 152–63.

32 On Racim, see R. Benjamin, *Orientalist Aesthetics: Art, Colonialism and French North Africa, 1880–1930* (Berkeley: University of California Press, 2003), 235–48.
33 Joseph Dancourt, "L'Andalousie au temps des Maures," *Le Livre d'or de l'exposition de 1900*, 2 (Paris: Edouard Cornély, 1900), 239.
34 See Georges Marçais, *La Vie musulman d'hier vue par Mohammed Racim* (Paris: Arts et Métiers graphiques, 1960), 45.
35 In Amin Maalouf's wonderfully atmospheric 1986 book *Leo the African*, trans. Peter Sluglett (London: Abacus, 1995), Boabdil is pudgy and irritable, disgraced for having chosen survival for himself (and his people) over annihilation.
36 Marçais, *La Vie musulman d'hier*, 77, "Danseuses orientales"; the Racim is illustrated in Roger Benjamin (ed.), *Orientalism: Delacroix to Klee* (Sydney: Art Gallery of New South Wales, 1997), 173.
37 See Zeynep Çelik and Leila Kinney, "Ethnography and Exhibitionism at the Expositions Universelles," *Assemblage*, 17 (December 1990), 35–59.
38 Dancourt, "L'Andalousie au temps des Maures," 240; this plate is illustrated in Jullian, *The Triumph of Art Nouveau*, 165.
39 Marius-Ary Leblond, "Les Expositions: L'Exposition des Orientalistes," *La Grande revue*, 47 (March 1908), 381.
40 Dancourt, "L'Andalousie au temps des Maures," 240.
41 See Benjamin, *Orientalist Aesthetics*, 62–5.
42 Staller, *A Sum of Destructions*, 303.
43 Ibid. 274.
44 The Dinet is illustrated in color in Benjamin, *Orientalist Aesthetics*, plate 7; see also Ghozzi, *L'Affiche orientaliste*, 97.
45 Philippe Hamon, *Expositions: Literature and Architecture in Nineteenth-Century France*, trans. Katia Sainson-Frank and Lisa Maguie (Berkeley: University of California Press, 1992).
46 La Celestina was the protagonist of a novel in dialog form attributed to Fernando de Rojas (1499). Thanks to Domingo Cordóba of the University of Sydney for identifying this inflection in Lunois's image.

Bibliography

Compiled by Hannah Williams

Books

À Fleur de peau: Le Moulage sur nature au XIXe siècle. (2002). Paris: Musée d'Orsay, Réunion des Musées Nationaux.

About, E. (1870). *Le Fellah: Souvenirs d'Egypte.* Paris: Hachette.

Ageron, C.-R. (1990). Peut-on parler d'une politique des "royaumes arabes" de Napoléon III? In M. Morsy (ed.). *Les Saint-Simoniens et l'Orient: Vers la modernité.* Aix-en-Provence: Édisud. 83–96.

Akarli, E. D. (1986). Abdülhamid II's Attempt to Integrate Arabs into the Ottoman System. In D. Kushner (ed.). *Palestine in the Late Ottoman Period: Political, Social, and Economic Transformations.* Jerusalem: Yad Izhak Ben-Zvi; Leiden: E. J. Brill. 74–89.

Aksel, M. (1960). *Anadolu Halk Resimleri.* Istanbul: Baha Matbaasi.

Alloula, M. (1986). *The Colonial Harem.* (M. Godzich and W. Godzich, trans.) Theory and History of Literature 21. Manchester: Manchester University Press.

Al-Sayyid, A. L. (1968). *Egypt and Cromer: A Study in Anglo-Egyptian Relations.* London: John Murray.

Ames, M. (2003). How to Decorate a House. In L. Peers and A. K. Brown (eds.). *Museums and Source Communities.* London: Routledge.

Assollant, A. (1867). La Femme fellah de M. Landelle. *L'Exposition Universelle de 1867 Illustrée: Publication Internationale autorisée par la Commission Impériale,* vol. ii. Paris: 106 Rue Richelieu. 115–16.

Baedeker, K. (1914). *Konstantinopel, Balkanstaaten, Kleinasien, Cypern. Handbuch für Reisende von Karl Baedeker.* (2nd edn.). Leipzig: Karl Baedeker.

Ballerini, J. (1987). Photography Conscripted: Horace Vernet, Gérard de Nerval and Maxime du Camp in Egypt. Ph.D. dissertation. New York: CUNY.

Barillari, D. (1995). *Raimondo D'Aronco.* Rome: Laterza.

Baron, B. (1994). *The Women's Awakening in Egypt: Culture, Society and the Press.* New Haven: Yale University Press.

Barringer, T. (2001). Imperial Visions: Responses to India and Africa in Victorian Art and Design. In J. Mackenzie (ed.). *The Victorian Vision: Inventing New Britain.* London: V&A Publications.

Barthe, C. (2003). 'Les Éléments de l'observation': Des daguerréotypes pour l'anthropologie. In *Le Daguerréotype français: Un objet photographique*, Musée d'Orsay, exhibition catalog (Paris: Réunion des Musées Nationaux, 2003), 73–86.

Barthe, C. (2004). Des modèles et des normes, allers-retours entre photographies, et sculptures ethnographiques. In *Charles Cordier, 1827–1905: L'autre et l'ailleurs*, Musée d'Orsay (exhibition catalog). Paris: Éditions de La Martinière. 93–113.

Barthes, R. (1981). *Camera Lucida: Reflections on Photography.* (R. Howard, trans.) New York: Hill & Wang.

Barthes, R. (1990). *New Critical Essays.* (R. Howard, trans.) Berkeley: University of California Press.

Bartholdi, F. A. (1984). *The Statue of Liberty Enlightening the World.* New York: N.Y. Bound (1st published 1885).

Batur, A. (1999). The Subject of Style in Ottoman Architecture at the End of the 19th Century. In *Art Turc/Turkish Art.* Geneva: Proceedings of the 10th International Congress of Turkish Art. 143–52.

Bayly, C. A. and Fawaz, L. T. (eds.) (2002). *Modernity and Culture: From the Mediterranean to the Indian Ocean.* New York: Columbia University Press.

Beaulieu, J. and Roberts, M. (eds.) (2002). *Orientalism's Interlocutors: Painting, Architecture, Photography.* Durham, NC: Duke University Press.

Becker, J. R. (1999). Auguste Rodin and Photography: Extending the Sculptural Idiom. In D. Kosinski (ed.). *The Artist and the Camera: Degas to Picasso.* Dallas: Dallas Museum of Art.

Benjamin, R. (ed.) (1997). *Orientalism: Delacroix to Klee.* Sydney: Art Gallery of New South Wales.

Benjamin, R. (2003). *Orientalist Aesthetics: Art, Colonialism and French North Africa, 1880–1930.* Berkeley: University of California Press.

Berchère, N. (1863). *Le Désert de Suez: Cinq mois dans l'isthme.* Paris: Hetzel.

Berger, J. (1975). *A Seventh Man.* Harmondsworth: Penguin.

Berk, N. (1950). *La Peinture turque.* Ankara: Direction Générale de la Presse et du Tourisme.

Berk, N. (1955). *Modern Painting and Sculpture in Turkey.* (B. Bather, trans.) Istanbul: Turkish Press, Broadcasting and Tourist Department.

Berman, M. (1982). *All That Is Solid Melts Into Air: The Experience of Modernity.* New York: Penguin Books.

Bernal, M. (1987). *Black Athena: The Afroasiatic Roots of Classical Civilisation*, vol. i: *The Fabrication of Ancient Greece, 1785–1985.* London: Free Association Press.

Bernal, M. (1991). *Black Athena: The Afroasiatic Roots of Classical Civilisation*, vol. ii: *The Documentary and Archaeological Evidence*. New Brunswick, NJ: Rutgers University Press.

Bhabha, H. K. (1994). *The Location of Culture*. London and New York: Routledge.

Boer, I. E. (1994). This Is Not the Orient: Theory and Postcolonial Practice. In M. Bal and I. E. Boer (eds.). *The Point of Theory: Practices of Cultural Analysis*. Amsterdam: Amsterdam University Press. 211–19.

Bohrer, F. N. (ed.) (1999). *Sevruguin and the Persian Image: Photographs of Iran, 1870–1930*. Washington, DC: Arthur M. Sackler Gallery, Smithsonian Institution.

Bohrer, F. N. (2003). *Orientalism and Visual Culture: Imagining Mesopotamia in Nineteenth Century Europe*. Cambridge: Cambridge University Press.

Brace, C. L., et al. (1996). Clines and Clusters Versus "Race": The Case of a Death on the Nile. In M. K. Lefkowitz and G. M. Rogers (eds.). *Black Athena Revisited*. Chapel Hill: University of North Carolina Press. 129–64.

Bull, D., Inepoğlu, G., Renda, G. and Nicolaas, E. S. (2003). *An Eyewitness of the Tulip Era: Jean-Baptiste Vanmour* (exhibition catalog). Topkapı Palace Museum and Rijksmuseum. Istanbul: Koçbank.

Burke, E. III (1996). Two Critics of French Rule in Algeria: Ismail Urbain and Frantz Fanon. In L. C. Brown and M. S. Gordon (eds.). *Franco-Arab Encounters*. Beirut: American University of Beirut. 329–44.

Burton, R. (1855). *Personal Narrative of a Pilgrimage to Al-Madinah and Meccah, 1855–56*. (2 vols.). New York: Dover Publications.

Carré, J. M. (1956). *Voyageurs et écrivains français en Egypte*. Cairo: Institut français d'archéologie orientale.

Catalogue des livres composants la bibliothèque de M. E. Viollet-le-Duc. (1880). Paris.

Caygill, M. L. and Leese, M. N. (1993). *A Survey of Visitors to the British Museum 1992–1993*. British Museum Occasional Paper 101, London.

Çelik, Z. (1986 and 1993). *The Remaking of Istanbul: Portrait of an Ottoman City in the Nineteenth Century*. Seattle: University of Washington Press, 1986; repr. Berkeley: University of California Press, 1993.

Çelik, Z. (1992). *Displaying the Orient: Architecture of Islam at Nineteenth-Century World's Fairs*. Berkeley: University of California Press.

Çelik, Z. (1997). *Urban Forms and Colonial Confrontations: Algiers under French Rule*. Berkeley: University of California Press.

Çelik, Z. (2000). Speaking Back to Orientalist Discourse at the World's Columbian Exposition. In H. Edwards (ed.). *Noble Dreams, Wicked Pleasures: Orientalism in America, 1870–1930*. Princeton, NJ: Princeton University Press. 77–9.

Çelik, Z. (2002). Speaking Back to Orientalist Discourse. In J. Beaulieu and M. Roberts (eds.). *Orientalism's Interlocutors: Painting, Architecture, Photography*. Durham, NC: Duke University Press. 26–31.

Chakrabarty, D. (2000). *Provincializing Europe: Postcolonial Thought and Historical Difference.* Princeton, NJ: Princeton University Press.

Charles Cordier 1827–1905: L'Autre et l'ailleurs. (2004). Paris: Musée d'Orsay, Éditions de La Martinière.

Charles-Roux, J. (1901). *L'Isthme et le Canal de Suez.* 2 vols. Paris: Hachette.

Châteaubriand, F. (1826). Les Aventures du dernier Abencérage. In *Œuvres complètes de Châteaubriand* (vol. iii), ed. M. Sainte-Beuve (1861). Paris: Garnier Frères.

"Une Circassienne" (pseud. Marguerite Pilon-Fleury) (1901). *Romance of a Harem.* (C. Forestier-Walker, trans.) London: Greening & Co.; 2nd edn. 1904.

"Une Circassienne" (pseud. Marguerite Pilon-Fleury) (1902). *The Woman of the Hill.* (C. Forestier-Walker, trans.) London: Greening & Co.

"Une Circassienne" (pseud. Marguerite Pilon-Fleury) and Barrucund, V. (1911). *Adile Sultane: Roman.* Paris.

Claire, H. (1996). *Reclaiming Our Pasts: Equality and Diversity in the Primary History Curriculum.* Stoke-on-Trent: Trentham Books.

Clark, J. (1998). *Modern Asian Art.* Sydney: Craftsman House.

Clifford, J. (1988). *The Predicament of Culture: Twentieth-Century Ethnography, Literature, and Art.* Cambridge, MA: Harvard University Press.

Codell, J. F. and Macleod, D. S. (eds.) (1998). *Orientalism Transposed: The Impact of the Colonies on British Culture.* Aldershot: Ashgate.

Crary, J. (1990). *Techniques of the Observer: On Vision and Modernity in the Nineteenth Century.* Cambridge, MA: MIT Press.

Crinson, M. (1996). *Empire Building: Orientalism and Victorian Architecture.* London: Routledge.

Crouse, M. E. (1907). *Algiers.* (A. B. Hyde, illustr.). London: Gay & Bird.

Le Daguerréotype français: Un objet photographique. (2003). Musée d'Orsay (exhibition catalog). Paris: Musée d'Orsay, Réunion des Musées Nationaux.

Danby, M. (1983). *The Islamic Perspective.* London: World of Islam Festival Trust.

Dancourt, J. (1900). L'Andalousie au temps des Maures. In *Le Livre d'or de l'exposition de 1900*, 2. Paris: Edouard Cornély.

Davison, R. H. (1990). *Essays in Ottoman and Turkish History, 1774–1923: The Impact of the West.* Austin: University of Texas Press.

De Leon, E. (1878). *The Khedive's Egypt, or The Old House of Bondage under New Masters.* New York: Harper & Brothers.

Deringil, S. (1999). *The Well-Protected Domains: Ideology and Legitimation of Power in the Ottoman Empire 1876–1909.* London: I. B. Tauris.

Des Godins de Souhesmes, G. (1893). *A Guide to Constantinople and its Environs* (G. P. Cacavas, trans.). Istanbul: A. Zellich.

Desprez, C. (1868). *Alger naguère et maintenant.* Algiers: Imprimerie du Maréchal.

Docker, J. (2001). *1492: The Poetics of Diaspora.* London: Continuum.

Douin, G. (1934). *Histoire du règne du Khédive Ismaïl: L'Apogée 1867–1873.* Rome: Stampata nell' Istituto Poligrafico.

Du Camp, M. (1877). *Le Nil, Egypte et Nubie.* Paris: Hachette (1st published 1854).

Ducuing, F. (ed.) (1867). Les Visites souveraines: Ismaïl Pacha. In *L'Exposition Universelle de 1867 Illustrée.* Paris: 106 Rue Richelieu.

Durand-Révillon, J. (1994). La Galerie anthropologique du Muséum national d'histoire naturelle et Charles-Henri-Joseph Cordier. In *La Sculpture ethnographique: De la Vénus hottentote à la Tehura de Gauguin.* Paris: Réunion des Musées Nationaux.

Edib, H. (1926). *Memoirs of Halidé Edib.* London: John Murray.

Edib, H. (1928). *The Turkish Ordeal: Being the Further Memoirs of Halidé Edib.* London: John Murray.

Edib, H. (1937). *Inside India.* London: George Allen & Unwin.

Edmond, C. [Chojecki, C.-E.] (1867). *L'Egypte à l'Exposition universelle de 1867.* Paris: Dentu.

Edwards, H. (ed.) (2000). *Noble Dreams, Wicked Pleasures: Orientalism in America, 1870–1930.* Princeton, NJ: Princeton University Press.

Ellison, G. (1915). *An Englishwoman in a Turkish Harem.* London: Methuen.

Ersoy, A. (1999). *Usul-i Mi'Mari-yi 'Osmani*: A Source of Revival in Ottoman Architecture. In *Art Turc/Turkish Art.* Geneva: Proceedings of the 10th International Congress of Turkish Art. 291–5.

Félicitations et Allégresse au sujet de l'entrée de S. M. Napoléon III à Alger: Poème composé par M'hammed el-Ouennas. (1867). Algiers: Imprimerie Typographique Bouyer.

Fisher, S. (2000). Exploring People's Relationships with Egypt: Qualitative Research for the Petrie Museum. Susie Fisher Group, unpublished document. Petrie Museum of Egyptian Archaeology.

Fornta, B. (2002). *Imperial Classroom: Islam, the State and Education in the Late Ottoman Empire.* Oxford: Oxford University Press.

Frampton, K. (1980). *Modern Architecture: A Critical History.* New York: Oxford University Press.

Freely, J. (1991). *Blue Guide: Istanbul.* London: A. & C. Black.

Frierson, E. B. (2000a). Cheap and Easy: The Creation of Consumer Culture in Late Ottoman Society. In D. Quataert (ed.). *Consumption Studies and the History of the Ottoman Empire 1550–1922.* New York: State University of New York Press.

Frierson, E. B. (2000b). Mirrors Out, Mirrors In: Domestication and Rejection of the Foreign in Late-Ottoman Women's Magazines. In D. F. Ruggles (ed.). *Women, Patronage, and Self-Representation in Islamic Societies.* New York: State University of New York Press.

Garber, M. (1997). The Chic of Araby: Transvestism and the Erotics of Cultural Appropriation. In *Vested Interests: Cross-Dressing and Cultural Anxiety.* New York: Routledge. 304–52.

Garnett, L. (1890–1). *The Women of Turkey and their Folk Lore.* (2 vols.). London: David Nutt.

Garnett, L. (1911). *Turkey of the Ottomans.* London: Sir Isaac Pitman & Sons.

Gautier, T. (1964). *Voyage en Espagne,* ed. J.-F. Revel. Paris: René Julliard (1st published 1843).

Gautier, T. (1991a). *Constantinople.* Paris: Christian Bourgeois (1st published 1853).

Gautier, T. (1991b). *Voyage en Egypte,* ed. P. Tortonese. Paris: La Boîte à Documents (1st published 1869).

Germaner, S. (1999). Le Mécénat dans l'art turc: Du Sérail à la République. In *Art Turc/Turkish Art.* Geneva: Proceedings of the 10th International Congress of Turkish Art. 345–7.

Germaner, S. and İnankur, Z. (1989). *Orientalism and Turkey.* Istanbul: The Turkish Cultural Service Foundation.

Germaner, S. and İnankur, Z. (2002). *Constantinople and the Orientalists.* Istanbul: Işbank.

Ghozzi, A. (1997). *L'Affiche orientaliste: Un siècle de publicité à travers la collection de la Fondation A. Slaoui.* Casablanca: Malika Editions.

Goethe, J. W. von. (1923). *West-Östlicher Divan.* In R. Müller-Freienfeld (ed.). *Goethes Werke.* Berlin: Wegweiser (1st published 1819).

Green, R. (1971). *John Frederick Lewis R.A. 1805–1876.* Newcastle-upon-Tyne: Laing Art Gallery.

Guégan, S., et al. (2003). *De Delacroix à Renoir: L'Algérie et les peintres.* Paris: Institut du Monde Arabe and Hazan.

Güvemli, Z. (1987). *The Art of Painting and Turkish Painting.* Istanbul: Akbank'ın bir kültür hizmeti.

Haikal, F. (2003). Egypt's Past Regenerated by its Own People. In S. MacDonald and M. Rice (eds.). *Consuming Ancient Egypt.* London: UCL Press.

Hamdy Bey, O. and de Launay, M. (1873). *Les Costumes populaires de la Turquie en 1873. Ouvrage Publié sous le Patronage de la Commission Impériale Ottomane pour l'Exposition Universelle de 1873 à Vienne.* Phototypie par P. Sébah. Constantinople: Imprimerie du Levant Times & Shipping Gazette.

Hamon, P. (1992). *Expositions: Literature and Architecture in Nineteenth-Century France.* (K. Sainson-Frank and L. Maguie, trans.) Berkeley: University of California Press.

A Handbook for Travellers in Turkey. (3rd edn., 1854). London: John Murray.

Hanioğlu, M. S. (1995). *The Young Turks in Opposition.* Oxford: Oxford University Press.

Harris, L. (2000). Ancient Egypt: Digging for Dreams: Museum Development Worker's Report. Unpublished document, Croydon Museum and Heritage Service.

Hassan, F. A. (1998). Memorabilia: Archaeological Materiality and National Identity in Egypt. In L. Meskell (ed.). *Archaeology under Fire: Nationalism, Politics and Heritage in the Eastern Mediterranean and the Middle East.* London: Routledge. 200–16.

Hélys, M. (pseud. Marie Léra) (1923). *L'Envers d'un roman: Le Secret des Désenchantées.* Paris: Perrin.

Herbert, J. D. (1998). Passing Between Art History and Postcolonial Theory. In M. A. Cheetham, M. A. Holly, and K. Moxey (eds.). *The Subjects of Art History: Historical Objects in Contemporary Perspective.* Cambridge: Cambridge University Press. 213–29.

Hilliard, A. G. (1994). Bringing Maat, Destroying Isfet: The African and African Diasporan Presence in the Study of Ancient KMT. In I. Van Sertima (ed.). *Egypt: Child of Africa.* New Brunswick, NJ: Transaction Publishers. 127–47.

Howe, K. S. (ed.) (1993). *Excursions Along the Nile: The Photographic Discovery of Ancient Egypt* (exhibition catalog). Santa Barbara: Santa Barbara Museum of Art.

Howe, S. (1998). *Afrocentrism: Imagined Pasts and Imagined Homes.* London: Verso.

Hueber, R. (ed.) (1990). *D'un album de voyage: Auguste Bartholdi en Egypte (1855–1856)* (exhibition catalog). Colmar: Musée Bartholdi.

Hueber, R. (1993). Les Salons d'Amilcar: Notes sur les dessins et tableaux orientalistes d'Auguste Bartholdi. *Annuaire de la Société d'Histoire et d'Archéologie de Colmar.* 75–137.

Hueber, R. (ed.) (1994). *Au Yemen en 1856: Photographies et dessins d'Auguste Bartholdi* (exhibition catalog). Colmar: Musée Bartholdi.

Hueber, R. (ed.) (1998). *Dahabieh, Almées et Palmiers: 52 Dessins du premier voyage en Orient 1855–56 d'Auguste Bartholdi* (exhibition catalog). Colmar: Musée Bartholdi.

İnankur, Z. (1999). Official Painters of the Ottoman Palace. In *Art Turc/Turkish Art.* Geneva: Proceedings of the 10th International Congress of Turkish Art. 381–8.

Irving, W. (1832). *Tales of the Alhambra.* Granada: Miguel Sanchez.

Jardine, L. and Brotton, J. (2000). *Global Interests: Renaissance Art between East and West.* London: Reaktion.

Johnson, G. A. (ed.) (1984). *Sculpture and Photography: Envisioning the Third Dimension.* Cambridge: Cambridge University Press.

Jones, O. and Gourey, J. (1836–45). *Plans, Elevations and Sections of the Alhambra.* London.

Jullian, P. (1974). *The Triumph of Art Nouveau: Paris Exhibition, 1900.* Oxford: Oxford University Press.

Kipling, R. (1899). The Ballad of East and West. In *Poems and Ballads.* New York: Caldwell (1st published 1889).

Klein, H. (1913). *Souvenirs de l'ancien et nouvel Alger.* Algiers: Imprimerie Orientale Fontate Frères.

Kuntay, M. C. (1944). *Namık Kemal Devrinin İnsanları ve Olayları Arasında* (vol. i). Istanbul: Maarif Mataasi. 311–39.

Lafont-Couturier, H. (2000). *Gérôme and Goupil: Art and Enterprise.* Paris: Éditions de la Réunion des Musées Nationaux.

Le Play, F. (1869). *Commission impériale. Rapport sur l'Exposition Universelle de 1867 à Paris. Précis des opérations et liste des collaborateurs avec un appendice sur l'avenir des expositions.* Paris: Imprimerie impériale.

Leïla Hanoum (pseud. Adriana Piazzi) (1883). *A Tragedy in the Imperial Harem at Constantinople.* (General R. E. Colston, trans.) London: Grübner & Co.

Levallois, M. (1990). Ismayl Urbain: Éléments pour une biographie. In M. Morsy (ed.). *Les Saint-Simoniens et l'Orient: Vers la modernité.* Aix-en-Provence: Édisud. 53–82.

Levey, M. (1975). *The World of Ottoman Art.* London: Thames & Hudson.

Lewis, J. F. (1835). *Sketches and Drawings of the Alhambra.* London.

Lewis, M. (1978). *John Frederick Lewis RA: 1805–1876.* Leigh-on-Sea: F. Lewis.

Lewis, R. (1996). *Gendering Orientalism: Race, Femininity and Representation.* London: Routledge.

Lewis, R. (2004). *Rethinking Orientalism: Women, Travel and the Ottoman Harem.* London: I. B. Tauris.

Loti, P. (pseud. Louis Marie Julien Viaud) (1989). *Aziyadé.* (M. Laurie, trans.) London: Routledge (1st published 1879).

Loti, P. (1906). *Les Désenchantées: Roman des harems turcs contemporains.* Paris: Calmann-Levy.

Loti, P. (1906). *Disenchanted (Désenchantées): A Romance of Harem Life.* (C. Bell, trans.) London: Macmillan.

Lott, E. (1866). *The English Governess in Egypt: Harem Life in Egypt and Constantinople.* London: R. Bentley.

Lott, E. (1867). *Nights in the Harem, or, The Mohaddeyn in the Palace of the Ghezire.* (2 vols.). London: Chapman & Hall.

Lott, E. (1869). *The Grand Pasha's Cruise on the Nile in the Viceroy of Egypt's Yacht.* (2 vols.). London: T. Cautley Newby.

Luthi, J.-J. (1998). *La Vie quotidienne en Egypte au temps des Khédives.* Paris: L'Harmattan.

Maalouf, A. (1995). *Leo the African.* (P. Sluglett, trans.). London: Abacus.

MacDonald, S., and Shaw, C. (2004). Uncovering Ancient Egypt. In N. Merriman (ed.). *Public Archaeology.* London: Routledge. 109–31.

MacKenzie, J. M. (1995). *Orientalism: History, Theory and the Arts.* Manchester: Manchester University Press.

Macleod, D. S. Cross-Cultural Cross-Dressing: Class, Gender and Modernist Sexual Identity. In J. F. Codell and D. S. Macleod (eds.). *Orientalism Transposed: The Impact of the Colonies on British Culture.* Aldershot: Ashgate. 63–85.

Magri, V. (1995). *Le Discours sur l'autre: À travers quatre récits de voyage en Orient.* Paris: Honoré Champion Éditeur.

Marçais, G. (1960). *La Vie musulman d'hier vue par Mohammed Racim.* Paris: Arts et Métiers graphiques.

Mardin, Ş. (1962). *The Genesis of Young Ottoman Thought: A Study in the Modernization of Turkish Political Ideals.* Princeton, NJ: Princeton University Press.

Mardin, Ş. (1969). *Continuity and Change in the Ideas of the Young Turks.* Ankara: Robert College School of Business Administration and Economics Occasional Papers.

Maugham. W. S. (1920). *Andalusia: Sketches and Impressions.* New York: Alfred A. Knopf.

Melek Hanoum, and Ellison, G. (1913). *Abdul Hamid's Daughter: The Tragedy of an Ottoman Princess.* London: Methuen.

Melman, B. (1992). *Women's Orients: English Women and the Middle East, 1718–1918. Sexuality, Religion and Work.* Basingstoke: Macmillan.

Merriman, N. (ed.) (1999). *Making Early Histories in Museums.* Leicester: Leicester University Press.

Miller, P. B. (2003). La Vision officielle de l'Algérie sous la règne de Napoléon III. In S. Guégan et al., *De Delacroix à Renoir: L'Algérie et les peintres.* Paris: Institut du Monde Arabe and Hazan. 152–63.

Montagu, Lady M. W. (1988). *Embassy to Constantinople: The Travels of Lady Mary Wortley Montagu,* ed. C. Pick; introd. Dervla Murphy. London: Hutchinson (1st published 1763).

MORI (2000). *Attitudes Towards the Heritage: Research Study Carried out for English Heritage.* London: English Heritage.

Moser, S., et al. (2003). Transforming Archaeology through Practice: Strategies for Collaborative Archaeology and the Community Archaeology Project at Quseir, Egypt. In L. Peers and A. K. Brown (eds.). *Museums and Source Communities.* London: Routledge.

Motawi, S. (1998). Egypt in the British Museum. MA dissertation. Institute of Archaeology, University College London.

Muirhead, L. R. (ed.) (1958). *The Blue Guides: Southern Spain, with Gibraltar, Ceuta and Tangier.* (2nd edn.). London: Ernest Benn.

Le Musée des Beaux-Arts d'Istanbul (n.p., n.d.).

Necipoğlu, G. (1995). *The Topkapi Scroll: Geometry and Ornament in Islamic Architecture.* Santa Monica, CA: Getty.

Neue Pinakothek München. (1982). Munich: Bayerische Staatsgemäldesammlungen.

Nir, Y. (1985). *The Bible and the Image: The History of Photography in the Holy Land, 1839–1899.* Philadelphia: University of Pennsylvania Press.

Nochlin, L. (1989). The Imaginary Orient. In *The Politics of Vision: Essays on Nineteenth-Century Art and Society.* New York: Harper & Row. 33–59.

O'Connor, D. and Reid, A. (2003). *Ancient Egypt in Africa.* London: UCL Press.

Öner, S. (1999). The Place of the Ottoman Palace in the Development of Turkish Painting and the Military Painters. In *Art Turc/Turkish Art.* Geneva: Proceedings of the 10th International Congress of Turkish Art. 517–23.

Oulebsir, N. (1998). Du politique à l'esthétique: L'Architecture néo-mauresque à Alger. In J. Dakhlia (ed.). *Urbanité arabe.* Arles: Sindbad/Actes Sud. 299–321.

Özdeniz, E. (1994). *Türk Deniz Subayı Ressamları.* Istanbul: Türk Deniz Kuvvetleri Komutanligi.

Özel, İ (1985).Tanzimatin Getirdiği "Aydin'." In *Tanzimat'tan Cumhuriyet'e Türkiye Ansiklopedisi,* vol. i. Istanbul: İletişim Yayınları. 65.

Özendes, E. (1999). *From Sébah and Joaillier to Foto Sabah: Orientalism in Photography.* Istanbul: Yapı Kredi Yayınları.

Öztuncay, B. (2000). *Vassilaki Kargopoulo: Photographer to His Majesty the Sultan.* Istanbul: Birieşik Oksijen Sanayi A. Ş.

Le Panorama. 1900 Exposition universelle. (1900). Paris: Ludovic Baschet.

Papet, E. (2002). Le Moulage sur nature au service de la science. In *A fleur de peau: Le Moulage sur nature au XIXe siècle* (exhibition catalog, Musée d'Orsay). Paris: Réunion des Musées Nationaux. 88–95.

Papet, E. (2004). Le Moulage sur nature ethnographique au XIXe siècle. In *Charles Cordier, 1827–1905: L'autre et l'ailleurs,* Musée d'Orsay (exhibition catalog). Paris: Éditions de La Martinière. 127–8.

Paris Exposition 1900. (1900). Paris: Librairie Hachette.

Peers, L. and Brown, A. K. (eds.) (2003). *Museums and Source Communities.* London: Routledge.

Peirce, L. (1993). *The Imperial Harem: Women and Sovereignty in the Ottoman Empire.* Oxford: Oxford University Press.

Peltre, C. (1998). *Orientalism in Art.* (J. Goodman, trans.) New York: Abbeville Press.

Perez, N. (ed.) (1988). *Focus East: Early Photography in the Near East (1839–1885).* New York: Harry N. Abrams.

Peters, T. F. (1996). *Building the Nineteenth Century.* Cambridge, MA: MIT Press.

Petrie, W. M. F. (1931). *Seventy Years in Archaeology.* London: Sampson Low.

Phillips, R. B. (2003). Community Collaboration in Exhibitions: Toward a Dialogic Paradigm. Introduction to L. Peers and A. K. Brown (eds.). *Museums and Source Communities.* London: Routledge.

Pollock, G. (1977). *Millet.* London: Oresko.

Pratt, M. L. (1986). Fieldwork in Uncommon Places. In J. Clifford and G. E. Marcus (eds.). *Writing Culture: The Poetics and Politics of Ethnography.* Berkeley: University of California Press.

Provoyeur, P. (1986). Artistic Problems. In *Liberty: The French-American Statue in Art and History.* New York Public Library (exhibition catalog). New York: Harper & Row.

Quataert, D. (1994). Part 4: The Age of Reforms 1812–1914. In H. Inalcik with D. Quataert. *An Economic and Social History of the Ottoman Empire, 1300–1914.* Cambridge: Cambridge University Press.

Raby, J. (2000). Opening Gambits: From Europe to Istanbul. In *The Sultan's Portrait: Picturing the House of Osman.* Istanbul: Topkapı Palace Museum.

Réau, L. (1924–33). *Histoire de l'expansion de l'art français* (4 vols). Paris: Van Oest.

Reichardt, A. (1908). *Girl-Life in the Harem: A True Account of Girl-Life in Oriental Climes.* London: John-Ouseley.

Reid, D. (2002). *Whose Pharaohs? Archaeology, Museums and the Egyptian National Identity from Napoleon to World War I.* Berkeley: University of California Press.

Renda, G. (2000). Portraits: The Last Century. In *The Sultan's Portrait: Picturing the House of Osman.* Istanbul: Topkapı Palace Museum. 442–542.

Renda, G., Erol, T., Turani, A., et al. (1988). *A History of Turkish Painting.* Seattle: University of Washington Press and London: Palasar SA.

Roberts, M. (1995). Travel, Transgression and the Colonial Harem: The Paintings of J. F. Lewis and the Diaries of British Women Travellers. Ph.D. dissertation, University of Melbourne.

Roberts, M. (2002). Contested Terrains: Women Orientalists and the Colonial Harem. In J. Beaulieu and M. Roberts (eds.). *Orientalism's Interlocutors: Painting, Architecture, Photography.* Durham, NC: Duke University Press. 179–203.

Roberts, M. (forthcoming). Harem Portraiture: Elisabeth Jerichau-Baumann and the Egyptian Princess Nazli Hanım. In D. Cherry and J. Helland (eds.). *Local/Global: New Narratives of Women's Art in the Nineteenth Century.* Aldershot: Ashgate.

Robinson, J. (1990). *Wayward Women: A Guide to Women Travellers.* Oxford: Oxford University Press.

Rosenblum, R., Stevens, M. and Dumas, A. (2000). *1900: Art at the Crossroads.* London: Royal Academy of Arts.

Roseyro, J. H. (1897). Unpublished letter to the Commissaire-Général de l'Exposition Universelle, Paris, 15 October. Archives nationales, F12–4355 ("Andalousie aux temps des Maures: Dossiers concernant des concessions diverses"). Paris.

Rushdie, S. (1995). *The Moor's Last Sigh.* London: Jonathan Cape.

Said, E. (1978). *Orientalism.* New York: Random House; Harmondsworth: Penguin.

Said, E. (1993). *Culture and Imperialism.* New York: Knopf.

Scarce, J. (1987). *Women's Costume of the Near and Middle East.* London: Unwin Hyman.

Scham, S. (2003). Ancient Egypt and the Archaeology of the Disenfranchised. In D. Jeffreys (ed.). *Views of Ancient Egypt since Napoleon Bonaparte: Imperialism, Colonialism and Modern Appropriations.* London: UCL Press.

Schick, I. (1999). *The Erotic Margin: Sexuality and Spatiality in Alteritist Discourse.* London: Verso.

Schiffer, R. (1999). *Oriental Panorama: British Travellers in 19th Century Turkey.* Amsterdam: Rodopi.

Schölch, A. (1981). *Egypt for Egyptians! The Socio-Political Crisis in Egypt 1878–1882.* London: Ithaca Press.

La Sculpture française au XIXe siècle. (1986). Paris: Réunion des Musées Nationaux.

Service des Monuments Historiques et des Sites. Fonds Viollet-le-Duc.

Shaw, W. M. K. (2003). *Possessors and Possessed: Museums, Archaeology, and the Visualization of History in the Late Ottoman Empire.* Berkeley: University of California Press.

Silvestre, A. (1900). *Guide Armand Silvestre de Paris et de ses environs et de l'Exposition de 1900.* Paris: A. Silvestre.

Simpson, M. (1996). *Making Representations: Museums in the Post-Colonial Era.* London: Routledge.

Slade, Captain A., RN FRAS, Admiral of the Turkish Fleet (Muchaver Pacha) (1854). *Records of Travels in Turkey, Greece etc. and of a Cruise in the Black Sea with the Captain Pacha.* London: Saunders & Otley.

Staller, N. (2002). *A Sum of Destructions: Picasso's Cultures and the Creation of Cubism.* New Haven and London: Yale University Press.

Stanton, J. E. (2003). Snapshots on the Dreaming: Photographs of the Past and Present. In L. Peers and A. K. Brown (eds.). *Museums and Source Communities.* London: Routledge.

Stevens, M. A. (ed.) (1984). *The Orientalists: Delacroix to Matisse. European Painters in North Africa and the Near East.* London: Royal Academy of Arts.

Stewart, S. (1994). *Crimes of Writing: Problems in the Containment of Representation.* Durham, NC: Duke University Press.

Stone, P. G. and Molyneaux, B. L. (eds.) (1994). *The Presented Past: Heritage, Museums and Education.* London: Routledge.

Stora, B. (1991). *Histoire de l'Algérie coloniale (1830–1954).* Paris: Éditions La Découverte.

The Sultan's Portrait: Picturing the House of Osman. (2000). Topkapı Palace Museum. Istanbul: Işbank.

Süreyya, M. (1996). *Sicill-i Osmanî* (vol. ii). Istanbul: Kültür Bakanliği ile.

Teissier, O. (1865). *Napoléon III en Algérie.* Paris: Challame, Ainé; Algiers: Bastide; Toulon: J. Renoux.

Ternar, Y. (1994). *The Book and the Veil: Escape from an Istanbul Harem.* Montreal: Véhicule Press.

Thackeray, W. M. (1869). *Notes on a Journey from Cornhill to Grand Cairo.* London: Smith Elder.

Thomas, N. (1994). *Colonialism's Culture: Anthropology, Travel, and Government.* Princeton, NJ: Princeton University Press.

Tinterow, G. and Lacambre, G. (2003). *Manet/Velázquez: The French Taste for Spanish Painting.* New York: Metropolitan Museum of Art.

Todorov, T. (1989). *Nous et les autres: La Réflexion française sur la diversité humaine.* Paris: Seuil.

Truman, N. (1962). Empire and the Dandies. In *Historic Costuming.* London: Sir Isaac Pitman & Sons. 87–92.

Tugay, E. F. (1963). *Three Centuries: Family Chronicles of Turkey and Egypt.* Oxford: Oxford University Press.

Turani, A. (1977). *Bati Anlayisina Dönük Türk Resim Sanati.* Ankara: Türkiye Iş Bankası Kültür Yayınları.

Türk Resim Sanatında: Şişli Atölyesi ve Viyana Sergisi. (1997). Istanbul: İstanbul Resim ve Heykel Müzeleri Derneği.

Vaka Brown, D. (1909). *Haremlik.* London: Constable.

Vaka Brown, D. (1911). *In The Shadow of Islam.* London: Constable.

Vaka Brown, D. (1923). *The Unveiled Ladies of Stamboul.* Boston: Houghton Mifflin.

Vidal, P. (2000). *Frédéric-Auguste Bartholdi: Par la main. Par l'esprit.* Paris: Les Créations du Pélican.

Viollet-le-Duc, E.-E. (1863). *Entretiens sur l'architecture.* (2 vols.). Paris: Ve A Morel et Cie.

Viollet-le-Duc, E.-E. (1873). Préface to J. Bourgoin, *Les Arts arabes.* Paris: Ve A Morel et Cie.

Viollet-le-Duc, E.-E. (1874). Préface to L. Parvillée, *Architecture et décoration turques au XVe siècle.* Paris: Ve A Morel et Cie.

Viollet-le-Duc, E.-E. (1877). *Art russe.* Paris: Ve A Morel et Cie.

Volney, C.-F. (1998). *Voyage en Syrie et en Egypte.* Paris: Fayard (1st published 1787).

Wagner, A. M. (1986). *Jean Baptiste-Carpeaux: Sculptor of the Second Empire.* New Haven: Yale University Press.

Wilson, E. (1985). Oppositional Dress. In *Adorned in Dreams: Fashion and Modernity.* London: Virago. 179–206.

Wright, A. (2004). *Matisse and the Subject of Modernism.* Princeton, NJ: Princeton University Press.

Yaman, Z. Y. (1999). The Theme of Peasants and Farmers in Turkish Painting. In *Art Turc/Turkish Art.* Geneva: Proceedings of the 10th International Congress of Turkish Art. 751–6.

Young, R. J. C. (1995). *Colonial Desire: Hybridity in Theory, Culture and Race.* London: Routledge.

Zeyneb Hanoum (1913). *A Turkish Woman's European Impressions, edited and with an introduction by Grace Ellison.* London: Seeley, Service & Co.

Zürcher, E. J. (1993). *Turkey: A Modern History.* New York: I. B. Tauris.

Articles

Adak, H. (2003). National Myths and Self-Na(rra)tions: Mustafa Kemal's *Nutuk* and Halide Edib's *Memoirs* and *The Turkish Ordeal. South Atlantic Quarterly,* 102/2–3, Spring/Summer, 511–29.

"Adalet" (1890a). A Voice from the Harem: Some Words about the Turkish Woman of Our Day. *The Nineteenth Century,* 28, August, 186–90.

"Adalet" (1890b). Life in the Harem. *The Nineteenth Century,* 28, December, 959–66.

Allen, W. (1984). The Abdul Hamid II Collection. *History of Photography,* 8/2, 119–45.

Anon. (1900). Les Attractions: Le Trocadéro. *Revue universelle,* 10, 298.

Beaulieu, J. (1996). "Voice of the People": The Monument to Corot at Ville-d'Avray. *Australian Journal of Art,* 8, 57–80.

Bhabha, H. K. (1984). Of Mimicry and Man: The Ambivalence of Colonial Discourse. *October,* 28, 125–33.

Bhabha, H. K. (1985). Signs Taken for Wonders: Questions of Ambivalence and Authority Under a Tree Outside Delhi, May 1817. *Critical Inquiry,* 12, 144–65.

Black, L. C. (1988–9). Baudelaire as Dandy: Artifice and the Search for Beauty. *Nineteenth-Century French Studies,* 17/1–2, Fall–Winter, 186–95.

Bohrer, F. N. (1996). Eastern Medi(t)ations: Exoticism and the Mobility of Difference. *History and Anthropology,* 9/2–3, 293–307.

Brown, M. R. (1987). The Harem Dehistoricized: Ingres' *Turkish Bath. Arts Magazine,* 61, 56–68.

Bustarret, C. (1989). Du Nil au Yémen: Bartholdi Photographe. *Histoire de l'art,* 7, October, 35–52.

Celal E. (1907). Osmanli Mimarisi. *Ikdam,* 3 January.

Çelik, Z. (1996). Colonialism, Orientalism, and the Canon. *Art Bulletin,* 78/2, 201–5.

Çelik, Z. (1999/2000). Colonial/Postcolonial Intersections: *Lieux de mémoire* in Algiers. *Third Text,* 49, Winter, 63–72.

Çelik, Z. and Kinney, L. (1990). Ethnography and Exhibitionism at the Expositions Universelles. *Assemblage,* 17, December, 35–59.

Concours pour la construction d'un Palais de Justice à Alger. (1867). *Revue générale de l'architecture et des travaux publics,* v/XXV.

Davies, R. (1925–6). John Frederick Lewis, R.A. (1805–1876). *The Old Watercolour Society's Club*, 3rd annual volume, 36–7.

Davison, R. H. (1986). Halil Şerif Paşa: The Influence of Paris and the West on an Ottoman Diplomat. *Osmanlı Araştırmaları (The Journal of Ottoman Studies)*, VI, Istanbul. 47–65.

De Baudot, A. (1867). Exposition Universelle de 1867. *Gazette des architectes et du bâtiment* (Paris, special issue).

De Mandach, C. (1913). Léon Belly (1827–1877). *Gazette des Beaux-Arts*, I, 73–84, 143–57.

Esad, Celal. (1907). Osmanli Mimarisi. *Ikdam*, January 3.

Frierson, E. B. (1995). Unimagined Communities: Woman and Education in the Late-Ottoman Empire. *Critical Matrix*, 9/2, 55–90.

Gestère (1865). Monument à élèver à Alger sur la Place Napoléon. *L'Illustration*, 2è semestre.

Green, N. (1987). Monuments, Memorials and the Framing of Individualism in Third Republic France. *New Formations*, 1, 127–43.

Grigsby, D. G. (1995). Rumor, Contagion, and Colonization in Gros's *Plague-Stricken of Jaffa* (1804). *Representations*, 51, 1–46.

Harbsmeier, M. (1985). On Travel Accounts and Cosmological Strategies: Some Models in Comparative Xenology. *Ethnos*, 50, 273–312.

Keita, S. O. Y. (1990). Studies of Crania from Northern Africa. *American Journal of Physical Anthropology*, 83, 35–48.

Keita, S. O. Y. (1992). Further Studies of Crania from Ancient Northern Africa: An Analysis of Crania from First Dynasty Egyptian Tombs, Using Multiple Discriminant Functions. *American Journal of Physical Anthropology*, 85, 245–54.

Leblond, M.-A. (1908). Les Expositions: L'Exposition des Orientalistes. *La Grande revue*, 47, March, 381–5.

Low, G. C.-L. (1989). White Skins/Black Masks: The Pleasures and Politics of Imperialism. *New Formations*, 9, Winter, 83–103.

MacDonald, S. (2002). An Experiment in Access. *Museologia*, 2, 101–8.

Makariou, S. and Martinez-Gros, G. (2001). L'Alhambra de Granada: Història d'un monument amb història. *L'Avenç* (Barcelona), 264, December, 12–19.

Malo, H. (1906). L'Exposition coloniale nationale de Marseille. *La Nouvelle Revue*, NS 43, 43–59.

McWilliam, N. (1987). Objets retrouvés. *Art History*, 10, 109–21.

Melek Hanoum. (1926). How I Escaped from the Harem and How I Became a Dressmaker. *The Strand Magazine*, February, 129–38.

Moser, S. (2003). Representing Archaeological Knowledge in Museums: Exhibiting Human Origins and Strategies for Change. *Public Archaeology*, 3, 3–20.

Petrie, W. M. F. (1986). A Digger's Life. *English Illustrated Magazine*, March, 440.

Reid, D. (1985). Indigenous Egyptology: The Decolonisation of a Profession. *Journal of the American Oriental Society*, 105, 233–46

Index

Page numbers in italic refer to illustrations.

Sekula, A. (1986). The Body and the Archive. *October*, 39, Winter, 3–64.

Stokes, H. (1929). John Frederick Lewis R.A. (1805–1876). *Walker's Quarterly*, 28, 22.

Trigger, B. G. (1984). Alternative Archaeologies: Nationalist, Colonialist, Imperialist. *Man*, 19, 355–70.

Weber, S. (1990). Der Marga-Platz in Damaskus. *Damaszener Mitteilungen*, 10, 316–17.

HAVERING COLLEGE OF F & H E
163107

WITHDRAWN